the smart palate

the smart palate

DELICIOUS RECIPES FOR A HEALTHY LIFESTYLE

Edited by

Tina Landsman Abbey,

Gail Goldfarb Karp, and

Dr. Joe Schwarcz

Published for

McGill | The Rosalind and Morris Goodman Cancer Research Centre

by McGill-Queen's University Press

Montreal & Kingston | London | Ithaca

© McGill-Queen's University Press 2014
ISBN 978-0-7735-4439-0

Legal deposit third quarter 2014
Bibliothèque nationale du Québec

Printed in Canada on acid-free paper.

McGill-Queen's University Press acknowledges the support of
the Canada Council for the Arts for our publishing program.
We also acknowledge the financial support of the Government
of Canada through the Canada Book Fund for our publishing
activities.

All recipes contained in this volume have been contributed
by individuals. Some recipes may have originated from other
sources or may have been inspired by other recipes. All
product and brand names are the property of their respective
trademark holders.

LIBRARY AND ARCHIVES CANADA CATALOGUING
IN PUBLICATION

The smart palate : delicious recipes for a healthy lifestyle /
edited by Tina Landsman Abbey, Gail Goldfarb Karp, and
Dr. Joe Schwarcz.

Includes index.
ISBN 978-0-7735-4439-0 (pbk.)

1. Cooking.   2. Low-fat diet – Recipes.   3. Cookbooks
I. Schwarcz, Joe, editor   II. Abbey, Tina, 1958–, editor
III. Karp, Gail Goldfarb, editor

TX714.S63 2014   641.5'63   C2014-903643-4

Food and prop stylists: Jacques Faucher and Luce Meunier

Photography: Tango Photographie (cover, pages 22–302);
Gary Munden (pages 3, 5, 7, 8, 9, 12, 14, 16); Courtesy of McGill
University (pages 2, 4)

Design consultant: CommDesign

Book design & typesetting: Garet Markvoort, zijn digital

Set in Hypatia Sans Pro, Sanchez, and Sanchez Condensed

To our unsung heroes

In honour of the professors, assistant professors, research associates, research assistants, postdoctoral fellows, graduate students, research technicians, and administrative staff at the GCRC who dedicate their lives to groundbreaking cancer research.

Proceeds of the sale of this cookbook will benefit the Rosalind and Morris Goodman Cancer Research Centre.

PART ONE

the rosalind and morris goodman cancer research centre

ROSALIND AND MORRIS GOODMAN

Why did more than fifty volunteers spend over a year creating this unique cookbook for healthy eating choices?

For the past five years, the Rosalind and Morris Goodman Cancer Research Centre (GCRC) has been running a successful free lecture series on various cancers. We wanted to thank our presenters for selflessly offering their time and expertise and felt that a healthy cookbook inspired by research would be an ideal gift. It would encourage readers to enhance their well-being with food choices that are not only wise but also delicious. As well, the process itself would engage our dedicated volunteers in an enjoyable and fulfilling activity as they created, tasted, and critiqued innovative, healthy recipes. In addition, it would provide a fundraising and awareness tool for the GCRC to help support researchers as they continue their groundbreaking work. It would be a means to honour cancer researchers everywhere and to thank them for devoting their life's work to the search for better ways to prevent, diagnose, treat, and cure cancer.

Our dream became a reality only when Tina Landsman Abbey and Gail Goldfarb Karp assumed leadership of the project. Their combined expertise, together with the generous participation of numerous volunteers as well as the discerning input of nutritionists Cindy Bassel Brown and Sharyn Katsof has resulted in this magnificent collection of over 180 recipes that look great, taste wonderful, and offer healthy choices.

We are grateful to our publisher, McGill-Queen's University Press, for helping us reach alumni around the world. We thank our sponsors and friends for underwriting the production costs of this book. Their generosity will allow the profits of each book to be directed toward basic cancer research, the essential foundation for the development of innovative and curative cancer drugs.

Enjoy your new cookbook. Use it often and take pride that you are supporting excellence in cancer research.

Rosalind Goodman, LLD, and Morris Goodman, LLD

Together, ordinary people can achieve extraordinary results.

BECKA SCHOETTLE

Knowledge is the food of the soul.

PLATO

DR. DAVID EIDELMAN

Cooking is more than just a means of nourishment; it is a universal art that brings people together, connecting them to one another and to their communities. These connections—together with the marrying of healthy ingredients with traditional and new approaches—create culinary masterpieces.

The same can be said of the collective strength of the research team at McGill's Rosalind and Morris Goodman Cancer Research Centre. Throughout its history, the GCRC has brought together outstanding expertise, rigorous science, and innovation to yield truly groundbreaking outcomes. Our investigators are world-renowned leaders in their fields who, in the last five years alone, have published some 650 research papers based on new discoveries. With its strong network of partners, here and internationally, the GCRC is helping us to decode the complexities of the disease and to open new pathways for better diagnostic procedures, treatments, and prognoses. Our success is being demonstrated through the impact on our patients, the hundreds of graduate and postgraduate scholars who have joined the GCRC corps, and the growing body of knowledge that has been generated as a result of these combined efforts.

Cancer has crossed borders and cultures to become a leading cause of death worldwide. Yet, now more than ever, scientific advances are making it possible for people with cancer to live longer and more productive lives. The GCRC is contributing to these advances not only through the leadership of researchers and staff, but also thanks to the vision and extraordinary support of our larger family of alumni and friends, such as Rosalind and Morris Goodman, who are helping us to move mountains to advance the GCRC's work.

Just as knowledge is food for the soul, in the hands of our GCRC community it is also nourishment for mind and body. This cookbook is a reflection of our shared hope, one that may serve as inspiration at your dinner table.

Enjoy.

David Eidelman, MDCM, FRCPC, FACP
Vice-Principal (Health Affairs)
Dean of the Faculty of Medicine
McGill University

DR. MORAG PARK

There is nothing more beautiful than coming together with family, colleagues, and friends at the table to celebrate, and to plan for a better future, over good food and sustenance. This cookbook is particularly special because it tells of the success that can be achieved through concerted effort. We are so very fortunate to know and collaborate with the many individuals who constitute the Rosalind and Morris Goodman Cancer Research Centre community. We have come together both by nature and design, motivated by a common goal: to vanquish cancer.

At this juncture, the Goodman Cancer Research Centre is celebrating the advances made since its inception, breakthroughs that are enabling us to better understand cancer at a cellular and molecular level, as well as how it progresses, spreads, and resists therapies. These, together with discoveries of new cancer genes, are opening up novel opportunities to personalize therapeutic strategies, alleviate suffering, and improve outcomes. We are privileged to count among our scientists many GCRC researchers who are recognized nationally and internationally—among them, Michel Tremblay, recently awarded the Robert L. Noble award, and Nahum Sonenberg, recipient of the Wolf prize and Gairdner award.

We are looking forward in the coming years to advancing our mission by reinforcing our foundation of internationally renowned scientists, providing an internationally recognized training ground for the next generation of researchers, and accelerating the translation of our discoveries into better cancer treatments.

The group at the core of the GCRC are working untiringly to further develop integrated networks in cancer biology, pre-clinical models, and personalized strategies for therapy, to alleviate suffering and improve outcomes for those with cancer. We aim to build on our strengths in breast and pancreatic cancers, to combat lung and other leading cancers, and to enhance and expand our capabilities to decipher the rich data we are now gleaning.

We thank you, the Goodman Cancer Research Centre community, for embarking on this journey with us, and all the exceptional supporters and volunteers who are behind the progress we make. The impetus you provide is immeasurable.

Alone we can do so little;
together we can do so much.
HELEN KELLER

So welcome to our table, and enjoy these recipes as inspiration for a better and healthier future, one in which, we hope, cancer will no longer exist in our everyday conversations.

Morag Park, PhD, FRSC
Director, Goodman Cancer Research Centre
Professor, Diane and Sal Guerrera Chair in Cancer Genetics

RESEARCHERS OF THE GOODMAN CANCER RESEARCH CENTRE

Sowing the seeds of hope

EMBRYONIC DEVELOPMENT AND CANCER

This group of researchers is examining the early mechanisms of cell movement, proliferation, organ formation, and gene regulation during mammalian embryonic development. By understanding more about cellular mechanisms during embryonic and postnatal development, these investigators can better understand how the pathways are re-engaged in certain cancers and how they can contribute to the malignancy of certain types of cancer.

left to right: Dr. Maxime Bouchard, Dr. Alain Nepveu, Dr. Xian Jiao Yang, Dr. Thomas Duchaine, Dr. Yojiro Yamanaka

Harvesting the kernels of wisdom

METABOLISM AND CANCER

This group is focusing their research on the energy requirements and building blocks needed by cancer cells to fuel uncontrolled growth. To accomplish this objective, the team has established an advanced plat-form for the profiling of metabolites from blood, tissue, and cellular extracts derived from animal models of cancer as well as from cancer patients. This platform allows researchers and physician-scientists to follow disease progression in patients and correlate it with specific metabolic changes, leading to the identification of unique bio-markers and potential targets for treatment.

left to right: Dr. Russell Jones, Dr. Nicole Beauchemin, Dr. Vincent Giguère, Dr. Arnim Pause, Dr. Julie St-Pierre

Thinking outside the box

STEM CELLS AND SIGNALLING

The scientists in this unit are studying the signalling pathways that are activated in healthy cells and comparing them with the pathways that are engaged in cancerous cells. Another interest of members within this group is the pathways that are active in stem cells and how these cells can be employed to treat numerous diseases and conditions, such as Alzheimer's disease, Parkinson's disease, spinal cord injuries, and heart disease. In addition, understanding how normal stem cells relate to cancer stem cells may reveal novel ways to target cancer stem cells, which are implicated in the formation of tumors and metastases.

left to right: Dr. Philippe Gros, Dr. José Teodoro, Dr. Michel L. Tremblay, Dr. Nahum Sonenberg, Dr. Jerry Pelletier

Getting to the root of a problem

DNA REPLICATION, DNA REPAIR, AND APOPTOSIS

All cells must carry out the fundamental process of DNA replication and repair and of apoptosis (programmed cell death). Interestingly, cancer cells have adopted strategies that render them resistant to apoptosis or that prevent them from dealing effectively with DNA damage. These mechanisms, once engaged in cancer cells, can make them refractory to current therapies or provide the means by which resistance to new therapies can develop. Researchers hope to exploit an understanding of these mechanisms in order to devise new ways to target cancer cells.

left to right: Dr. Maria Zannis-Hadjopoulos, Dr. Phil Branton, Dr. Gordon Shore, Dr. Imed Gallouzi

Searching for the sweetness of success

PANCREATIC CANCER

Until recently, research opportunities in the field of pancreatic cancer have been rare. As a result, relatively little is known about the causes of and risk factors for this type of cancer. The goals of this research team are to learn more about the biology of pancreatic cancer, as well as patient lifestyle and environmental factors that may affect risk for this cancer type, hereditary factors associated with pancreatic cancer in some families, and how our ability to detect pancreatic cancer earlier can be improved.

Dr. George Zogopoulos

Benefiting from the fruits of our labour

BREAST CANCER

The GCRC has an integrated research program focused on deciphering the molecular basis of breast cancer progression and metastasis. The group employs cell-based models, pre-clinical animal models, and patient-derived tumor material that can be propagated in mice to investigate specific molecules and signalling pathways that influence tumor growth, metastasis, and resistance to therapies. This unit has also established high-quality serum and tissue banks that permit researchers in the group to validate their findings using clinical material.

left to right: Dr. Luke McCaffrey, Dr. William Muller, Dr. Morag Park, Dr. Peter Siegel, Dr. Michael Hallett

PART TWO

notes to our readers

The best kind of dining features
great taste accompanied by
a serving of science.

DR. JOE SCHWARCZ

DR. JOE SCHWARCZ

Given my background in chemistry, my long-standing interest in food and cooking is perhaps no surprise. After all, food is nothing more than an amazing collage of chemical compounds, and cooking is a matter of altering them to achieve a change in texture and flavour. Food, of course, is also the source of everything we are made of, so there can be no question that what we eat has an impact on our health. Neither can there be a question about the pleasure we derive from eating. I have certainly experienced novel delights by trying the likes of Cauliflower Apple Mash and Spinach Arugula Pear Strudel, to name only a couple of the recipes included here.

So, what should we have for dinner? It seems a simple question, but it is so difficult to answer! Unfortunately, what pleases our palate is not always pleasing to our health. Our taste buds may celebrate a meeting with sugar, butter, or salt, while the rest of our body responds to such encounters with less enthusiasm, preferring to deal with broccoli or alfalfa sprouts.

We have been struggling to find the appropriate balance between taste and health ever since Hippocrates laid the foundation for the science of nutrition over two thousand years ago with his oft-quoted statement, "Let food be thy medicine." The struggle is complicated: a diet conducive to weight loss might not be ideal for reducing the risk of heart disease and might also differ from one that reduces the risk of cancer. And then we have the conundrum that, in spite of data gleaned from thousands of studies, there is no universal agreement on what constitutes the best diet either for weight loss or for optimal health.

There's certainly no shortage, either, of nutritional information, or of opinions about what we should eat. Dr. Robert Lustig, a pediatric neuroendocrinologist at the University of California, believes that many health problems, particularly obesity, can be traced to consuming too much fructose. University of Missouri professor Frederick vom Saal is of the opinion that obesity can be linked to bisphenol A, a chemical that can leach from the lining of canned foods. In his book *Deadly Dairy Deception*, dermatologist Dr. Robert Bibb makes a case for dairy products being the cause of prostate and breast cancer. Dr. Neal Barnard, president of the US-based Physicians Committee for Responsible Medicine, goes even further in *Eat Right, Live Longer* by claiming that salvation lies in avoiding all animal products.

Cardiologist Dr. William Davis sees no problem with meat, but views wheat as the real bogeyman. According to Davis, the grain's polypeptides cross the blood-brain barrier and interact with opiate receptors to induce a mild euphoria that in turn causes addiction to wheat, resulting in fluctuating blood sugar levels that in turn create hunger and lead to obesity as well as numerous other health problems. Journalist Gary Taubes maintains that not only wheat but all carbohydrates need to be limited. In *Good Calories, Bad Calories* he has gathered a massive amount of information to "prove" that excessive consumption of carbohydrates is the cause of heart disease, cancer, Alzheimer's disease, and type-2 diabetes. He advises against a low-fat diet. Dr. Dean Ornish, author of *Eat More, Weigh Less*, would take issue with Taubes. He puts his cardiac patients on an extremely low-fat, high-complex-carbohydrate diet and claims that deposits in their arteries actually regress. In *Soy Smart Health*, Dr. Neil Solomon claims that eating soy can decrease the risk of breast cancer, heart disease, and osteoporosis, while in *The Whole Soy Story*, Dr. Kaayla Daniel links soy to malnutrition, digestive problems, thyroid dysfunction, cognitive decline, reproductive disorders, heart disease, and cancer. Go figure.

The "experts" can't all be right. When I throw all the divergent opinions into my mental flask and distill the essence, I come up with something like the "Okinawa Diet Plan" or its close relative, "The Mediterranean Diet." Looking at the Japanese islands of Okinawa, we have our sights on a people whose unusual longevity and good health is well documented. So is the fact that Okinawans do not gain significant weight as they age! Why? Because they consume 1600 calories a day—at least 500 less than we do. And they do this while eating half a pound more food. It's all a matter of what *sort* of food. No hamburgers, hot dogs, or smoked meat here. And no soda pop. But plenty of food with few calories per gram. The lower the "calorie density," the more food can be eaten without gaining weight. For example, broccoli, mushrooms, and carrots check in at about 0.4 calories per gram, tofu at 0.7, bread and meat, of which Okinawans eat very little, at about 3.0, and oils at 8.8 calories per gram. Similarly, the Mediterranean diet emphasizes olive oil, legumes, unrefined cereals, fruits, vegetables, and fish coupled with the moderate consumption of cheese, yogurt, and wine, and a low consumption of meat.

The recipes in this book are in line with current nutritional knowledge, although in the world of nutrition we are constantly saddled with the problem that what is deemed healthy today may be shown tomorrow to be not so healthy after all. Let's remember also that taste can be a source of great pleasure, and that there's more to life than evaluating every morsel of food in terms of whether it is good for us. So cook up a storm and educate your palate with these delicious recipes for a healthy lifestyle.

Joe Schwarcz, PhD
Director
McGill Office for Science and Society

TINA LANDSMAN ABBEY AND GAIL GOLDFARB KARP

The Smart Palate is a celebration of good food as well as of friendship. Tina was up to her elbows in flour and sugar baking honey cakes for the Jewish New Year when she received a phone call from Rosalind Goodman. Rosalind wanted to know whether Tina would be interested in working on a project to honour the Goodman Cancer Research Centre scientists. Roz recognized that Tina, who had recently completed a cookbook for another organization, was the right person for the job. Never one to fret about how much salt, sugar, and fat were needed to make a recipe delicious, Tina was being offered the challenge of creating a book full of delectable international recipes made healthier by incorporating fresh ingredients while limiting additives and preservatives and moderating the use of sugar in all its forms. Additionally, the idea was to familiarize readers with *untried* foods available today that taste great and are beneficial to health.

Tina wanted a partner in this venture, and immediately thought of Gail, her friend of 50 years, who had recently been diagnosed with cancer. Not a nice bit of news, of course, but a battle Gail was prepared to fight and win. So many people were offering unsolicited advice about how to beat this dreadful disease, but instead of taking their recommendations on faith, Gail decided to educate herself about how to tip the odds in her favour. While she had always tried to "eat healthy," it was becoming increasingly clear that almost all of the nutrients that promote health are available not in a vitamin bottle but by eating the right foods.

We were up for the challenge of finding new recipes and adapting some of our favourites into healthier ones by reducing sugar and additives and increasing the amount of nutrients without compromising the taste. While we share a keen interest in cooking and baking, we are pretty much opposites in our food preferences. Gail likes things crunchy and tart; Tina likes them sweet and rich. Gail loves vanilla with chocolate; Tina prefers chocolate with chocolate. Gail likes savoury seasonings; Tina loves spicy heat. The list goes on, but there is one area where our inclinations coincide: we both have a passion for great food and for the process of creating and perfecting recipes. You can be certain that once a recipe was tested, tasted, re-tested, and finally agreed upon by the nutritionists and us to be included in the book, it was a winner.

To eat is a necessity, but to
eat intelligently is an art.

LA ROCHEFOUCAULD

Gail Goldfarb Karp (left) and
Tina Landsman Abbey

The Smart Palate is in no way a diet cookbook aimed at people who want to lose weight. Nor was it designed exclusively for people with cancer or any other disease. Rather, it was written to educate readers on healthy eating and to familiarize them with many of the foods available today that not only taste great but are good for us. To that end, we knew it was necessary to include a wide variety of foods—sometimes uncommon ones—from nutty grains to hearty beans, that can be both nutritious and delicious when prepared using an array of herbs and seasonings. We are not advocating cutting out butter, white flour, or even sugar entirely, but we are suggesting that these ingredients, when used in moderation, can be incorporated into a healthy diet. There are no "bad" foods, but there are better ones that taste great and can actually boost your health. Although many people propose cutting out red meat, it might just be that it is both the type of meat chosen (i.e., lean cuts such as flank steak) and the portion size (yes, no bigger than a deck of cards) that need to be considered. Likewise, if we skip the salad smothered in blue cheese dressing in favour of a tasty lentil citrus salad or replace the buttery mashed potatoes with a creamy cauliflower apple mash, we'll have a much healthier meal. And there lies the secret to healthy eating: balance and moderation. We can achieve both by making the right choices. Finally, we believe that everyone can learn to perfect the art of cooking if they are taught some basic skills and encouraged with some creative prodding.

It has taken almost two years, but our project has reached its conclusion. Throughout, we brainstormed ideas, ate, tested, researched, and educated ourselves about different cultures, foods, nutritional facts, and cooking methods. Still, it was not always easy. Although we had many successes, there were almost as many flat-out failures. Perfecting the Grandma's Chicken Soup and the Tandoori Fish recipes drove us crazy, and it took four women and at least fifteen trial batches of the Morning Glory Bars to arrive at a version that was approved for inclusion in the book.

We pinched ourselves at how fortunate we were to have Dr. Joe Schwarcz on board to answer our myriad questions and to share his wealth of knowledge. Not only is he a man of great wisdom, but he also shares our passion for great food and home cooking. Dr. Schwarcz provided all the "Smart Facts" and even offered one of his own healthy recipes (Vegetarian Goulash).

Food preparation and the experience of eating are perhaps two of the most pleasurable routines of our daily lives. Food transcends cultural and linguistic boundaries. When we think about our favourite family recipes, comforting memories often accompany those thoughts. So, although it is nice to treat yourself to a dinner out, nothing spells love as clearly as home-cooked meals shared among family and friends. Better still, by preparing food yourself, you can customize recipes by adding any of your flavour preferences and omitting certain ingredients, including unhealthy additives and allergens. All of our recipes are, in fact, simply guidelines, and the word "optional" in many of them means that you can and should make adjustments according to the availability of ingredients and individual taste. You can substitute cilantro for parsley, soy nuts for almonds, apples for pears, tarragon for rosemary, cumin for chili, and so on. You can even try adding ingredients that we do not mention as a way to experiment and have fun with the whole cooking experience.

Today is an occasion to celebrate: our book has found its way into your hands. Not only do we get to share our cherished project with you, but you can begin to learn about all the wonderfully nutritious foods available to you and how best to prepare them. Making the same recipes over and over again can become quite boring, so use this book to create dishes that will wow anybody and everybody. We hope we have provided enough information so that you can truly understand the importance of including fresh produce, whole grains, fibre, protein, complex carbohydrates, and healthy fats in your daily diet. Once you master the art of eating everything in moderation, even dessert will be something you no longer have to feel guilty about. Remember, you are what you eat—so eat responsibly!

Tina Landsman Abbey, BComm, and Gail Goldfarb Karp, BA

The field of nutrition is dynamic.

CINDY BASSEL BROWN
AND SHARYN KATSOF

Cindy Bassel Brown (left)
and Sharyn Katsof

CINDY BASSEL BROWN AND SHARYN KATSOF

Food, cooking, and eating give us great pleasure and should be celebrated. But sorting out what healthy eating means is a challenge and can be confusing. As professionals in this field, we often have the daunting task of revising our recommendations on the basis of new scientific findings. However, some basic guidelines stand no matter what science uncovers. These guidelines include

- eating in moderation
- eating a variety of foods
- realizing that no single "super" food exists
- accepting that different people have different dietary needs
- acknowledging that healthy eating is a *lifestyle,* not a *recipe*

The starting-point for eating healthy is choosing foods that are fresh, mostly plant-based, and minimally processed. The recipes in *The Smart Palate* start with the same premise. You will find novel ways of preparing well-known favourites and discover some new foods with which to expand your culinary repertoire. In the spirit of discovery, we chose to eliminate the chapter dedicated to vegetarian choices and disperse these plant-based recipes (identified by the green plant-based icon) throughout the other chapters in the book. There is occasion for sweets and treats, but the vitamins, minerals, and phytochemicals we need are found in vegetables, fruits, whole grains, nuts, seeds, and animal products, and these nutritious foods should make up the bulk of our diet. The recipes found in *The Smart Palate* were scrutinized and reworked to maximize nutrition without compromising on flavour.

ABOUT THE NUTRIENT ANALYSIS

Each recipe is accompanied by a nutrient analysis. The serving sizes used for the analysis may not be representative of your personal choice but were chosen to be consistent with the current Health Canada recommendations (www.hc-sc.gc.ca/fn-an/index-eng.php).

At a glance, some recipes may appear high in energy (calories). It is important, however, to consider the recipe's nutrient density. In essence, how much of a bang (nutrients) are you getting for your buck (calories)? For example, a snack of 100 calories from nuts offers more nutrients than 100 calories from a sugar candy.

In the nutrient analysis, we chose to list the total fat and saturated fat content of each recipe. There are virtually no trans-saturated fats in any of the recipes, and so this information was not included.

The nutrient analysis also includes the fibre content of each recipe. Our typical North American diet has made achieving the recommended 30 g of fibre a day an effort. The benefits of fibre cannot be undersold, and we encourage you to explore some of the recipes that provide a generous amount of fibre (> 5 g per serving).

The sodium content of the recipes provoked philosophical exchanges and compromises. At present, Health Canada recommends that adults aim for an adequate intake of 1500 mg/day of sodium and advises the population not to exceed an upper limit of 2300 mg/day (www.hc-sc.gc.ca/fn-an/nutrition/sodium/index-eng.php-a2). We set a flexible limit of 300 mg sodium per serving in a given recipe. However, consideration was given to soups and other items that were more likely to require salt to produce a flavourful dish. Moderation and variety in our diets ensures that sodium-high dishes are balanced by lower-sodium choices. Cooks with a heavier hand with the salt shaker may find the recipes less flavourful than those they are used to. Our suggestion is to follow the recipes as they are written and to add extra salt on one's own plate according to preference. Let the flavours of the recipe's ingredients stimulate your taste buds. The recipes in the book were analyzed using eaTracker.ca (an interactive web tool used by Dietitians of Canada) according to the following principles:

- The serving size for a recipe was based on the largest number of servings when a range of yields is given: that is, for a recipe that serves 6 to 8 people, the nutrient analysis is based on one-eighth of the total yield.
- The nutritional analysis used the first ingredient listed when a choice is given for ingredients.
- Garnishes or ingredients listed as optional are not included in the analysis.
- The icons identifying recipes as gluten free, nut free, and plant based were determined using the first-choice ingredients in the list when options were given and do not include optional ingredients or garnishes.
- For calculations, low-sodium stocks were used.
- Nutrient analysis does not include salt "to taste."
- Calculations of meat recipes assumed that only the lean portion was eaten and that the skin from poultry was not consumed.
- The classifications "good" and "excellent" with respect to sources of nutrients were identified using the guidelines outlined in the Canadian Food Inspection Agency's "Guide to food labelling and advertising" (2011) and the Recommended Daily Intakes for Canadians (updated November 2010).

It has been a pleasure to work with Tina and Gail on this project. It is not often that nutritionists have an opportunity to work so closely with cooks. Our work together validates our belief that healthy eating does not have to be complicated or compromising. The recipes that follow in *The Smart Palate* are proof that wholesome, unprocessed foods combined with interesting herbs, spices, and homemade condiments can result in tasty and nutritious dishes.

Happy and healthy cooking!

Cindy Bassel Brown, BComm, BSc(NutrSc), PDt, and Sharyn Katsof, BSc, BSc(FSc)

ESSENTIAL NUTRIENTS FOR GOOD HEALTH

NUTRIENT	COMMONLY KNOWN FUNCTIONS	EXAMPLES OF FOOD SOURCES
Vitamin A	Vitamin A is important for normal vision, the immune system, and reproduction. It also helps the heart, lungs, kidneys, and other organs to work properly. Vitamin A is considered an antioxidant.	• Dairy products • Green leafy vegetables and other green, orange, and yellow vegetables, such as broccoli, carrots, and squash • Fruits, including cantaloupe, apricots, and mangoes • Some types of fish, such as salmon • Beef liver and other organ meats
Vitamin B$_6$	The body needs vitamin B$_6$ for energy metabolism and maintenance of a healthy immune system. It may protect against heart disease.	• Bananas, prune juice, avocado, and potatoes • Chickpeas • Fish, poultry, and organ meats
Vitamin B$_{12}$	Vitamin B$_{12}$ helps keep the body's nerve and blood cells healthy, helps prevent anemia, and helps make DNA. It may play a role with vitamin B$_6$ to prevent heart disease.	• Egg yolks • Milk and other dairy products • Nutritional yeast • Fish, poultry, meats, beef liver, and shellfish
Vitamin C	Vitamin C acts as an antioxidant. It promotes wound healing, improves the absorption of iron from plant-based foods, and ensures proper functioning of the immune system.	• Sweet peppers, broccoli, and Brussels sprouts • Citrus fruits and other fruit such as strawberry, kiwi, and cantaloupe
Vitamin D	Vitamin D is important for bone maintenance, muscle movement, and message transmission through the nerves. It also plays an important role in the immune system.	• Fortified milk • Fatty fish such as salmon
Vitamin E	Vitamin E is an antioxidant. It boosts the immune system and lowers the risk of coronary artery disease.	• Wheat germ and vegetable oils, such as sunflower and safflower oil • Nuts such as almonds, peanuts, and hazelnuts • Seeds such as sunflower seeds • Green vegetables such as spinach and broccoli
Thiamin (Vitamin B$_1$)	Thiamin helps with energy metabolism. It is essential for healthy brain and nerve cells, as well as for heart function.	• Enriched, fortified, and whole-grain products such as bread, cereals, rice, pasta, and flour • Eggs • Legumes and peas • Nuts and seeds • Beef liver and pork
Riboflavin (Vitamin B$_2$)	Riboflavin helps with energy metabolism. It is important for growth and for red blood cell production.	• Dairy products such as milk • Eggs • Green leafy vegetables • Legumes • Nuts • Lean meats

NUTRIENT	COMMONLY KNOWN FUNCTIONS	EXAMPLES OF FOOD SOURCES
Niacin (Vitamin B$_3$)	Niacin helps the digestive system, skin, and nerves to function. It is also important for energy metabolism.	• Dairy products • Eggs • Enriched breads and cereals • Legumes • Nuts • Fish, poultry, and lean meats
Folate	Folate helps to make DNA and other genetic material. It is needed for the formation of hemoglobin. Folate is also needed for the body's cells to divide.	• Vegetables such as asparagus, Brussels sprouts, and dark green leafy vegetables • Fruits and fruit juices, such as oranges and orange juice • Nuts, beans, and peas, such as peanuts, black-eyed peas, and kidney beans • Whole grains and fortified cold cereals • Beef and chicken liver
Calcium	Calcium helps to maintain and support strong bones and teeth. It is involved in muscle movement and in message transmission through the nerves. It helps in blood transport and in the release of hormones and enzymes.	• Dairy products such as milk, yogurt, and cheese • Kale, broccoli, and Chinese cabbage • Fish with soft bones, such as canned sardines and salmon
Potassium	Potassium helps balance the pH of the body's fluids. It is vital for muscle contraction, nerve impulses, the functioning of the heart and kidneys, and the regulation of blood pressure. It helps move nutrients into cells and waste products out of cells. It may help to offset some of sodium's harmful effects on blood pressure.	• Soy products and beans • Vegetables such as broccoli, peas, lima beans, tomatoes, potatoes (especially their skins), sweet potatoes, winter squashes, and avocado • Fruits such as citrus fruits, cantaloupe, bananas, kiwi, prunes, dried apricots, and figs • Milk and yogurt • Nuts • Fish such as salmon, cod, flounder, and sardines • Meat and chicken
Iron	Iron is involved in oxygen transport in the blood. It is also essential for the regulation of cell growth and differentiation.	• Egg yolk • Green leafy vegetables • Lentils, beans, and legumes • Dried fruit • Red meats, poultry, and fish
Fibre	Fibre serves to normalize and maintain bowel health. It also lowers blood cholesterol levels and controls blood sugar levels. Fibre can help achieve a healthy body weight.	• Fruits and vegetables • Whole grains • Legumes

This resource is provided as a source of additional information and is believed to be reliable and accurate at the time of publication. References: US National Institute of Health website; Wellness Foods A to Z, UC Berkeley Wellness Letter

USING THIS COOKBOOK

To make life in the kitchen easier and more successful, we offer the following suggestions:

- Read a recipe in its entirety before you begin. Nothing is more frustrating than discovering part way through preparing a dish that you are missing some ingredients. Be on the lookout for the time icon to prevent finding out too late that you should have started the recipe the night before.
- Prepare your *mise en place* ("put in place") for all the required ingredients, as this will allow you to cook without pausing to get ingredients ready. Your ingredients should be measured out, washed, chopped, and placed in individual bowls. Prepare the equipment you will need and preheat your oven if necessary.
- Cook only with ingredients that are fresh.
- Taste and season as you go along, adding small amounts of salt and pepper throughout the cooking process.
- Egg quantities are based on large eggs.

We use the following terms throughout the book:

- julienned: thin strips ⅛ inch thick and 1 to 2 inches long (3 mm × 2.5 to 5 cm)
- sliced: the classic width is about ¼ inch (5 mm)
- minced: chop item as finely as possible; smaller than ⅛ inch (3 mm)
- finely chopped: uniformity and appearance are not important: cut into pieces smaller than ¼ inch (5 mm)
- coarsely or roughly chopped: uniformity and appearance are not important: cut into pieces slightly larger than ¼ inch (5 mm)
- diced small: cut into uniform pieces about: ¼ inch (5 mm) square
- diced medium: cut into uniform pieces about: ½ inch (1 cm) square
- diced large: cut into uniform pieces about: ¾ inch (2 cm) square

To simplify the preparation of many of our recipes, we suggest investing in three kitchen tools: a good zester, a mandoline, and an immersion blender!

The following icons are used. Note that optional ingredients and garnishes are not considered in the designation of recipes as nut free or gluten free:

Time

Nut Free

Gluten Free

Plant Based

Freezable

SMART TIP

DR. JOE'S SMART FACT

recipes

Breakfast can boost your brain power. After fasting all night, your body and your brain need to be refuelled.

breakfast & beverages

homemade granola

This delicious mixture will be a morning delight for the whole family. Personalize it by adding lemon or orange zest before baking or by adding chocolate chips once the mixture has cooled. Experimentation is encouraged! Serve with milk, sprinkle over yogurt, or enjoy on its own.

DRY INGREDIENTS

6 cups (1.5 L) mixed rolled oats, Kamut flakes, rye flakes, spelt flakes, and bran
½ cup (125 ml) raw almonds
⅓ cup (75 ml) unsweetened coconut flakes (optional)
⅓ cup (75 ml) sunflower and/or pumpkin seeds
¼ cup (60 ml) mixed chia seeds, ground flax, and hemp seeds
2 teaspoons (10 ml) ground cinnamon

WET INGREDIENTS

¾ cup (175 ml) Almond or Cashew Butter (see page 296)
½ cup (125 ml) honey
2 tablespoons (30 ml) lightly packed brown sugar
1 tablespoon (15 ml) pure vanilla extract
½ teaspoon (2 ml) salt

DRIED FRUIT

2 cups (500 ml) roughly chopped mixed dried fruits (e.g., apricots, blueberries, cherries, cranberries, dates, figs, and prunes)

Position racks in upper and lower thirds of oven and preheat to 300°F (150°C). Line 2 rimmed baking sheets with parchment paper.

In a large bowl, combine dry ingredients.

In a small bowl, whisk together wet ingredients. Pour wet ingredients over dry ingredients and mix well.

Divide the mixture between the baking sheets and spread into thin, even layers.

Bake for 15 minutes, toss the mixture, and switch positions of pans. Bake for an additional 10 to 15 minutes until the granola has a fragrant, toasty aroma and is golden brown. Lower oven temperature to 275°F (140°C) if granola browns too quickly.

Remove the trays from the oven and let cool on a wire rack. Once the mixture has cooled, add the dried fruit.

Granola will keep in an airtight container for 6 to 8 weeks.

Makes 28 to 30 half-cup servings ‖ NUTRITION (per ½ cup dry granola): energy 209 kcal | total fat 8 g | saturated fat 1 g | carbohydrate 31 g | fibre 4 g | protein 5 g | sodium 38 mg | good source of thiamin

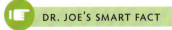

SMART TIP

To make portioning quick, easy, and mindful, keep a small measuring scoop inside your jar of granola.

DR. JOE'S SMART FACT

Although dried fruit is high in sugar, it is low on the glycemic index scale, meaning that it has a low impact on blood sugar. Too much blood sugar can lead to weight gain and subsequently diabetes, so making sure that blood sugar remains balanced is an important step in the prevention of heart disease.

build-your-own instant oatmeal

A comforting and nutritious breakfast can be had almost instantly when this delightful oatmeal mix is on hand, ready for the microwave. By creating your own oatmeal at home, you can eliminate unwanted additives and use a variety of your preferred accents.

BASE INGREDIENTS

4 cups (1 L) rolled oats
½ cup (125 ml) wheat germ
⅓ cup (75 ml) oat bran
¼ cup (60 ml) lightly packed brown sugar
1 teaspoon (5 ml) salt
½ teaspoon (2 ml) ground cinnamon

FRUIT AND NUT MIXTURE

1½ to 2 cups (375 to 500 ml) mixed:
    nuts—almonds, pecans, and walnuts, toasted and roughly chopped
    dried fruit—apricots, cranberries, and dates, roughly chopped
    seeds—chia, pumpkin, and sunflower
Roasted Coconut (see page 298)

Preheat oven to 350°F (180°C).

Spread oats, wheat germ, and oat bran on a rimmed baking sheet and bake for 10 to 15 minutes, stirring every 5 minutes until lightly toasted. Let cool.

Pulse 1 cup of toasted oat mixture in a blender or food processor until finely chopped. Remove to a large bowl and stir in remaining oat mixture and base ingredients.

Add fruit and nut mixture and stir until well combined. Store in an airtight container.

To make your own hot oatmeal, measure ⅓ cup (75 ml) of oatmeal mix into a mug or small bowl, add ¾ cup (175 ml) milk or water and microwave on high for 1 to 2 minutes.

Makes 12 servings ‖ **NUTRITION** (for ⅓ cup oatmeal base ingredients with ¾ cup skim milk): energy 334 kcal | total fat 10 g | saturated fat 4 g | carbohydrate 49 g | fibre 6 g | protein 16 g | sodium 287 mg | excellent source of thiamin, riboflavin, vitamin D, vitamin B12 | good source of calcium, niacin, iron, vitamin E

DR. JOE'S SMART FACT

Oats are a smart breakfast option because of their ability to keep you feeling full longer. In a study comparing oatmeal to a sugary, flaked cereal, researchers found that participants who ate oatmeal at breakfast consumed one-third fewer calories for lunch, thus helping with weight management. Beta-glucan is a form of soluble fibre found in oats and has been shown to lower blood cholesterol.

quinoa porridge

To take the chill out of fall and winter days, start off right with this delicious, protein-packed, and gluten-free alternative to traditional porridge.

BASE INGREDIENTS

½ cup (125 ml) dry quinoa (black, red, or white), rinsed and sorted
¼ teaspoon (1 ml) ground cinnamon
1½ cups (375 ml) almond or dairy milk
½ cup (125 ml) water
2 tablespoons (30 ml) honey
1 teaspoon (5 ml) pure vanilla extract
pinch of kosher salt

FRUIT AND NUT MIXTURE

1 cup (250 ml) mixed sunflower seeds, nuts, dried apricots, cherries, cranberries, dates, and prunes, coarsely chopped as needed
½ cup (125 ml) berries, fresh or thawed from frozen (optional)

Mix quinoa and cinnamon in a medium saucepan over medium heat, stirring frequently, about 3 minutes until toasted.

Add remaining base ingredients and fruit and nut mixture (except berries), stir until mixed, and bring to a boil. Reduce heat, cover pot, and continue to cook for about 35 minutes, stirring occasionally, until porridge is thick and quinoa is tender. If porridge is too thick, add more water.

Sprinkle on berries, if using, and serve.

Serves 4 ‖ **NUTRITION** (per serving): energy 287 kcal | total fat 12 g | saturated fat 0 g | carbohydrate 40 g | fibre 4 g | protein 7 g | sodium 74 mg | excellent source of vitamin E, thiamin | good source of iron, niacin, folate, vitamin B$_6$

Quinoa can help prevent a spike in blood sugar after consumption and can help keep you feeling full until your next meal.

breakfast burrito

Fuel the beginning of your day with this Mexican-influenced wrap. It's protein-packed, flavour-filled, and has fewer calories and less fat than an all-dressed burrito. So enjoy without the guilt.

INGREDIENTS

1 medium sweet potato, peeled, diced small
1 tablespoon (15 ml) canola oil
1 red bell pepper, diced small
2 scallions, thinly sliced
4 large eggs, lightly beaten
¼ cup (60 ml) low-fat plain Greek yogurt
½ teaspoon (2 ml) kosher salt
¼ teaspoon (1 ml) freshly ground pepper
2 tablespoons (30 ml) finely chopped fresh dill
6 small whole-grain tortillas
⅓ cup (75 ml) shredded low-fat mozzarella cheese

Preheat oven to 375°F (190°C).

Place diced sweet potato in a steam basket in a medium pot and fill with 2 cups (500 ml) of water. Bring to a boil, reduce heat, and simmer. Cover and steam about 10 to 15 minutes until tender. Remove from heat.

While potatoes are cooking, heat oil in a large, non-stick skillet over medium heat and sauté red bell pepper and scallions about 3 to 5 minutes until softened. Add eggs, stirring frequently until combined and just set. Remove from heat and transfer to a large bowl.

Add steamed sweet potato, yogurt, dill, salt, and pepper to egg mixture and stir until combined.

Wrap tortillas in foil and warm in oven for 2 to 3 minutes to soften. Lay warm tortillas on work surface and evenly divide egg mixture into centre of each wrap. Top with cheese. Fold top edge up and over filling, tuck sides in, and roll toward you.

Wrap each burrito, seam side down, in aluminum foil and place on baking sheet.

Bake for about 15 minutes, or until hot throughout and cheese is melted.

Serves 6 || **NUTRITION** (per serving): energy 222 kcal | total fat 9 g | saturated fat 2 g | carbohydrate 25 g | fibre 2 g | protein 10 g | sodium 413 mg | excellent source of vitamin A, folate, vitamin B12 | good source of vitamin C, thiamin, riboflavin, niacin, vitamin E

spinach baked eggs

Abundant with cheese and egg, these omelets are fluffy and unique, creating a stunning presentation. The perfect choice to serve for brunch or any time you wish to impress.

INGREDIENTS

8 ounces (225 g) fresh baby spinach, trimmed
½ teaspoon (2 ml) kosher salt, plus more for seasoning
¼ teaspoon (1 ml) freshly ground pepper, plus more for seasoning
8 large eggs
2 to 3 drops of Tabasco sauce, to taste
2 tablespoons (30 ml) shredded low-fat cheddar or mozzarella cheese
3 tablespoons (45 ml) finely chopped fresh chives
About 8 cups (2 L) boiling water

Preheat oven to 350°F (180°C). Grease four 3-inch (7.5 cm) ramekins; place ramekins in a deep baking dish.

Steam spinach 2 to 3 minutes until wilted. Cut into small pieces and squeeze to remove excess moisture. Add salt and pepper. Divide spinach among ramekins.

In a medium bowl, lightly whisk together eggs, Tabasco, and a pinch of salt and pepper. Fill ramekins with egg mixture and sprinkle with cheese and chives.

Pour boiling water into baking dish to reach halfway up sides of ramekins. Bake about 25 to 30 minutes until set.

Serve immediately.

Serves 4 ‖ NUTRITION (per serving): energy 176 kcal | total fat 11 g | saturated fat 4 g | carbohydrate 3 g | fibre 2 g | protein 15 g | sodium 404 mg | excellent source of vitamin A, riboflavin, folate, vitamin C, vitamin D, vitamin E, vitamin B12 | good source of calcium, iron, niacin

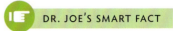

SMART TIP

To test eggs for freshness, gently drop the uncooked egg into a glass of water; if it sinks, it's fresh; if it floats, it's not!

DR. JOE'S SMART FACT

Lutein, a natural antioxidant present in the macula of the eye, protects against macular degeneration. Researchers looked at the role of lutein in the diet and how it might have an effect on the risk of eye disease. They quickly learned from retrospective studies that people who ate more foods that were high in lutein had a lower risk of eye disease. This was particularly so for spinach, the most significant source of lutein in our diet. Cooked spinach was better than raw, since cooking breaks down plant cell walls, allowing nutrients to be released more readily.

shakshuka

Shakshuka is a North African breakfast dish made with eggs simmered in a spicy tomato sauce. Often included on the menus at Middle Eastern restaurants, it is becoming increasingly popular. Serve with multi-grain bread or a pita to soak up every last bit of deliciousness!

INGREDIENTS

1 tablespoon (15 ml) extra-virgin olive oil
1 large onion, diced small
1 large red bell pepper, stems and seeds removed, diced small
3 large garlic cloves, chopped
1 teaspoon (5 ml) ground cumin
1 teaspoon (5 ml) chili powder
¼ teaspoon (1 ml) crushed red pepper flakes
2 or 3 large tomatoes, finely chopped, or one 28-ounce (793 g) can whole plum tomatoes
1 cup (250 ml) lightly packed fresh baby spinach
½ teaspoon (2 ml) kosher salt, plus more for seasoning
¼ teaspoon (1 ml) freshly ground pepper, plus more for seasoning
5 ounces (142 g) feta or goat cheese, crumbled (optional)
6 large eggs
sprigs of finely chopped fresh cilantro, dill, or parsley for garnish

Preheat oven to 375°F (190°C).

Heat oil in a large ovenproof skillet over medium-low heat. Add onions and bell pepper and sauté about 5 minutes until softened. Add garlic and cook 1 to 2 minutes until tender. Stir in cumin, chili powder, and red pepper flakes. Cook for 1 minute.

Pour in tomatoes and spinach and season with salt and pepper. Simmer about 10 minutes until sauce thickens. Sprinkle with feta (optional).

Make six little indentations in sauce and gently break eggs, one by one, into grooves; sprinkle with a pinch of salt and pepper.

Transfer skillet to oven, uncovered, and cook another 10 to 12 minutes until eggs are just set.

Garnish with fresh herbs and let sit for a couple of minutes to settle.

Bring skillet to table and divide into 6 servings.

Serves 6 ‖ **NUTRITION** (per serving): energy 140 kcal | total fat 8 g | saturated fat 2 g | carbohydrate 9 g | fibre 3 g | protein 8 g | sodium 241 mg | excellent source of vitamin C, vitamin A, vitamin E, folate, vitamin B12 | good source of riboflavin, vitamin D, vitamin B6

new age eggs benedict

A refined take on eggs Benedict, this recipe replaces traditional ingredients with healthy and vibrant alternatives. For diversity, try scrambled or soft-boiled eggs, as they work well here too!

SMART TIP

Poaching eggs in water with a small amount of vinegar helps the eggs maintain a nice shape.

INGREDIENTS

1 avocado, halved and pitted
1 teaspoon (5 ml) Hot Mustard (see page 299) or whole-grain mustard
1 teaspoon (5 ml) fresh lime juice
¼ teaspoon (1 ml) kosher salt, plus more for seasoning
¼ teaspoon (1 ml) freshly ground pepper, plus more for seasoning
4 slices multi-grain bread, lightly toasted
1 tomato, sliced
1 tablespoon (15 ml) vinegar
4 large eggs
1 cup (250 ml) lightly packed arugula or spinach

Scoop flesh from avocado into a medium bowl. Add mustard, lime juice, salt, and pepper. Mash and stir with a fork until combined and almost smooth, leaving some small chunks.

Divide avocado mixture among toast slices, spreading evenly. Top avocado with tomato slices.

In a large deep skillet over medium-high heat, bring 4 inches (10 cm) of water to almost boiling. Stir in vinegar. Crack 1 egg first into a small cup and then gently drop the egg into water. Repeat with remaining eggs. Cover and turn off the heat. Let eggs sit undisturbed until whites are firm and yolks are still runny, about 3 to 4 minutes (for firmer yolks, poach 1 to 2 minutes more).

Carefully remove eggs from water with a slotted spoon, allowing excess water to drain off. Place 1 egg on each prepared slice of toast. Taste, adding more salt and pepper if necessary.

Garnish with arugula or spinach and serve immediately.

Serves 4 ‖ **NUTRITION** (per serving): energy 234 kcal | fat 14 g | saturated fat 3 g | carbohydrate 18 g | fibre 6 g | protein 11 g | sodium 315 mg | excellent source of riboflavin, folate, vitamin E, vitamin B12 | good source of thiamin, vitamin D, niacin, vitamin B6

carrot walnut muffins

Using a combination of whole-grain flours adds depth and makes these muffins completely satisfying. They are especially delicious when served warm.

DRY INGREDIENTS

1½ cups (375 ml) whole-wheat flour
¾ cup (175 ml) spelt flour
¼ cup (60 ml) granulated sugar
2 teaspoons (10 ml) baking powder
1 teaspoon (5 ml) baking soda
2 teaspoons (10 ml) ground cinnamon
½ teaspoon (2 ml) salt
½ cup (125 ml) coarsely chopped raw walnuts
½ cup (125 ml) roughly chopped pitted dates

WET INGREDIENTS

1 cup (250 ml) buttermilk
¼ cup (60 ml) honey
3 tablespoons (45 ml) canola oil
2 large eggs
1 tablespoon (15 ml) fresh orange juice
1 teaspoon (5 ml) finely grated orange zest
2 cups (500 ml) carrots, julienned
cinnamon for sprinkling

Preheat oven to 475°F (240°C). Lightly grease a 12-cup muffin tin.

Combine dry ingredients in a large bowl.

In a separate bowl, whisk together wet ingredients (except carrots) until well mixed. Stir in carrots.

Pour wet ingredients into dry ingredients and stir until just moistened; do not over-mix.

Pour batter into muffin tin, filling each three-quarters full. Sprinkle tops with cinnamon and place on middle rack in oven.

Turn oven down to 350°F (180°C) and bake for 15 to 20 minutes until muffin tops spring back when touched. Cool on wire rack in tin before removing.

Makes 12 muffins ‖ NUTRITION (per muffin): energy 242 kcal | total fat 9 g | saturated fat 1 g | carbohydrate 37 g | fibre 4 g | protein 6 g | sodium 287 mg | good source of vitamin A, vitamin E

beet and berry muffins

Children and adults alike will love these muffins as a sweet and healthy treat any time of day. The combination of beets and berries makes these muffins visually appealing and hard to resist.

DRY INGREDIENTS

2 cups (500 ml) multi-grain pastry flour
2 teaspoons (10 ml) baking powder
1 teaspoon (5 ml) baking soda
½ teaspoon (2 ml) ground allspice, cinnamon, or cardamom
½ teaspoon (2 ml) salt

WET INGREDIENTS

⅓ cup (75 ml) granulated sugar
⅓ cup (75 ml) canola oil
⅓ cup (75 ml) non-fat plain Greek yogurt
2 large eggs
1 teaspoon (5 ml) finely grated lemon zest
1 teaspoon (5 ml) pure vanilla extract

FILLING

2 small beets or 1 medium beet, finely grated
1 cup (250 ml) assorted berries, fresh or thawed from frozen

Preheat oven to 475°F (240°C). Lightly grease a 12-cup muffin tin.

Combine dry ingredients in a large bowl.

In a separate bowl, whisk wet ingredients until well combined.

Pour wet ingredients into dry ingredients and stir until just moistened. Batter will be thick; do not overmix.

Gently fold in beets and berries.

Divide batter into prepared muffin tin and place on middle rack in oven.

Turn oven down to 375°F (190°C) and bake for 12 to 15 minutes until muffin tops spring back when touched.

Cool on wire rack in tin before removing. Serve warm or at room temperature with a dollop of yogurt.

Makes 12 muffins || NUTRITION (per muffin): energy 173 kcal | total fat 7 g | saturated fat 1 g | carbohydrate 22 g | fibre 2 g | protein 5 g | sodium 259 mg | good source of vitamin E

SMART TIP

The perfect muffin dome is achieved by preheating the oven to 475°F (240°C) and turning the heat down to the specified temperature as soon as you place the muffins in the oven. The initial high heat causes the batter to rise rapidly during the first few minutes of baking, creating high and springy muffin tops.

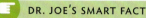
morning glory bars

These breakfast bars are an easy on-the-go alternative to granola. No bowl, spoon, or milk necessary. Packed with a delicious assortment of goodies, they will power you through your morning routine.

DRIED FRUIT

½ cup (125 ml) roughly chopped dried cranberries
½ cup (125 ml) roughly chopped dried pitted prunes

DRY INGREDIENTS

2½ cups (625 ml) rolled oats
½ cup (125 ml) roughly chopped raw cashews, almonds, or soy nuts
½ cup (125 ml) raw pumpkin seeds and/or sunflower seeds
¼ cup (60 ml) chia, ground flax, and/or hemp seeds
¼ teaspoon (1 ml) salt

WET INGREDIENTS

¼ cup (60 ml) honey
⅓ cup (75) Sunflower Seed Butter (see page 297)
1 teaspoon (5 ml) pure vanilla or almond extract
½ teaspoon (2 ml) ground cardamom or cinnamon, or a pinch of nutmeg
2 egg whites

Soak dried fruit in enough hot water to cover, about 15 to 20 minutes.

While the fruit is soaking, preheat oven to 300°F (150°C). Line a 9-inch (23 cm) square baking pan with parchment paper, leaving an overhang on two parallel sides.

In a large bowl, whisk wet ingredients until smooth.

Finely grind ½ cup oats in a food processor. Transfer to wet ingredients bowl and stir in remaining dry ingredients until thoroughly coated.

Drain soaked fruit; add to batter and stir until incorporated.

Transfer mixture into prepared pan and spread into an even layer, compressing firmly with a piece of wax paper or greased spatula.

Bake about 45 to 50 minutes until granola bars are golden, rotating pan halfway through baking.

Let granola bars cool in pan on wire rack for 15 minutes and then cut into bars or squares. Let cool for about an hour to room temperature. Remove from pan by lifting overhanging parchment paper. Transfer bars to cutting board and, using a sharp knife, recut bars following original cuts.

Granola bars can be stored at room temperature in an airtight container for up to 1 week or in the freezer for up to 3 months.

Makes 21 bars or 42 squares ‖ **NUTRITION** (per bar): energy 142 kcal | total fat 5 g | saturated fat 1 g | carbohydrate 22 g | fibre 3 g | protein 4 g | sodium 31 mg

eggless banana loaf

This scrumptious eggless loaf is perfectly balanced with its crispy exterior and moist and light centre. Sweetened with a bountiful array of dried fruit, it makes a satisfying breakfast or dependable dessert.

DRY INGREDIENTS

2 cups (500 ml) whole-wheat flour, plus 1 teaspoon (5 ml) to coat the flavour add-ins
2 teaspoons (10 ml) baking powder
2 teaspoons (10 ml) baking soda
¼ teaspoon (1 ml) ground cinnamon
¼ teaspoon (1 ml) salt

WET INGREDIENTS

½ cup (125 ml) canola oil
½ cup (125 ml) honey
⅔ cup (150 ml) milk (dairy, soy, or almond)
1 teaspoon (5 ml) pure vanilla extract

FLAVOUR ADD-INS

⅔ cup (150 ml) roughly chopped raw walnuts, toasted
½ cup (125 ml) roughly chopped mix of dried dates, figs, prunes, and/or raisins
½ cup (125 ml) semi-sweetened chocolate chips (optional)
3 ripe bananas, coarsely mashed

Preheat oven to 350°F (180°C). Line one large 9 × 5 inch (23 × 18 cm) or two small 7 × 3¼ inch (0.75 L) loaf pans with parchment paper, leaving an overhang on the long sides. Lightly grease to prevent sticking.

In a large bowl, combine dry ingredients.

In a medium bowl, combine wet ingredients.

In a small bowl, toss walnuts, dried fruit, and chocolate chips, if using, with one teaspoon of flour.

Add wet ingredients to dry ingredients and stir until batter is smooth. Add coated nut, dried fruit, and chocolate mixture and stir until evenly distributed. Gently fold in bananas.

Fill prepared pan(s) halfway with batter and bake until bread is golden and springs back when touched, about 60 to 70 minutes for a large loaf pan or 40 to 50 minutes for small loaf pans. Rotate pan(s) halfway through baking.

Cool pan(s) on a wire rack for 15 to 20 minutes. Gently run knife around edges and lift out of pan with overhanging parchment paper.

Store, wrapped in plastic, in the refrigerator or freezer.

Serves 20 || **NUTRITION** (per serving): energy 177 kcal | total fat 9 g | saturated fat 1 g | carbohydrate 24 g | fibre 2 g | protein 3 g | sodium 187 mg | excellent source of vitamin E

SMART TIP

For squares and loaf cakes, let the parchment paper overhang on two sides, forming a sling; this makes removing the baked goods a breeze.

DR. JOE'S SMART FACT

Increased potassium levels in the diet are associated with a decreased risk of stroke and cardiovascular disease. It is possible that an increase of potassium may also have a beneficial effect on blood pressure in children, but more data are needed to support this type of conclusion.

breakfast seed loaf

Nothing beats the aroma of fresh baked bread wafting through the kitchen in the early morning. Rich and moist, this loaf is the perfect way to start your day.

SMART TIP

There are a few ways to make sure a loaf or cake has cooked all the way through. A toothpick inserted in the centre should come out clean. The top of the loaf or cake should spring back when lightly touched, and the sides of the cake should be starting to pull away from the sides of the pan.

MILK AND SEED MIXTURE

1 cup (250 ml) milk (dairy, soy, or almond)
2 tablespoons (30 ml) ground flax seeds (or flax meal)
2 tablespoons (30 ml) chia seeds
2 tablespoons (30 ml) raw sunflower seeds
2 teaspoons (10 ml) anise seeds (optional)

DRY INGREDIENTS

1½ cups (375 ml) whole-wheat or multi-grain flour
1 teaspoon (5 ml) baking soda
1 teaspoon (5 ml) baking powder
1 teaspoon (5 ml) ground cinnamon or ground cardamom
finely grated zest from 1 lemon

WET INGREDIENTS

½ cup (125 ml) granulated sugar
½ cup (125 ml) unsweetened applesauce
⅓ cup (75 ml) canola or melted coconut oil
3 tablespoons (45 ml) fresh lemon juice

FLAVOUR ADD-IN

6 Medjool dates, pitted and chopped

Heat oven to 350°F (180°C). Line a 9 × 5 inch (2 L) loaf pan with parchment paper, leaving an overhang on the long sides. Lightly grease.

Combine milk and seeds in a small bowl. Stir gently to combine and let sit for 10 to 15 minutes.

In a medium bowl, combine dry ingredients.

In a large bowl, combine wet ingredients. Add milk and seed mixture and stir to combine.

Add dry ingredients, stir together until just combined, and then gently stir in dates.

Pour batter into prepared pan and bake for 45 minutes or until loaf is golden and springs back when touched.

Cool on a wire rack for 15 to 20 minutes. Lift from pan with overhanging parchment paper.

Serves 12 ‖ NUTRITION (per serving): energy 209 kcal | total fat 8 g | saturated fat 1 g | carbohydrate 33 g | fibre 4 g | protein 4 g | sodium 143 mg | excellent source of vitamin E

Shown with Pear Butter (see page 297)

blueberry buttermilk buckwheat pancakes

Pancakes can be served with many toppings. Try them with one of our Fruit Compotes (see page 281). You can convert this recipe into a savoury version by omitting the blueberries and adding grated zucchini, chopped chives, and a pinch of Parmesan cheese.

DRY INGREDIENTS

1 cup (250 ml) whole-wheat flour
1 cup (250 ml) buckwheat flour
2 teaspoons (10 ml) baking powder
¾ teaspoon (4 ml) baking soda
½ teaspoon (2 ml) ground cinnamon
½ teaspoon (2 ml) salt

WET INGREDIENTS

2 cups (500 ml) buttermilk
2 tablespoons (30 ml) honey
1 large egg
1 tablespoon (15 ml) canola oil, plus additional for cooking
finely grated zest from 1 lemon

2 to 3 cups (500 to 750 ml) blueberries, fresh or thawed from frozen

Preheat a large skillet over medium-high heat.

In a large bowl, whisk dry ingredients together until thoroughly combined.

In a separate bowl, mix 1 tablespoon of dry mixture with blueberries and set aside.

In a medium bowl, beat wet ingredients together. Pour wet ingredients over dry ingredients and whisk very gently until just combined. Do not over-mix; some lumps should remain in batter. Fold in blueberries.

Preheat oven to 200°F (95°C). Set a wire rack on a baking sheet.

Add 1 teaspoon of oil to preheated skillet and brush to coat. Ladle batter onto skillet. When small bubbles appear across surface of pancake, flip and continue cooking until pancakes are golden brown, about 1½ minutes per side. Transfer pancakes to prepared rack and place in oven. Repeat with remaining batter, using additional oil only if necessary.

Makes 12 pancakes ‖ NUTRITION (per 2 pancakes): energy 315 kcal | total fat 8 g | saturated fat 1 g | carbohydrate 52 g | fibre 5 g | protein 10 g | sodium 535 mg | excellent source of vitamin E, folate | good source of iron, thiamin, niacin, riboflavin, vitamin B12

 SMART TIP

To save time in the morning, mix the dry and wet ingredients separately the night before. In the morning, stir them together and cook.

mango lassi

INGREDIENTS

2 ripe mangoes, peel and stones removed, cut into chunks
1 cup (250 ml) low-fat plain Greek yogurt
1 tablespoon (15 ml) honey
2 cups (500 ml) ice cubes
½ teaspoon (2 ml) ground cardamom (optional)
1 tablespoon (15 ml) fresh basil leaves and additional leaves for garnish

Place all ingredients in a blender and process for 3 to 4 minutes until ice is crushed and drink is frothy.

Pour into glasses (with additional ice if desired) and garnish with finely chopped fresh basil leaves.

Serves 4 ‖ **NUTRITION** (per serving): energy 123 kcal | total fat 0 g | saturated fat 0 g | carbohydrate 23 g | fibre 2 g | protein 7 g | sodium 33 mg | good source of vitamin C, riboflavin

pb & j smoothie

INGREDIENTS

2 tablespoons (30 ml) Almond Butter (see page 296)
2 frozen bananas, thawed 15 minutes, peeled and quartered
1 cup (250 ml) milk (dairy, soy, or almond)
1 cup (250 ml) berries and/or stone fruits, fresh or frozen

Process all ingredients in a blender until smooth. Scrape down sides of blender with spatula as needed.

Pour into glasses and serve.

Serves 3 ‖ **NUTRITION** (per serving): energy 152 kcal | fat 3 g | saturated 0 g | carbohydrate 31 g | fibre 3 g | protein 5 g | sodium 38 mg | good source of riboflavin, vitamin B6, vitamin B12

abc juice

EXTRACTOR METHOD

Pulse all ingredients, one at a time, through the extractor into a small pitcher. Stir to blend.

Pour into glasses (with additional ice if desired) and serve.

HIGH-PERFORMANCE BLENDER METHOD

Cut apple and carrot into large chunks.

Peel beet, lemon, and ginger. Cut beet in half.

Process all ingredients along with 1 cup (250 ml) of water in blender until smooth. Add more water if mixture is too thick.

Pour into glasses (with ice if desired) and serve.

Serves 1 to 2 ‖ NUTRITION (per serving): energy 93 kcal | total fat 1 g | saturated fat 0 g | carbohydrate 23 g | fibre 5 g | protein 3 g | sodium 87 mg | excellent source of vitamin A, vitamin C, folate | good source of vitamin E, potassium, iron

INGREDIENTS

1 Granny Smith apple
1 large beet
1 large carrot
1 lemon
1-inch (2.5 cm) piece fresh ginger
1 cup (250 ml) lightly packed fresh spinach leaves
1 cup (250 ml) parsley, stems removed

> **SMART TIP**
>
> To dry washed glasses without streaks or spots, rest glasses upside down on two chopsticks laid out on a drying mat.

green goddess juice

EXTRACTOR METHOD

Pulse all ingredients one at a time through the extractor into a pitcher. Stir to blend.

BLENDER METHOD

Blend half of the kale leaves with coconut or honey water in a blender until smooth. Add remaining kale and blend until all leaves are completely broken down and the mixture is smooth.

Add remaining ingredients and process until the drink is frothy, about 2 minutes.

Pour into tall glasses (with ice if desired) and serve.

Serves 4 ‖ NUTRITION (per serving): energy 89 kcal | total fat 1 g | saturated fat 0 g | carbohydrate 23 g | fibre 3 g | protein 2 g | sodium 50 mg | excellent source of vitamin A, vitamin C

INGREDIENTS

2 cups (500 g) kale, centre ribs and stems discarded, leaves coarsely chopped
½ cup (125 ml) 100% pure coconut water, or ½ cup (125 ml) water plus 1 teaspoon (5 ml) honey
½ cup (125 ml) fresh lemon juice (extractor method: 2 lemons, peeled)
2 Granny Smith apples, cored and cut into chunks
1 cup (250 ml) coarsely chopped fresh pineapple
2 tablespoons (30 ml) minced fresh ginger

watermelon berry lemonade

INGREDIENTS

2 pounds (900 g) seedless watermelon, cut in
   large chunks
1 cup (250 ml) fresh raspberries and/or
   strawberries, plus a handful for garnish
1 cup (250 ml) 100% pure coconut water, or 1 cup
   (250 ml) water plus ½ tablespoon (7 ml) honey
½ cup (125 ml) fresh lemon juice
2 cups (500 ml) crushed ice, for serving

Process all ingredients in a blender until
smooth. Refrigerate until cold, about 2 to
3 hours.

Serve in tall glasses with ice. Garnish
with berries.

Serves 6 ‖ **NUTRITION** (per serving): energy
70 kcal | total fat 1 g | saturated fat 0 g | carbohydrate
17 g | fibre 3 g | protein 2 g | sodium 46 mg | good
source of vitamin C

iced chai

INGREDIENTS

3 chai tea bags
3 cups (750 ml) boiling water
½ tablespoon (7 ml) brown sugar (optional)
1½ cups (375 ml) cranberry juice
1½ cups (375 ml) apple cider
½ cup (125 ml) fresh berries (optional)
1 orange, thinly sliced
1 lemon, thinly sliced
2 cups (500 ml) crushed ice, for serving

Place tea bags in a large pitcher. Pour in boiling water and sugar, if using. Allow tea to steep for 10 to 15 minutes. Remove tea bags.

Add juice, cider, berries, and lemon and orange slices; stir to blend. Refrigerate about 2 to 3 hours until cold.

Serve in tall glasses with ice.

Serves 4 to 5 ‖ **NUTRITION** (per serving): energy 73 kcal | total fat 0 g | saturated fat 0 g | carbohydrate 19 g | fibre 0 g | protein 0 g | sodium 5 mg | excellent source of vitamin C

DR. JOE'S SMART FACT

Chai is a blend of black tea with various spices, commonly cardamom, ginger, cinnamon, fennel, cloves, and black pepper, which some believe improve digestion, enhance the immune system, and fight inflammation.

Smart snacking can help
keep your energy up
throughout the day.

snacks & tapas

taro root chips

Taro root can be found at most grocery stores that specialize in Asian produce. Full of natural sugars, this wonderful vegetable has a sweet and nutty flavour. Baked instead of fried, these chips have a crunchy texture without being greasy.

Position racks in the upper and lower thirds of the oven and preheat oven to 375°F (190°C). Lightly coat two large baking sheets with cooking spray.

Using a mandoline or hand-held slicer, slice taro root into very thin rounds (about 1/16 inch thick).

Place slices on paper towels in a single layer. Sprinkle with sea salt, let stand for 15 minutes, and blot dry.

Working in batches, place slices in a single layer on prepared baking sheets; slices may touch but should not overlap. Bake for 10 to 12 minutes. After 8 minutes, check every 2 minutes to make sure they do not burn. (Cooking times will vary depending on thickness of slices.) Remove from oven and sprinkle with additional salt, if desired.

Let cool on baking sheet for 5 minutes. Transfer to a bowl and wipe baking sheets clean. Repeat with more cooking spray and remaining taro root slices.

Serves 8 ‖ NUTRITION (per serving): energy 29 kcal | total fat 0 g | saturated fat 0 g | carbohydrate 7 g | fibre 1 g | protein 0 g | sodium 3 mg

INGREDIENTS

1 taro root, peeled
sea salt
olive oil cooking spray

 **SMART TIP**

Using a mandoline is a quick way to achieve very thin, uniform slices without the need for great knife skills, translating into even cooking and an impressive presentation.

DR. JOE'S SMART FACT

Taro is a root vegetable similar to the potato but is richer in potassium and has a significantly lower glycemic index. It must always be cooked or baked to reduce levels of naturally occurring calcium oxalate, a compound implicated in the formation of kidney stones.

beet dip

With a smooth texture and stunning fuchsia colour, this dip is as impressive as it is simple to prepare.

Preheat oven to 425°F (220°C).

Place beets and garlic on a double layer of aluminum foil. Drizzle with 1 tablespoon of the canola oil and sprinkle with salt and pepper. Fold up foil to seal. Transfer to a baking sheet and bake 60 to 70 minutes. When beets and garlic are cool enough to handle, rub beets with a paper towel to remove skins. Coarsely chop into cubes. Remove tip of roasted garlic clove and squeeze to release from peel.

Place chopped beets, roasted garlic, and chickpeas in food processor and pulse until combined. Add remaining ingredients and process until smooth.

If dip is too thick, thin by adding water, 1 tablespoon at a time, while the processor is running.

Serve at room temperature.

Makes about 3 cups ‖ NUTRITION (per 2 tablespoons): energy 28 kcal | total fat 2 g | saturated fat 0 g | carbohydrate 2 g | fibre 0 g | protein 1 g | sodium 47 mg

INGREDIENTS

2 medium beets, scrubbed
  and trimmed
4 large garlic cloves
2 tablespoons (30 ml) canola oil
½ cup (125 ml) cooked chickpeas
juice and finely grated zest of
  1 lemon
2 tablespoons (30 ml) tahini
1 teaspoon (5 ml) ground cumin
½ teaspoon (2 ml) kosher salt
¼ teaspoon (1 ml) freshly ground
  pepper

eggplant hummus

This hummus features eggplant as its main ingredient, creating a robust flavour that can't be beat. Grilling the eggplant adds a smoky nuance to this sophisticated snack.

INGREDIENTS

1 large eggplant
½ cup (125 ml) cooked chickpeas
juice and finely grated zest of 1 lemon
1 tablespoon (15 ml) tahini
1 garlic clove, minced
1 tablespoon (15 ml) roughly chopped fresh flat-leaf parsley
1 teaspoon (5 ml) kosher salt, plus more for seasoning
½ teaspoon (2 ml) freshly ground pepper, plus more for seasoning

Preheat oven to 350°F (180°C).

Pierce eggplant in 4 to 6 places with a fork. Place on rimmed baking sheet and bake for 30 minutes. Turn and continue to bake for an additional 30 to 45 minutes until eggplant is very soft. Alternatively, place on a hot barbecue and grill on medium-high heat, covered, for 15 to 20 minutes. Turn and barbecue for additional 15 minutes.

Remove from oven (or barbecue) and let stand until cool enough to handle.

Process chickpeas in a food processor until minced.

Slice cooked eggplant in half and scoop flesh into food processor (discard skin and juice). Add remaining ingredients and purée until mixture is almost smooth. Season to taste with salt and pepper.

Eggplant hummus can be stored in an airtight container in the refrigerator for up to 5 days.

Makes about 2 cups ‖ **NUTRITION** (per 2 tablespoons): energy 23 kcal | total fat 1 g | saturated fat 0 g | carbohydrate 4 g | fibre 2 g | protein 1 g | sodium 150 mg

Poppy seeds are a source of natural opiates (opium-containing drugs), but the levels are low. Although there have been cases of positive urine tests for opiates in people who consumed large amounts of poppy seeds, this merely demonstrates the sensitivity of the tests: no opiate-induced symptoms of any kind have been linked with the consumption of foods flavoured with poppy seeds.

sweet potato hummus

Sweet potato adds a whole new dimension to the hummus we know and love. This variation creates a rich and velvety dip or spread.

MICROWAVE METHOD

Microwave sweet potato on high 8 to 10 minutes until soft when pierced with a fork. Pause microwave halfway through cooking to flip and rotate sweet potato to ensure even cooking. Allow to cool, remove skin, and cut into pieces.

OVEN METHOD

Preheat oven to 400°F (200°C). Line a rimmed baking sheet with aluminum foil. Pierce sweet potatoes with a fork, place on prepared baking sheet, and bake for 45 to 60 minutes until soft. Allow to cool, remove skin, and cut into pieces.

Drop garlic through feed tube of food processor while machine is running. Add chickpeas and process until minced. With machine running, add tahini, lemon juice, salt, and ⅓ cup of stock through feed tube; process about 2 to 3 minutes until a very creamy and smooth paste is achieved. (For a thinner consistency, add more stock 2 tablespoons at a time.)

Serve at room temperature.

INGREDIENTS

1 medium to large sweet potato
3 garlic cloves, peeled
2 cups (500 ml) cooked chickpeas
2 tablespoons (30 ml) tahini
3 tablespoons (45 ml) fresh lemon juice
1 teaspoon (5 ml) kosher salt, plus more for seasoning
⅓ to ½ cup (75 to 125 ml) Vegetable Stock (see page 80) or water

Makes 3 cups ‖ **NUTRITION** (per 2 tablespoons): energy 21 kcal | total fat 1 g | saturated fat 0 g | carbohydrate 3 g | fibre 1 g | protein 1 g | sodium 88 mg

lavosh

These crackers can easily be customized for any taste or occasion. Other possibilities for toppings include sea salt, red pepper flakes, onion flakes, and sharp cheddar cheese.

Preheat oven to 400°F (200°C). Line a large baking sheet with parchment paper.

Using an electric stand mixer or a large bowl and a hand mixer, combine flour(s), sugar, and salt on low speed. Attach dough hook; add water, oil, and 1 egg white. Mix on medium speed about 5 to 7 minutes until dough is smooth and elastic.

In a small bowl, mix seeds together; set aside.

Turn dough out onto lightly floured surface and knead by hand to form a smooth, round ball. Divide dough into 4 equal pieces, brush with oil, and cover with a dishtowel or plastic wrap. Let rest at room temperature for 1 hour.

Divide each ball into 2 or 3 pieces. Using a rolling pin, roll each ball on a lightly floured work surface until thin. Transfer to prepared baking sheet. Brush with remaining egg white and sprinkle with seed mixture.

Bake about 12 to 15 minutes until browned, rotating pan halfway through baking.

Lavosh can be stored at room temperature in an airtight container for up to 2 weeks.

INGREDIENTS

2½ cups (625 ml) whole-wheat, rye, or multi-grain flour (or a combination of all three)
1 teaspoon (5 ml) granulated sugar
½ teaspoon (2 ml) salt
⅔ cup (150 ml) water
2 tablespoons (10 ml) olive oil, plus extra for brushing
2 large egg whites, in separate bowls
1 tablespoon (15 ml) sesame seeds
½ tablespoon (7 ml) each poppy seeds and caraway seeds

Makes 8–12 crackers ‖ **NUTRITION** (per cracker): energy 138 kcal | total fat 3 g | saturated fat 0 g | carbohydrate 23 g | fibre 3 g | protein 6 g | sodium 107 mg | good source of niacin

apple pomegranate guacamole

INGREDIENTS

2 ripe avocados, halved and pitted
¼ cup (60 ml) finely chopped white onion
1 serrano chili pepper, diced very small (include seeds)
½ teaspoon (2 ml) kosher salt, plus more for seasoning
¼ cup (60 ml) fresh lime juice
½ cup (125 ml) pomegranate seeds
1 Granny Smith apple, diced small
¼ cup (60 ml) finely chopped fresh herbs, according to preference: dill, cilantro, flat-leaf parsley

This guacamole is as good as it gets. The richness of avocado blended with the tartness of apples results in an explosion of tastes and textures. Retire the classic version; this one's a keeper!

Scoop flesh from avocados into a large bowl; coarsely mash until as smooth or as chunky as desired. Stir in onion, chilies, salt, and lime juice. Gently fold in remaining ingredients.

Taste and adjust with additional salt and lime juice if necessary.

Makes 1½ cups ‖ NUTRITION (per 2 tablespoons): energy 70 kcal | total fat 5 g | saturated fat 1 g | carbohydrate 7 g | fibre 3 g | protein 1 g | sodium 82 mg

rosemary almond crackers

INGREDIENTS

½ cup (125 ml) ground flax seed
¼ cup (60 ml) water
2 cups (500 ml) ground raw almonds
2 tablespoons (30 ml) finely chopped fresh rosemary
½ teaspoon (2 ml) salt
1 tablespoon (15 ml) extra-virgin olive oil
1 large egg

Easy to make, these gluten-free crackers are seasoned to perfection with fresh rosemary and have a subtle nutty flavour.

Preheat oven to 350°F (180°C). Line a large baking sheet with two layers of parchment paper.

Mix flax seeds and water and let sit about 15 minutes until water is absorbed.

In a large bowl, combine almonds, rosemary, and salt.

In a small bowl, whisk oil and egg together and add flax seed and water mixture; stir to combine.

Pour egg and flax seed mixture into almond mixture and stir until thoroughly combined.

Transfer dough onto a pan lined with parchment paper. Cover dough with a second sheet of parchment paper. Using the palm of your hand or a rolling pin, push and spread dough to form an even layer about ⅛-inch (3 mm) thick.

Remove top piece of parchment paper and cut dough into desired shapes using a knife, pizza wheel, or cookie cutter.

Bake for 15 to 20 minutes until lightly golden.

Let crackers cool on baking sheet.

Makes about 60 crackers ‖ NUTRITION (per 5 crackers): energy 140 kcal | total fat 12 g | saturated fat 1 g | carbohydrate 5 g | fibre 4 g | protein 5 g | sodium 86 mg | excellent source of vitamin E | good source of riboflavin

SMART TIP

To prevent discoloration, firmly pat guacamole into container to eliminate air pockets. Pour ½ inch of water over surface, cover with tight-fitting lid, and place in refrigerator. When ready to use, remove water and stir.

DR. JOE'S SMART FACT

The fat content of avocados, although high, is mostly of the monounsaturated and poly-unsaturated varieties, which do not increase the risk of heart disease. In fact, preliminary studies indicate that high avocado intake can lower blood cholesterol.

peaches 'n "cream" crostini

Grilled peaches make a refreshing topping for this delicious snack. The recipe for a lighter "cheese spread" can be used to turn a slice of apple or pear into a wonderful hors d'oeuvre.

CHEESE SPREAD

½ cup (125 ml) feta cheese
¼ cup (60 ml) ricotta cheese, room temperature
1 tablespoon (15 ml) extra-virgin olive oil
1 tablespoon (15 ml) fresh lemon juice
½ tablespoon (7 ml) finely grated lemon zest
¼ teaspoon (1 ml) freshly ground pepper

PEACH TOPPING

2 ripe but firm peaches, cut in half and pitted
extra-virgin olive oil for brushing
1 tablespoon (15 ml) finely chopped fresh thyme leaves

1 small whole-wheat or multi-grain baguette, cut on the diagonal
    into ½-inch (1 cm) slices
honey for drizzling

Pulse feta and ricotta cheeses in a food processor until mixed. Add remaining spread ingredients and process until smooth.

Preheat barbecue or grill pan to medium-low heat. Brush peach halves lightly with oil. Grill peaches for about 8 minutes until lightly charred and softened, turning once halfway through cooking. Remove from heat, let cool several minutes, and then dice. While peaches are cooling, preheat oven to 425°F (220°C).

Place bread slices on baking sheet and lightly brush with oil. Bake for 5 to 7 minutes until lightly browned. Remove from oven and spread each slice of bread with ricotta and feta mixture.

Using a spoon, place peaches on top of cheese spread. Transfer to serving platter and sprinkle with thyme and honey.

Serve immediately.

Makes 24 crostini || NUTRITION (per serving): energy 64 kcal | total fat 2 g | saturated fat 1 g | carbohydrate 8 g | fibre 1 g | protein 3 g | sodium 123 mg

leek zucchini pesto flatbread

Flatbread is typically made without yeast and rolled out into a thin layer before baking. Brimming with an assortment of tasty ingredients, this version is truly yummy!

INGREDIENTS

2 teaspoons (10 ml) canola oil
1 large leek, white and pale green part only, thinly sliced
1 zucchini, julienned
kosher salt and freshly ground pepper
one 12-inch (30 cm) whole-wheat flatbread or thin pizza crust
⅓ cup (75 ml) Low-Fat Pesto (see page 302)
1 cup (250 ml) lightly packed fresh spinach leaves
¼ cup (60 ml) feta cheese, crumbled (optional)
2 tablespoons (20 ml) finely chopped fresh basil for garnish
finely grated zest of 1 lemon

Preheat oven to 450°F (230°C). Line a large baking sheet with parchment paper.

Heat oil in a large, non-stick saucepan over medium heat. Add leeks and zucchini and sauté, stirring, about 8 to 10 minutes until bright green and wilted. Season with salt and pepper.

Lay flatbread on prepared baking sheet and spread with pesto, leaving a 1-inch (2.5 cm) border. Scatter spinach leaves over top and cover with leeks, zucchini and feta, if using.

Bake for 5 to 7 minutes until the edges are golden and leeks have started to crisp.

Let cool on a wire rack. Just before serving, slice flatbread, transfer to serving platter, and sprinkle with chopped basil and lemon zest.

Serves 6 as an appetizer ‖ NUTRITION (per serving): energy 59 kcal | total fat 3 g | saturated fat 1 g | carbohydrate 6 g | fibre 1 g | protein 2 g | sodium 112 mg

DR. JOE'S SMART FACT

Like garlic and onions, leeks are a member of the allium family. Flavonoids, a type of antioxidant, are present in leeks but are most concentrated in the lower leaf and bulb portion.

mini mac 'n cheese

Kids and adults alike will love these scrumptious mini "muffins." Packed with spinach, these nutritious treasures are made healthier with whole grain pasta and ricotta cheese. Light on fat, full on flavour!

FILLING

1 pound (455 g) dry whole-wheat elbow macaroni
2 large eggs
1½ cups (370 ml) low-fat evaporated milk
2 cups (500 ml) low-fat ricotta cheese
1 tablespoon (15 ml) Dijon mustard
1½ teaspoons (7 ml) salt
½ teaspoon (2 ml) freshly ground pepper
8 ounces (225 g) fresh baby spinach
1 tablespoon (15 ml) olive oil
a few grape tomatoes and fresh herbs for garnish

Preheat oven to 375°F (190°C). Grease 2 mini muffin tins liberally.

Bring a large pot of water to a boil. Add macaroni and cook for about 6 minutes until just tender. Drain pasta well.

In a medium bowl whisk eggs, evaporated milk, ricotta, mustard, 1 teaspoon salt, and ½ teaspoon pepper. Set aside.

Heat oil in a large skillet over medium heat. Add spinach and ½ teaspoon of salt and cook about 1 to 2 minutes until spinach begins to wilt. Reduce heat to low. Add drained pasta and cheese mixture and stir about 5 minutes until creamy.

Working in batches (if necessary), fill each muffin cup to the rim with the mixture. Bake about 10 to 15 minutes until sauce is bubbling.

Unmould muffins using a sharp knife. Serve warm on a platter garnished with tomatoes and herbs.

Store leftover muffins in the freezer. Reheat in oven or microwave.

Makes 48 mini or 24 regular "muffins" ||
NUTRITION (per 2 mini "muffins"): energy 121 kcal | total fat 3 g | saturated fat 1 g | carbohydrate 18 g | fibre 2 g | protein 7 g | sodium 200 mg | good source of niacin

grilled avocado seafood salad

This salad makes a nice light lunch or hearty afternoon snack. Grilling avocados takes them to a whole new level, and they can be stuffed with virtually anything. Be adventurous!

SEAFOOD SALAD

½ pound (225 g) pre-cooked lobster, lump crab meat, or tuna
¼ cup (60 ml) low-fat plain Greek yogurt
¼ cup (60 ml) celery, diced small
2 tablespoons (30 ml) finely chopped chives
juice and finely grated zest of 1 lemon
½ teaspoon (2 ml) Sriracha sauce, or more to taste
kosher salt and freshly ground pepper, to taste

2 avocados, halved and pitted
olive oil for brushing
kosher salt and freshly ground pepper

In a medium bowl, combine all ingredients for seafood salad. Cover and refrigerate until ready to use.

Preheat barbecue to medium-high.

Brush avocado halves with olive oil and sprinkle with salt and pepper. Grill, cut-side down, for about 3 to 5 minutes. Transfer to serving platter.

Using a slotted spoon, place about ¼ cup (125 ml) of seafood salad (or other filling) into each avocado half.

Serve immediately.

Serves 4 ‖ NUTRITION (per serving): energy 228 kcal | total fat 15 g | saturated fat 2 g | carbohydrate 11 g | fibre 7 g | protein 16 g | sodium 238 mg | excellent source of niacin and vitamin B12 | good source of potassium, vitamin E, riboflavin, folate, and vitamin B6

veggie dumplings with soy dipping sauce

These pillowy Asian-inspired parcels are sure to impress! They are delicious in any broth or served warm and accompanied by an aromatic dipping sauce. Double the recipe for a crowd or keep frozen for when guests arrive unexpectedly.

Combine all ingredients for soy dipping sauce in a small bowl and set aside.

Cut tofu in half horizontally and place on a flat surface covered with several layers of paper towel. Cover with paper towel; place a weight on top and let stand at least 20 minutes, allowing excess water to drain.

Coarsely chop cabbage, carrot, red pepper, and scallions in a food processor. Transfer to a bowl.

Drop garlic and ginger through feed tube and process until minced. Add drained tofu, egg, soy sauce, oil, cilantro, salt, and pepper and process until well blended. Return reserved chopped vegetables and pulse until mixture is well combined and coarsely minced.

Line a large baking sheet with parchment paper.

Remove 6 wonton wrappers from the package, covering remainder with a damp clean dishcloth. Place 1 full teaspoon of mixture in centre of each wrapper. Dip a pastry brush in water and moisten edge of wrappers. Bring sides of wrapper up and over filling and press edges together to seal. If dumpling does not seal, moisten edges with a little more water. Set finished dumplings on prepared baking sheet, making sure none are touching, and repeat until all filling is used.

Dumplings should be steamed or boiled immediately or stored in freezer for future use. Freeze on baking sheet and transfer to storage container when frozen.

To steam, line the bottom of the steamer compartment with a banana leaf. Arrange dumplings in a single layer on leaf. Steam over high heat for 10 to 15 minutes.

To boil, place dumplings in a large pot of rapidly boiling salted water for about 5 to 7 minutes until dumplings rise to surface.

Serve warm with soy dipping sauce.

SOY DIPPING SAUCE

2 tablespoons (30 ml) low-sodium
   soy sauce
1 tablespoon (15 ml) seasoned
   rice vinegar
1 tablespoon (15 ml) honey
1 teaspoon (5 ml) hot chili oil
1 teaspoon (5 ml) fresh garlic,
   minced
1 teaspoon (5 ml) fresh ginger,
   minced

DUMPLINGS

8 ounces (225 g) firm tofu
½ cup (125 ml) napa cabbage
1 large carrot, peeled and
   cut in thirds
¼ red bell pepper, seeds removed
   and cut in chunks
1 scallion, cut in thirds
2 cloves garlic, peeled
1-inch (2.5 cm) piece of fresh
   ginger, peeled
1 egg
1 tablespoon (15 ml) low-sodium
   soy sauce
2 teaspoons (10 ml) sesame oil
1 tablespoon (15 ml) fresh cilantro
½ teaspoon (2 ml) salt
¼ teaspoon (1 ml) freshly
   ground pepper
1 package round dumpling
   wrappers or small won ton
   wrappers, thawed from frozen
1 banana leaf for steaming,
   available frozen at most Asian
   food stores (optional)

Makes 40 dumplings ‖ NUTRITION (per dumpling): energy 33 kcal | total fat 1 g | saturated fat 0 g | carbohydrate 5 g | fibre 0 g | protein 2 g | sodium 86 mg

vegetarian quesadillas

This flavourful version of a Mexican specialty will satisfy carnivores and vegetarians alike. Olé!

BEAN MIXTURE

2 tablespoons (30 ml) canola oil, divided
½ small red onion, finely chopped
2 scallions, finely chopped
3 garlic cloves, minced
¾ cup (175 ml) cooked black beans
¾ cup (175 ml) corn kernels, fresh or frozen

CARROT MIXTURE

1 medium carrot, diced small
½ red bell pepper, diced small
1 jalapeño pepper, seeded and diced small
2 tablespoons (30 ml) finely chopped fresh cilantro
1 tablespoon (15 ml) finely chopped fresh flat-leaf parsley
1½ tablespoons (22 ml) fresh lemon juice
pinch of cayenne pepper
pinch of ground cumin
pinch of chili powder

four 9-inch (23 cm) whole-wheat flour tortillas
½ cup (125 ml) Stone Fruit Salsa (see page 301)
½ cup (125 ml) grated low-fat cheddar cheese
vegetable oil cooking spray

Preheat oven to 350°F (180°C). Lightly grease a large baking sheet with cooking spray.

Heat 1 tablespoon of oil in a large skillet over medium heat. Add onions, scallions, and garlic, and sauté about 5 minutes until softened. Stir in cooked beans and cook until heated through. Remove from heat and transfer to a large bowl. Purée one-third of the bean mixture in a blender or food processor, then return mixture to bowl.

Heat remaining tablespoon of oil in skillet over medium heat. Sauté carrots, red bell pepper, and jalapeño about 5 minutes until tender. Remove from heat and add cilantro, parsley, lemon juice, and seasonings. Mix well. Transfer to bean mixture and combine.

Lay tortillas on baking sheet. Spread a couple of tablespoons of the bean and carrot mixtures on one half of each tortilla. Cover with two tablespoons of salsa and sprinkle with a tablespoon of cheese. Fold other half over to cover. Repeat with remaining tortillas.

Bake for 6 to 8 minutes, or until tortillas are hot and cheese has melted.

Makes 4 quesadillas ‖ NUTRITION (per quesadilla): energy 313 kcal | total fat 10 g | saturated fat 1 g | carbohydrate 45 g | fibre 7 g | protein 12 g | sodium 115 mg | excellent source of fibre, vitamin C, vitamin E, folate | good source of vitamin A, calcium, thiamin, niacin, vitamin B6

Shown with Stone Fruit Salsa (page 301)

spicy nuts and seeds

Nuts are loaded with protein, healthy fats, and fibre, making them a beneficial snack food when eaten in moderation. This irresistible mixture is both sweet and piquant.

Preheat oven to 300°F (150°C). Line a large, rimmed baking sheet with parchment paper. Lightly grease parchment paper.

Combine spices in a large bowl. Add nuts and seeds; toss until coated.

Spread nuts on prepared sheet in a single layer. Bake, stirring every 5 minutes until lightly toasted, about 15 to 20 minutes.

Remove from oven and let cool. Store in an airtight container for up to 2 weeks, or in the freezer for up to 3 months.

Makes 3 cups ‖ NUTRITION (per 2 tablespoons): energy 90 kcal | total fat 8 g | saturated fat 1 g | carbohydrate 4 g | fibre 1 g | protein 3 g | sodium 21 mg | good source of vitamin E

SEASONING

2 tablespoons (30 ml) finely chopped fresh rosemary
½ teaspoon (2 ml) ground cumin
¼ teaspoon (1 ml) kosher salt
pinch of finely crushed red pepper flakes or cayenne powder
2 tablespoons (30 ml) pure maple syrup

NUTS AND SEEDS

½ cup (125 ml) raw almonds
½ cup (125 ml) raw walnuts
½ cup (125 ml) raw hazelnuts
½ cup (125 ml) raw cashews
¼ cup (60 ml) raw pistachios
¼ cup (60 ml) raw pumpkin seeds
¼ cup (60 ml) raw sunflower seeds

SMART TIP

Because nuts contain a lot of oil, they spoil quickly and should be kept in airtight containers or resealable plastic bags in the freezer.

DR. JOE'S SMART FACT

People who eat nuts are not nutty. Yes, nuts have a lot of fat, but these are of the beneficial polyunsaturated and monounsaturated variety. Eating nuts does not appear to cause weight gain and can make you feel satiated and less likely to overeat. A handful of walnuts contain almost twice the antioxidants by weight as an equivalent amount of any other commonly consumed nut.

roasted chickpeas

The perfect crunchy and savoury snack, this is sure to appease any late-afternoon craving.

INGREDIENTS

1 cup (250 ml) dry chickpeas
1 tablespoon (15 ml) canola oil
2 teaspoons (10 ml) dried oregano
1 teaspoon (5 ml) chili powder
1 teaspoon (5 ml) curry powder
1 teaspoon (5 ml) kosher salt
¼ teaspoon (1 ml) freshly ground pepper

Soak dry chickpeas in water for 6 hours or overnight.

Preheat oven to 400°F (200°C). Lightly grease a rimmed baking sheet.

Drain chickpeas and pat with a dishcloth until dry.

Combine remaining ingredients in a large bowl. Add chickpeas and toss until coated. Spread chickpeas on prepared sheet in a single layer.

Bake on middle rack of oven for 30 minutes, tossing after 20 minutes. Turn off oven and let chickpeas sit for 15 minutes. Check often, as they burn easily. Remove from oven and cool on a wire rack.

Roasted Chickpeas can be stored for up to 2 weeks in an airtight container, or in the freezer for up to 3 months.

Makes 2½ cups ‖ NUTRITION (per 2 tablespoons): energy 106 kcal | total fat 4 g | saturated fat 0 g | carbohydrate 14 g | fibre 3 g | protein 4 g | sodium 248 mg | excellent source of folate | good source of vitamin E

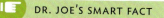 DR. JOE'S SMART FACT

Chickpeas, particularly when sprouted, are a source of isoflavones, which are natural estrogens. Current animal research suggests that isoflavones isolated from chickpea sprouts can curb bone loss. This has suggested to researchers that such extracts may have potential for the treatment of human menopausal symptoms and osteoporosis related to estrogen deficiency.

Pepitas, the Spanish culinary term for shelled pumpkin seeds, are a source of L-tryptophan, the body's precursor for serotonin, a neurotransmitter with anti-anxiety properties. They are also a good source of protein, iron, zinc, manganese, magnesium, phosphorus, copper, and potassium. Only 25 grams of pepitas can provide over 20% of the recommended daily iron intake.

multi-seed squares

Light as a feather, these sweet and salty squares have a delightful crunch. Packed with protein, they are perfect for keeping your energy levels stable throughout the day.

Preheat oven to 200°F (95°C). Line a 10-inch (25 cm) square baking pan with parchment paper, leaving an overhang on two parallel sides.

Mix all ingredients in large bowl until well combined.

Pour mixture into prepared pan. Wet hands and press mixture into an even layer.

Bake about 3 to 3½ hours until dry. Turn off oven and let cool in oven for 1 hour.

When completely cool, cut into 1-inch (2.5 cm) squares.

Store in an airtight container at room temperature or in the refrigerator or freezer.

Makes 90 to 100 squares ‖ **NUTRITION** (per square): energy 43 kcal | total fat 3 g | saturated fat 1 g | carbohydrate 3 g | fibre 1 g | protein 2 g | sodium 10 mg

INGREDIENTS

3 cups (750 ml) raw pumpkin seeds
1 cup (250 ml) dried cherries, roughly chopped
½ cup (125 ml) raw sunflower seeds
½ cup (125 ml) white sesame seeds
½ cup (125 ml) coarsely ground flax seeds
½ teaspoon (2 ml) salt
5 tablespoons (75 ml) honey

SMART TIP

Keep healthy snacks up front in the pantry or refrigerator so they are an easy grab!

no-bake powerballs

This no-bake snack is perfect for any time of day, but especially for a late-afternoon boost.

In a large bowl, combine all dry ingredients.

In a separate large bowl, combine wet ingredients. Add dry ingredients to wet ingredients and mix until well blended.

Place in refrigerator for about 30 minutes.

Remove from fridge. Working with slightly wet hands, form into balls by squeezing a heaping tablespoon of mixture and then rolling it into a ball. If the mixture is too sticky, add a little more oat bran.

Store in an airtight container in refrigerator or freezer.

Makes 24 balls ‖ **NUTRITION** (per ball): energy 79 kcal | total fat 4 g | saturated fat 1 g | carbohydrate 10 g | fibre 2 g | protein 3 g | sodium 2 mg

DRY INGREDIENTS

1 cup (250 ml) rolled oats
¼ cup (60 ml) unsweetened coconut flakes
¼ cup (60 ml) lightly ground flax seeds
¼ cup (60 ml) oat bran
¼ cup (60 ml) raw sunflower seeds
¼ cup (60 ml) raw pumpkin seeds
1 to 2 teaspoons (5 to 10 ml) ground cinnamon or ground cardamom

WET INGREDIENTS

½ cup (125 ml) Almond or Cashew Butter (see page 296)
⅓ cup (75 ml) honey
1 teaspoon (5 ml) pure vanilla extract
pinch of kosher salt

Nourish the body and nurture the soul. Eat soup in all its forms.

soups

vegetable stock

A flavourful stock is the key to successful soups. This one is so easy to make that you will never use store-bought stock again! It is a good idea to use equal portions of vegetables to give your stock a balanced flavour. Vegetables slightly past their prime have a deeper flavour and are a good choice to use, but avoid any that are too far gone, as they will impart a bitter taste. Chop your vegetables well so the flavours can be more quickly and easily drawn out.

SMART TIP

Prevent the stock from becoming cloudy by skimming it frequently as it cooks, especially during the first hour. Use a ladle to remove impurities and fat that rise to the surface.

INGREDIENTS

3 tablespoons (45 ml) extra-virgin olive oil
1 medium onion, peeled
1 leek, rinsed and roughly chopped
3 carrots, roughly chopped
3 celery stalks, roughly chopped
1 cup (250 ml) roughly chopped mushrooms
2 garlic cloves, peeled and sliced
8 to 10 cups (2 to 2.3 L) water
10 sprigs fresh parsley
8 sprigs fresh thyme
½ teaspoon (2 ml) whole peppercorns
2 bay leaves

Heat oil in a large pot over medium-high heat. Add onion and leek and cook, stirring often, about 10 to 15 minutes until they begin to brown. Add remaining vegetables and garlic and cook, stirring occasionally, for about another 10 minutes until vegetables are tender and lightly browned. Add water, cover, and bring to a low boil. Reduce heat to medium-low.

Cook, uncovered, for 1 to 1½ hours. Skim surface to remove any impurities or fat. Stir occasionally.

Remove pot from stove and set aside until cool enough to handle.

Pour vegetables and stock through a fine sieve set over a large bowl and press vegetables to extract as much liquid as possible. Discard solids.

Cool stock for a while and divide into small containers, ice-cube trays, or freezer-safe resealable bags. When completely cool, transfer to refrigerator or freezer. Stock will keep for 2 to 3 days refrigerated, or for several months in the freezer

Makes about 8 cups || **NUTRITION** (per 1½ cups): energy 20 kcal | total fat 0 g | saturated fat 0 g | carbohydrate 11 g | fibre 0 g | protein 1 g

chicken stock

There is an incredible difference between homemade and store-bought chicken stock. This recipe is easy and makes your house smell yummy!

INGREDIENTS

5 pounds (2.2 kg) chicken parts, such as backs, necks, giblets, and wings
16 cups (4 L) water
2 medium leeks, rinsed and roughly chopped
2 carrots, roughly chopped
2 celery stalks, roughly chopped
2 parsnips, roughly chopped
10 sprigs fresh parsley
10 sprigs fresh dill
8 sprigs fresh thyme
10 whole peppercorns

Place chicken parts and water in a large stockpot over medium-high heat and bring to a boil. Skim off any scum that comes to the surface.

Add remaining ingredients and reduce heat to a gentle simmer. Cook, uncovered, skimming frequently, for 1½ to 2½ hours. Stir occasionally.

Remove pot from stove and set aside until cool enough to handle. Pour stock through a sieve set over a large bowl. Discard solids. Refrigerate at least 8 hours to allow fat to accumulate at the top. Skim off and discard fat.

Divide stock into small containers, ice-cube trays, or freezer-safe resealable bags. When completely cool, transfer to refrigerator or freezer. Stock will keep for 2 to 3 days refrigerated, or for several months in the freezer.

Makes between 8 and 12 cups ‖ **NUTRITION** (per 1½ cups): energy 20 kcal | total fat 0 g | saturated fat 0 g | carbohydrate 11 g | fibre 0 g | protein 1 g

SMART TIP

Always save backs and necks from chicken and store them in the freezer. When your storage bag is full, it is time to make stock.

emerald summer soup

A medley of green vegetables and fruit infused with mint and citrus, this chilled soup is sure to awaken your palate on a hot summer day.

INGREDIENTS

½ English cucumber, cut into large chunks
½ green bell pepper, seeded and cut in half
2 celery stalks, cut into large slices
6 scallions, white and pale green parts only, cut into large slices
1 cup (250 ml) seedless green grapes
1 cup (250 ml) lightly packed fresh baby spinach
2 tablespoons (30 ml) fresh mint leaves
2 cups (500 ml) white grape juice
zest and juice from 1 lime
1 ripe avocado, pit and peel removed
1 teaspoon (5 ml) kosher salt, plus more for seasoning
½ teaspoon (2 ml) white pepper, plus more for seasoning
mint sprigs for garnish

Place cucumber in food processor and pulse until finely chopped. Do not purée completely. Transfer to a large mixing bowl. Process green bell pepper, celery, scallions, grapes, spinach, and mint, each in turn separately.

Place grape juice, lime zest, avocado, salt and pepper in food processor and pulse until combined. Return vegetables to processor and process until smooth. Taste, adding more salt and pepper if necessary.

Transfer to container, cover and chill at least 4 hours.

To serve, ladle soup into chilled soup bowls and garnish with a dollop of yogurt and a mint sprig.

Serves 8 to 10 ‖ **NUTRITION** (per serving): energy 106 kcal | total fat 4 g | saturated fat 0 g | carbohydrate 18 g | fibre 3 g | protein 2 g | sodium 316 mg

SMART TIP

To get the most juice a lime has to offer, roll the lime on a countertop to soften the membranes slightly, then slice in half and squeeze out the juice!

chickpea soup with chunky gazpacho topping

The main attraction of this tasty soup is, without a doubt, its stunning presentation. A sprinkling of crumbled feta adds just enough substance to turn this soup into a wonderful light lunch.

GAZPACHO TOPPING

1 cup (250 ml) diced medium English cucumber, divided
1 cup (250 ml) red, yellow, and purple cherry tomatoes, quartered
½ cup (125 ml) diced medium red and yellow bell peppers
3 tablespoons (45 ml) finely chopped red onion
3 tablespoons (45 ml) pitted kalamata olives, quartered
¼ cup (60 ml) finely chopped fresh herbs: cilantro, flat-leaf parsley, or dill
1 teaspoon (5 ml) kosher salt
½ teaspoon (2 ml) freshly ground pepper

SOUP

3 cups (750 ml) cooked chickpeas
1 tablespoon (15 ml) extra-virgin olive oil
3 tablespoons (45 ml) fresh lemon juice
3 tablespoons (45 ml) tahini
2 garlic cloves, peeled and coarsely chopped
½ teaspoon (2 ml) ground cumin
½ teaspoon (2 ml) cayenne pepper
¼ teaspoon (1 ml) coarse salt
¼ teaspoon (1 ml) white pepper
¾ cup (175 ml) crumbled feta cheese for garnish
kosher salt and freshly ground pepper

In a small bowl, combine ⅔ cup (150 ml) diced cucumber and remaining topping ingredients. Sprinkle with salt and pepper; set aside.

In a blender, combine remaining cucumber and soup ingredients (except cheese).

Gradually add 2 to 3 cups (500 to 750 ml) water and blend until smooth and thin enough to pour.

Taste and adjust seasoning if necessary. Pour soup into a large pitcher.

Divide gazpacho topping into individual serving bowls. Bring bowls, soup pitcher, and feta cheese to table. Pour soup over vegetables and top with feta.

Serves 8 ‖ **NUTRITION** (per serving): energy 168 kcal | total fat 7 g | saturated fat 1 g | carbohydrate 22 g | fibre 4 g | protein 7 g | sodium 398 mg | excellent source of folate | good source of iron, vitamin C

grandma's chicken soup

An apple, the secret ingredient, provides a hint of sweetness to this soup, making this recipe just what the doctor ordered.

INGREDIENTS

4 to 5 pound (1.8 to 2.2 kg) kosher chicken, divided into quarters, fat trimmed and discarded
2 pounds (1 kg) chicken bones
12 cups (3 L) water
4 carrots, peeled and sliced in half lengthwise
4 parsnips, peeled and sliced in half lengthwise
2 leeks, white and pale-green part only, halved lengthwise
2 celery stalks (with leaves), halved
1 medium onion
1 Macintosh apple
½ bunch flat-leaf parsley
½ bunch fresh dill, plus additional for garnish
1 teaspoon (5 ml) coarse salt, plus more for seasoning
½ teaspoon (2 ml) freshly ground pepper, plus more for seasoning

Bring chicken and water to a boil in a large soup pot over high heat. Skim off the fat. Reduce heat and add vegetables. Place apple on top of soup, cover, and let simmer gently for 2 to 3 hours. Add more water as necessary to cover chicken and vegetables.

Remove and discard apple, leeks, celery, and onion. Remove carrots, parsnip, and chicken from pot. Transfer to a large bowl. When cool enough to handle, slice carrots and parsnips, remove meat from bones, and return to pot if serving with soup, or save for another use.

Taste and adjust seasoning with salt and pepper as needed.

Ladle hot soup into serving bowls and sprinkle with finely chopped dill.

Serves 12 to 14 || **NUTRITION** (per serving, including chicken, carrots, and parsnips): energy 176 kcal | total fat 5 g | saturated fat 1 g | carbohydrate 12 g | fibre 2 g | protein 21 g | sodium 284 mg | excellent source of vitamin A, niacin, vitamin B6 | good source of riboflavin

SMART TIP

Freezing expands liquids, so always allow at least 1 inch of space at the top of container before placing it in the freezer.

carrot ginger soup

An abundance of sweet carrots contrasted with the tartness of apple is what sets this soup apart. A feast for the eyes and the palate.

INGREDIENTS

1 pound (455 g) carrots, peeled and roughly chopped
2 teaspoons (10 ml) ground cumin or sweet smoked paprika
1 tablespoon (15 ml) canola oil, plus more for drizzling
½ cup (125 ml) coarsely chopped onion
3 tablespoons (45 ml) coarsely chopped fresh ginger
1 medium apple, peeled, cored, and diced medium
1 tablespoon (15 ml) finely grated orange zest
6 cups (1.5 L) Vegetable Stock (see page 80)
fresh chives, finely chopped, for garnish
¼ cup (60 ml) roughly chopped raw pistachios, toasted,
   for garnish
kosher salt and freshly ground pepper, to taste

Preheat oven to 375°F (190°C).

Place carrots on a rimmed baking sheet, sprinkle with 1 teaspoon of cumin, and salt and pepper to taste, then drizzle with oil. Toss well to coat. Bake about 45 minutes until tender and slightly browned. Toss at least once during baking.

Meanwhile, heat 1 tablespoon of oil in a large soup pot over medium heat. Add onions and sauté about 5 minutes until softened.

Add ginger, apple, orange zest, and remaining teaspoon of cumin and sauté for another 3 minutes.

Add roasted carrots and stock, bring soup to a boil, then reduce heat to low and simmer for 40 to 50 minutes.

Remove from heat and purée soup with an immersion blender or in batches using a blender or food processor. Add more vegetable stock, if needed, to thin. Taste, adding more salt and pepper if necessary.

Ladle soup into serving bowls and garnish with chives and pistachios.

Serves 10 ‖ **NUTRITION** (per serving): energy 53 kcal | total fat 2 g | saturated fat 0 g | sodium 117 mg | carbohydrate 9 g | fibre 2 g | protein 1 g | excellent source of vitamin C

indo-mex soup

Is this a Mexican chili, or an Indian curry soup? Either way, this eclectic soup is perfectly balanced and deliciously hearty.

INGREDIENTS

½ tablespoon (7 ml) canola oil
1½ cups (375 ml) finely chopped onion
4 garlic cloves, minced
2 tablespoons (30 ml) minced fresh ginger
1 to 2 jalapeño or Thai chili peppers (depending on desired heat), seeded and finely chopped
1 teaspoon (5 ml) ground cumin
2 teaspoons (10 ml) ground curry powder
¼ teaspoon (1 ml) ground turmeric
5 cups (1.25 L) Vegetable or Chicken Stock (see pages 80 and 81) or water
28-ounce (796 ml) can chopped plum tomatoes, with juice
2 cups (500 ml) cooked kidney beans
2 cups (500 ml) cooked black beans
1 teaspoon (5 ml) kosher salt, plus more for seasoning
½ teaspoon (2 ml) freshly ground pepper, plus more for seasoning
1 tablespoon (15 ml) finely chopped chives for garnish
Roasted Chickpeas (see page 75) for garnish

Heat oil in a large soup pot over medium heat. Add onions and sauté about 5 minutes until soft and golden.

Add ginger, chili peppers, and spices. Let cook, stirring occasionally, about 30 seconds until fragrant. Add stock, tomatoes, beans, salt, and pepper. Bring to a boil, reduce heat, and let simmer about 10 minutes until thickened slightly.

Remove from heat and purée soup with an immersion blender, or in batches using a food processor, leaving a bit of texture. Taste, adding more salt and pepper if necessary.

Ladle soup into serving bowls and garnish with roasted chickpeas.

Serves 10 ‖ **NUTRITION** (per serving): energy 153 kcal | total fat 2 g | saturated fat 0 g | carbohydrate 29 g | fibre 7 g | protein 7 g | sodium 528 mg | excellent source of folate, vitamin B6 | good source of iron, thiamin

Shown with Roasted Chickpeas (see page 75)

DR. JOE'S SMART FACT

What makes the chili pepper so hot? Capsaicin. The more capsaicin, the hotter the pepper, and the hotter the pepper, the higher the antioxidant level. Depending on the tongue's nerve cells, people either love or hate the spiciness of peppers. Interestingly enough, the presence of capsaicin is likely an evolutionary adaptation to ward off foraging animals.

soupe au pistou

Pistou is similar to pesto in that it is a cold sauce made from fresh garlic, basil, and olive oil, but unlike pesto it contains no pine nuts. It is added to the bowl only upon serving. This pistou soup makes for a complete meal. *Bon appétit!*

SOUP

1 teaspoon (5 ml) canola oil
2 leeks, white and pale-green part only, diced small
2 shallots, diced small
1 skinless and boneless chicken breast, cubed
2 large carrots, peeled and diced small
4 cups (1 L) Vegetable Stock (see page 80)
2 cups (500 ml) cooked white beans
1 cup (250 ml) green beans, diced small
1 large tomato, seeded and diced small

PISTOU

2 garlic cloves
½ cup (125 ml) fresh basil leaves
½ teaspoon (2 ml) kosher salt
¼ teaspoon (1 ml) freshly ground pepper
1 tablespoon (15 ml) extra-virgin olive oil

Heat oil in a large, non-stick skillet over medium heat. Add leeks and shallots and sauté about 5 minutes until soft and golden.

Add chicken and carrots and let cook, stirring occasionally, for 2 minutes. Transfer to a large soup pot, add stock, and bring to a gentle simmer. Cover and reduce heat to maintain a gentle simmer and continue to cook for 30 minutes.

Add white beans, green beans, and tomatoes and continue to simmer, covered, for 15 minutes.

Meanwhile, in a small processor, prepare the pistou by processing the garlic, basil, salt, and pepper in oil until a paste is formed.

Ladle soup into serving bowls and place a teaspoon of pistou on top. Serve immediately.

Serves 4 to 6 ‖ NUTRITION (per serving, including 1 tablespoon of pistou): energy 203 kcal | total fat 2 g | saturated fat 0 g | carbohydrate 31 g | fibre 8 g | protein 15 g | sodium 163 mg | excellent source of vitamin A, iron, niacin, vitamin B6 | good source of potassium, vitamin E, thiamin, folate

The texture of puréed soups can be as smooth or as chunky as you desire, depending on the equipment you use. A blender or an immersion blender will produce the smoothest, creamiest texture. A food processor will provide a less refined texture.

DR. JOE'S SMART FACT

Curry powder is a combination of spices used in Indian cuisine and varies widely in composition depending on its region of origin. Some have suggested that the lowered incidence of Alzheimer's disease in India is connected to the large amounts of curry consumed. This is currently under scientific investigation.

mulligatawny soup

The name "mulligatawny" derives from the Tamil words for pepper and water. Turmeric, which is considered a "wonder spice" because of its healing benefits, is what gives this traditional curried Indian soup its yellow colour. This unconventional version includes banana, which imparts a delicious sweetness.

INGREDIENTS

1 tablespoon (15 ml) canola oil
2 medium onions, coarsely chopped
2 garlic cloves, minced
1 tablespoon (15 ml) minced fresh ginger
½ cup (125 ml) unsweetened shredded coconut
1 tablespoon (15 ml) curry powder
1 tablespoon (15 ml) ground turmeric
1 teaspoon (5 ml) ground cumin
¼ teaspoon (1 ml) cayenne pepper
8 cups (2 L) Vegetable Stock (see page 80)
2 carrots, peeled and coarsely chopped
2 celery stalks, coarsely chopped
2 ripe bananas, peeled and coarsely chopped, divided
kosher salt and freshly ground pepper to taste
½ cup (125 ml) low-fat plain yogurt for garnish
cilantro sprigs for garnish
almond slices or soy nuts (for nut-free version), toasted, for garnish

Heat oil in a large soup pot over medium heat. Add onions and sauté about 5 minutes until soft and golden. Add garlic, ginger, coconut, and spices. Stir about 2 minutes until fragrant.

Gradually whisk in stock. Add carrots, celery, and one banana, and stir. Increase heat to medium-high and bring to a boil. Cover, reduce heat, and let simmer about 20 minutes until vegetables are tender.

Remove from heat and purée until smooth all at once with an immersion blender, or in batches using a blender or food processor. Return to heat. Add second banana and adjust seasoning with salt and pepper if necessary.

Ladle soup into serving bowls and top with a dollop of yogurt. Sprinkle with cilantro and nuts. Serve immediately.

Serves 8 ‖ **NUTRITION** (per serving): energy 123 kcal | total fat 6 g | saturated fat 4 g | carbohydrate 17 g | fibre 4 g | protein 2 g | sodium 164 mg

bean and barley soup

This humble soup is sure to become addictive during chilly winter days. While the beauty lies in its simplicity, it is far from ordinary. Keep in the fridge to be enjoyed as a hearty snack or light meal any day of the week.

INGREDIENTS

½ cup (125 ml) pearl barley
2 bay leaves
1 tablespoon (15 ml) canola oil
1 leek, white and pale-green parts only, diced small
1 medium onion, diced small
2 garlic cloves, minced
2 large carrots, peeled and diced small
2 stalks celery, diced small
1 cup (250 ml) sliced mushrooms
½ cup (125 ml) finely chopped tomatoes
1 cup (250 ml) cooked white kidney beans
⅔ cup (150 ml) finely chopped fresh dill, plus a few sprigs for garnish
4 cups (1 L) Vegetable or Chicken Stock (see pages 80 and 81)
1 teaspoon (5 ml) coarse salt, plus more for seasoning
½ teaspoon (2 ml) freshly ground pepper, plus more for seasoning
2 cups (500 ml) coarsely chopped Swiss chard, centre ribs and stems discarded (can also use kale or spinach)

Place barley and bay leaves in a large pot and cover with several inches of cold water. Bring to a boil, lower heat, and simmer 30 to 40 minutes until barley is almost cooked. If necessary, adjust the heat and add more water. Remove from heat and rinse with cold water.

Meanwhile, heat oil in a large soup pot over medium heat. Add leek and onion and sauté about 5 minutes until softened.

Add garlic, carrots, and celery. Sauté for another 3 minutes.

Add mushrooms, tomatoes, beans, dill, and stock. Bring to a boil, cover, and reduce heat to maintain a gentle simmer. Continue to cook for another 20 to 30 minutes until vegetables are tender.

Add Swiss chard, return barley to pot, and simmer for 5 minutes. Taste and adjust seasoning with salt and pepper.

Ladle soup into serving bowls, garnish with reserved dill sprigs, and serve.

Serves 10 ‖ NUTRITION (per serving): energy 119 kcal | total fat 2 g | saturated fat 0 g | carbohydrate 20 g | fibre 4 g | protein 6 g | sodium 293 mg | excellent source of vitamin A | good source of vitamin C, thiamin, riboflavin, folate, niacin

SMART TIP

Another method to store fresh herbs is to place them in a jar or glass filled with a few inches of water. When you are ready to use them, blot the herbs dry. Chop with a very sharp knife to avoid bruising the leaves.

roasted "cream" of tomato soup

For anyone who enjoys a good aromatic Italian dish infused with lots of garlic and tomato, this soup will surely whet the appetite. Adding milk merely enhances its indescribable richness.

SMART TIP

Make your own herbed croutons by cutting 6 pieces of multi-grain bread into cubes. Toss with 1 tablespoon of canola oil on a rimmed baking sheet. Place in a preheated 350°F (180°C) oven and bake about 9 to 10 minutes until golden. Toss with a heaping tablespoon of chopped fresh herbs such as parsley, basil, or thyme.

DR. JOE'S SMART FACT

Tomatoes contain lycopene, a carotenoid that belongs to a family of pigments responsible for giving fruits and vegetables their vibrant colours. It is a powerful antioxidant that can trap free radicals that damage DNA and other cell structures. Lycopene has been shown to reduce the risk of prostate cancer and, according to a 2012 Finnish study, high lycopene levels in the blood significantly lower the risk of stroke and blood clots.

INGREDIENTS

1 small eggplant, peeled and sliced
olive oil, for brushing
kosher salt, for sprinkling
6 cups (1.5 L) cherry tomatoes
1 small onion, coarsely chopped
2 garlic cloves, minced
1 stalk celery, coarsely chopped
4 cups (1 L) Vegetable or Chicken Stock (see pages 80 and 81)
1 teaspoon (5 ml) coarse salt, plus more for seasoning
¼ teaspoon (1 ml) freshly ground pepper, plus more for seasoning
½ cup (125 ml) milk (dairy or soy)
2 tablespoons (30 ml) Parmesan cheese, grated (optional)
2 tablespoons (30 ml) finely chopped fresh basil for garnish
2 tablespoons (30 ml) finely chopped fresh flat-leaf parsley for garnish
herbed croutons (see SMART TIP at left) for garnish

Preheat oven to 400°F (200°C).

Lightly brush both sides of the eggplant slices with oil. Place in a single layer on a large baking dish and sprinkle with salt. Roast for 20 to 25 minutes until softened and golden. Remove from oven, then place tomatoes, onion, garlic, and celery on top of eggplant and continue to roast for 15 to 20 minutes until vegetables are soft and browned. Can be made in advance and refrigerated.

Meanwhile, bring stock to a boil in a large pot over medium-high heat. Transfer roasted vegetables to pot, add salt and pepper, and mix well. Bring to a boil, cover, reduce heat to low and simmer for 10 minutes.

Remove from heat and purée soup all at once with an immersion blender or in batches using a blender or food processor, slowly adding milk and cheese (optional). Purée until tomato skins are pulverized. Soup should retain some texture. Taste and adjust seasoning with salt and pepper.

Ladle soup into serving bowls, sprinkle with basil, parsley, and croutons and serve.

Serves 8 to 10 ‖ NUTRITION (per serving): energy 70 kcal | total fat 1 g | saturated fat 0 g | carbohydrate 12 g | fibre 4 g | protein 4 g | sodium 351 mg | good source of vitamin C, niacin, folate

roasted cauliflower soup

Anyone with a fondness for pronounced flavours will embrace this sumptuous soup. Roasting the vegetables before adding them to the pot amplifies their natural sweetness. The citrus and aromatic seasonings make this soup irresistibly good.

 **SMART TIP**

One medium lemon will yield about 1 teaspoon of grated zest and 3 to 4 tablespoons of lemon juice.

INGREDIENTS

1 large head of cauliflower, outer leaves and core removed, cut into large pieces
1 Vidalia onion, coarsely chopped
1 tablespoon (15 ml) canola oil
1 teaspoon (5 ml) herbes de Provence
½ tablespoon (7 ml) ground cumin
½ tablespoon (7 ml) ground coriander
½ tablespoon (7 ml) garlic powder
1 teaspoon (5 ml) coarse salt, plus more for seasoning
¼ cup (60 ml) cognac (optional)
4 cups (1 L) Vegetable Stock (see page 80)
¼ cup (60 ml) pure maple syrup
1 teaspoon (5 ml) pure vanilla extract
juice and finely grated zest from 1 lemon
freshly ground pepper
lemon slices and fresh dill sprigs for garnish

Preheat oven to 375°F (190°C).

Toss cauliflower, onions, oil, herbes de Provence, cumin, coriander, garlic, and salt in a large bowl until well mixed. Transfer to a large baking dish and bake about 25 to 30 minutes until browned.

Add cognac (optional) and continue baking for about another 10 minutes until cauliflower is brown and caramelized.

Meanwhile, bring stock and water to a boil in a large pot over medium-high heat. Transfer roasted cauliflower mixture to pot and mix well. Return to a boil, reduce heat to low, and simmer, covered, for 10 to 15 minutes.

Remove from heat and purée soup all at once with an immersion blender or in batches using a blender or food processor. Add water if soup is too thick. Return to heat and stir in maple syrup, vanilla, lemon juice, and zest. Taste and adjust seasoning with salt and pepper if necessary.

Ladle soup into serving bowls, garnish with lemon slices and dill sprigs, and serve.

Serves 8 ‖ **NUTRITION** (per serving): energy 91 kcal | total fat 2 g | saturated fat 0 g | carbohydrate 17 g | fibre 4 g | protein 3 g | sodium 401 mg | excellent source of vitamin C, folate | good source of riboflavin, niacin, vitamin B6

hearty lentil vegetable soup

Nourishing and substantial, this is a perfect meal for the winter months. Lentils and vegetables are the main attraction in this soup, which can be made even heartier by adding more lentils and using less water.

INGREDIENTS

2 tablespoons (30 ml) olive oil
1 large onion, diced small
4 garlic cloves, minced
1 small sweet potato, peeled and diced medium
1 pound (455 g) carrots, thinly sliced
2 celery stalks, thinly sliced
1½ cups (375 ml) dry red lentils, rinsed and drained (for a thinner soup, use fewer lentils)
1 tablespoon (15 ml) tomato paste
½ teaspoon (2 ml) ground turmeric
3 drops Tabasco sauce, or more to taste
2 teaspoons (10 ml) kosher salt, divided, plus more for seasoning
¼ teaspoon (1 ml) freshly ground pepper, plus more for seasoning
8 cups (2 L) Vegetable Stock (see page 80) or water
1 teaspoon (5 ml) grated fresh ginger
6 cups (1.5 L) lightly packed dark kale, centre ribs and stems discarded, chopped (can also use Swiss chard or spinach)
2 cups (500 ml) cooked kidney beans

Heat oil in a large soup pot over medium heat. Add onion and sauté about 5 minutes until softened.

Add garlic and cook for 2 or 3 minutes. Then add sweet potato, carrots, and celery and cook for 5 minutes. Stir in lentils and cook for 2 minutes.

Add tomato paste, turmeric, Tabasco, 1 teaspoon salt, and pepper, stirring well for 1 to 2 minutes to combine. Add stock and ginger.

Bring soup to a boil, reduce heat, and gently simmer for 10 minutes. Add kale, beans, and remaining teaspoon of salt. Simmer for an additional 10 to 15 minutes.

Taste and adjust seasonings, adding more stock if necessary.

Serve as a stew with crusty bread, or as a soup garnished with Roasted Chickpeas (see page 75).

Serves 16 as soup, 12 as stew ‖ NUTRITION (per serving): energy 147 kcal | total fat 2 g | saturated fat 0 g | carbohydrate 24 g | fibre 5 g | protein 8 g | sodium 373 mg | excellent source of vitamin A, thiamin, folate | good source of potassium, iron

SMART TIP

Du Puy or Le Puy green lentils, tiny legumes from Auvergne, France, are prized for having a distinctive nutty taste and less starch than other types of lentils. They cook quickly and remain firm after cooking.

DR. JOE'S SMART FACT

Sweet potatoes are high in fibre, have virtually no fat, and have more beta-carotene (the body's precursor for vitamin A) than any other food. What more can you ask for? Taste? They have that too!

squash and sweet potato soup with seared scallops

Delicious, delicious, delicious! Like the sun, the taste and colour of this soup will awaken your senses. Whether served alone or with scallops, this is certain to satisfy even the heartiest appetite.

SOUP

2 teaspoons (10 ml) canola oil
1 small yellow onion, chopped
3 cloves garlic, minced
1 tablespoon (15 ml) minced fresh ginger
2 cups (500 ml) peeled, seeded and chopped butternut squash
2 cups (500 ml) peeled and chopped sweet potato
4 cups (1 L) Vegetable or Chicken Stock (pages 80 and 81)
1 teaspoon (5 ml) curry powder
½ teaspoon (2 ml) ground cumin or smoked paprika (optional)
1 teaspoon (5 ml) coarse salt, plus more for seasoning
½ teaspoon (2 ml) freshly ground pepper, plus more for seasoning
½ cup (125 ml) low-fat coconut milk

SCALLOPS

6 large scallops, side muscle removed and rinsed well
kosher salt and freshly ground pepper
1 tablespoon (15 ml) canola oil
¼ cup (60 ml) finely chopped fresh chives for garnish

Heat oil in a large soup pot over medium heat.

Add onions, garlic, and ginger and sauté until softened, about 5 minutes.

Add remaining ingredients except coconut milk. Reduce heat to low, cover, and simmer for 30 minutes.

Remove soup from heat and purée all at once with an immersion blender, or in batches using a blender or food processor, until creamy and smooth.

Return to heat, stir in coconut milk, and blend well. Taste and adjust seasoning with salt and pepper.

Just before serving, pat scallops dry and sprinkle both sides with salt and pepper to taste. Heat oil in a large sauté pan over medium-high heat about 1 minute until hot. Without crowding pan, sear scallops about 2 minutes until well browned. Turn scallops and cook 30 seconds to 1 minute longer (depending on their size) until sides of scallop are firm and middle is opaque.

Ladle soup into each bowl, placing one scallop, seared side up, on top and sprinkle with chives and freshly ground pepper. Serve very hot.

Serves 6 ‖ NUTRITION (per serving): energy 178 kcal | total fat 7 g | saturated fat 2 g | cholesterol 7 mg | carbohydrate 22 g | fibre 3 g | protein 8 g | sodium 603 mg | excellent source of vitamin A, vitamin E | good source of niacin, vitamin B_{12}

SMART TIP

To peel a butternut squash, trim ends and cut squash in two at base of neck. Remove thin skin with a vegetable peeler. Halve each section lengthwise and scoop out seeds from bottom. Slice or dice as directed in recipe.

DR. JOE'S SMART FACT

The antioxidant and anti-inflammatory compounds in winter squash give this food clear potential in the area of cancer prevention and cancer treatment. However, most of the research on winter squash and inflammation has been conducted in animals or has focused on laboratory studies of cellular activity. Prostate cancer has been of greatest research interest, followed by colon cancer, breast cancer, and lung cancer. But, even then, such studies do not involve everyday amounts of winter squash consumed in food, but concentrated amounts in food extracts. Given the antioxidant and anti-inflammatory benefits of winter squash, further investigation is warranted.

Eating salads as a side or main dish is a sure way to get the necessary daily intake of certain essential nutrients.

salads

buying, storing, and preparing vegetables

Always try to buy locally grown produce, since vegetables begin to lose nutrients as soon as they are picked. It might be wise to choose recipes according to the freshness of available ingredients.

Storing vegetables properly helps to preserve their taste and nutritional value. Most vegetables stay freshest when stored loosely in the refrigerator. If you use plastic bags, they should be perforated to allow for good air flow. Peppers, mushrooms, and leafy greens keep well in the fridge when wrapped, unwashed, in paper towels. Herbs keep longest when their stems are immersed in water. Potatoes, onions, winter squash, and garlic should never be refrigerated, but should be stored in a cool dry place, where they will keep for up to a month. Keep them separated from each other so their flavours and smells do not mingle. Tomatoes should be kept at room temperature

Do not store fruits and vegetables together, as the natural ripening agent found in some fruits will increase the speed with which certain vegetables spoil.

Although it is tempting to wash and trim your vegetables before storing, doing so speeds their deterioration. An exception is the leafy ends attached to root vegetables. These should be removed and discarded or, in the case of beets, stored separately to use as greens.

The peel contains many nutrients and fibre, so leave it on whenever possible. Scrub your potatoes, cucumbers, and zucchini well just before using to minimize pesticide residues and waxy preservatives.

Save any vegetable ends to use later when making stocks and sauces.

To keep the bright green colour in vegetables such as broccoli, never cook them with acidic ingredients such as lemon, and always cook them uncovered.

SMART TIP

Water or fruit juice (apple, white grape, or orange) can be used to replace some of the oil in a salad dressing or marinade.

These multi-purpose vinaigrettes are a combination of interesting and complex flavours. Mix and match ingredients to complement your favourite recipes.

not-so-basic vinaigrette

Place all ingredients (except oil) in a blender and purée until smooth. Gradually add oil and blend until emulsified.

Pour dressing into a jar and keep refrigerated.

Makes ¾ cup || **NUTRITION** (per tablespoon): energy 33 kcal | total fat 3 g | saturated fat 0 g | carbohydrate 1 g | fibre 0 g | protein 0 g | sodium 20 mg

INGREDIENTS

¼ cup (60 ml) water
3 tablespoons (45 ml) red wine vinegar
2 tablespoons (30 ml) Hot Mustard (see page 299)
1 tablespoon (15 ml) honey
2 tablespoons (30 ml) finely chopped fresh herbs, such as dill, basil, rosemary, and thyme
kosher salt and freshly ground pepper, to taste
¼ cup (60 ml) extra-virgin olive oil

maple balsamic vinaigrette

Place all ingredients (except oil) in a blender and purée until smooth. Gradually add oil and blend until emulsified. Taste, adding more salt and pepper if necessary.

Pour dressing into a jar and keep refrigerated.

Makes 1 cup || **NUTRITION** (per tablespoon): energy 41 kcal | total fat 4 g | saturated fat 1 g | carbohydrate 2 g | fibre 0 g | protein 0 g | sodium 61 mg

INGREDIENTS

¼ cup (60 ml) balsamic vinegar
¼ cup (60 ml) water
2 tablespoons (30 ml) fresh lemon juice
2 tablespoons (30 ml) pure maple syrup
½ teaspoon (2 ml) kosher salt
¼ teaspoon (1 ml) freshly ground pepper
¼ cup (60 ml) extra-virgin olive oil

asian carrot ginger dressing

Mince carrot in a food processor. Add ginger and garlic and pulse until minced. Add remaining ingredients (except oil) and process for 5 to 10 seconds. Add oil through feed tube and process for 1 minute. Taste, adding salt and pepper if necessary.

Pour dressing into a jar and keep refrigerated.

Makes just under 2 cups || **NUTRITION** (per tablespoon): energy 39 kcal | total fat 4 g | saturated fat 0 g | carbohydrate 1 g | fibre 0 g | protein 0 g | sodium 38 mg

INGREDIENTS

1 large carrot, peeled and cut into chunks
1-inch (2.5 cm) piece fresh ginger, peeled
1 large garlic clove, peeled
1 tablespoon (15 ml) honey
2 tablespoons (30 ml) low-sodium soy sauce
½ cup (125 ml) seasoned rice vinegar
¼ cup (60 ml) water
½ cup (125 ml) canola oil
kosher salt and freshly ground pepper

lime vinaigrette

INGREDIENTS

juice and finely grated zest from 3 limes
1 tablespoon (15 ml) red wine vinegar
4 garlic cloves, minced
1 teaspoon (5 ml) ground cumin
½ teaspoon (2 ml) chili powder
pinch of cayenne pepper
½ teaspoon (2 ml) salt, plus more for seasoning
¼ teaspoon (1 ml) freshly ground pepper, plus more for seasoning
3 tablespoons (45 ml) extra-virgin olive oil

Place all ingredients (except oil) in a blender and purée until smooth. Gradually add oil and blend until emulsified.

Pour dressing into a jar and keep refrigerated.

Makes 1 cup ‖ NUTRITION (per tablespoon): energy 27 kcal | total fat 3 g | saturated fat 0 g | carbohydrate 1 g | fibre 0 g | protein 0 g | sodium 61 mg

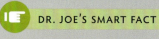 DR. JOE'S SMART FACT

The term "vinegar" comes from the French *vin*, wine, and *aigre*, sour. It was discovered long ago when a cask of wine, past its time, turned sour.

apple cider vinaigrette

INGREDIENTS

3 tablespoons (45 ml) Dijon mustard
3 tablespoons (45 ml) apple cider vinegar
2 tablespoons (30 ml) honey
¼ cup (60 ml) water
½ teaspoon (2 ml) kosher salt
¼ teaspoon (1 ml) freshly ground pepper
3 tablespoons (45 ml) canola oil

Place all ingredients (except oil) in a blender and purée until smooth. Gradually add oil and blend until emulsified.

Pour dressing into a jar and keep refrigerated.

Makes 1 cup ‖
NUTRITION (per tablespoon): energy 31 kcal | total fat 3 g | saturated fat 0 g | carbohydrate 2 g | fibre 0 g | protein 0 g | sodium 59 mg

sesame miso dressing

This dressing works on salads and grains and as a marinade for fish and chicken.

INGREDIENTS

1 tablespoon (15 ml) minced fresh ginger
1 large garlic clove, peeled
1 tablespoon (15 ml) miso paste
1 tablespoon (15 ml) tahini
1 tablespoon (15 ml) honey
¼ cup (60 ml) rice vinegar
¼ cup (60 ml) water
1 tablespoon (15 ml) sesame oil
3 tablespoons (45 ml) canola oil

Place all ingredients (except oils) in a blender and purée until smooth. Gradually add oils and blend until emulsified. As the dressing rests, it will thicken. Add additional water, one tablespoon at a time, and stir until desired consistency is reached.

Pour dressing into a jar and keep refrigerated.

Makes 1 cup ‖ NUTRITION (per tablespoon): energy 44 kcal | total fat 4 g | saturated fat 0 g | carbohydrate 2 g | fibre 0 g | protein 0 g | sodium 42 mg

---

📌 **SMART TIP**

Miso is a good substitute for salt, soy sauce, or anchovy paste. It is very concentrated: a little goes a long way.

a salad for all seasons

This salad is a bounty of fresh produce from the farmers' market. Substituting or adding ingredients according to seasonal availability will result in charming and unexpected flavours. To make this salad a main dish, simply add tuna, sliced egg, chicken, or any other meat.

INGREDIENTS

2 to 3 medium beets, stems removed (if available, use beets of different colours)
2 to 3 Jerusalem artichokes, scrubbed with skin left on, very thinly sliced
3 tablespoons (45 ml) olive oil
1 tablespoon (15 ml) finely grated zest from 1 orange
kosher salt and freshly ground pepper for seasoning
6 asparagus spears, cut on diagonal into 1-inch (2.5 cm) pieces
3 or 4 kale leaves, centre ribs and stems discarded, finely chopped
½ cup (125 ml) sugar snap peas, cut on diagonal into ½-inch (1 cm) pieces
½ cup (125 ml) shaved fresh fennel
1 yellow zucchini, julienned
1 endive, sliced
2 clementines, peeled and pith removed
⅓ cup (75 ml) cooked navy beans
⅓ to ½ cup (75 to 125 ml) Apple Cider Vinaigrette (see page 110)
¼ cup (60 ml) very thinly sliced red onion rounds
¼ cup (60 ml) pine nuts, toasted, for garnish
¼ cup (60 ml) feta cheese, crumbled, for garnish

Preheat oven to 400°F (200°C).

Prepare a foil packet by placing beets on a large sheet of heavy aluminum foil. Drizzle with 2 tablespoons of oil, orange zest, salt, and pepper. Fold up and seal. Roast about 45 to 60 minutes until beets are easily pierced with a fork. Let sit until cool enough to handle. Peel skins and cut into ¼-inch cubes.

Spread sliced Jerusalem artichokes on a rimmed baking sheet lined with aluminum foil, drizzle with remaining tablespoon of oil, and roast alongside beets for 10 to 15 minutes until lightly browned. Sprinkle with salt (optional). Cool on a wire rack.

Blanch asparagus and sugar snap peas in boiling water for 1 to 2 minutes. Rinse under very cold water to stop cooking process. Dry well.

Massage kale leaves to soften. Place in a large serving bowl. Add all ingredients and mix gently.

Divide salad among serving plates. Garnish with pine nuts and feta.

Surround with a small amount of dressing.

Serves 6 to 8 ‖ NUTRITION (per serving): energy 152 kcal | total fat 8 g | saturated fat 1 g | carbohydrate 19 g | fibre 4 g | protein 3 g | sodium 100 mg | excellent source of vitamin C | good source of vitamin A, thiamin, folate

deconstructed beet salad

Everything blends beautifully in this modern salad. The coupling of pears and beets is certain to delight any palate.

INGREDIENTS

3 small beets, stems removed (if available, use beets of different colours)
extra-virgin olive oil for drizzling
kosher salt for sprinkling
one 4-ounce (115 g) cylinder soft unripened goat cheese
¼ cup (60 ml) finely chopped pecans, toasted, plus additional pecan pieces for garnish
1 Anjou or Bosc pear, very thinly sliced
½ cup (125 ml) lightly packed mesclun salad mix or arugula leaves (optional)
white balsamic vinegar for drizzling
sea salt
1 tablespoon (15 ml) chopped thyme for garnish
small handful of sunflower sprouts or pea shoots for garnish

Preheat oven to 400°F (200°C).

Place beets on a large sheet of heavy aluminum foil. Drizzle with oil and sprinkle with salt. Fold up and seal foil to form a packet. Roast about 45 to 60 minutes until easily pierced with a fork. Let sit until cool enough to handle. Peel skins, cut into very thin rounds, and set aside.

Cut the goat cheese into equal rounds. Roll into a ball and then dredge goat cheese in pecans, pressing lightly so that the nuts adhere.

Assemble salad by arranging a row of beet slices across plate. Overlap a second row in a contrasting colour next to the first. Continue in the same fashion with pear and remaining beets. Lay coated goat cheese balls on top. Add mesclun mix or arugula leaves as desired.

Drizzle salad with oil and balsamic vinegar. Sprinkle with sea salt and garnish with fresh herbs and sprouts.

Serves 4 to 6 as an appetizer ‖ NUTRITION (per serving): energy 130 kcal | total fat 9 g | saturated fat 3 g | carbohydrate 9 g | fibre 2 g | protein 5 g | sodium 104 mg | good source of vitamin E

SMART TIP

Using unwaxed dental floss makes cutting soft goat cheese an easy task.

DR. JOE'S SMART FACT

According to some studies, beets can raise levels of nitric oxide in the bloodstream, helping to increase blood flow and allowing blood vessels to respond to blood pressure changes with a reduced risk of damage.

Serves 6 to 8 || **NUTRITION** (per serving): energy 145 kcal | total fat 9 g | saturated fat 2 g | carbohydrate 12 g | fibre 7 g | protein 8 g | sodium 135 mg | excellent source of vitamin A, vitamin C, potassium, calcium, folate, riboflavin | good source of iron, thiamin, niacin, vitamin B6

untraditional caesar salad

A culinary exercise in the art of juxtaposition: the sweetness of tomatoes against the spiciness of pepper, and the richness of cheese contrasted with the tartness of lemon, work to create a perfect balance. Spinach and kale add a crunchy texture to this untraditional salad.

CAESAR DRESSING

1 egg
2 garlic cloves, peeled
2 anchovies, chopped, or 2 teaspoons (10 ml) anchovy paste
3 tablespoons (45 ml) fresh lemon juice
1 tablespoon (15 ml) Dijon mustard
½ teaspoon (2 ml) Worcestershire sauce
¼ teaspoon (1 ml) crushed red chili pepper flakes
¼ cup (60 ml) water
⅓ cup (75 ml) extra-virgin olive oil
3 tablespoons (45 ml) Parmesan cheese, grated

SALAD

2 romaine hearts, roughly torn
8 cups (2 L) loosely packed fresh baby spinach, trimmed
3 to 4 kale leaves, centre ribs and stems discarded, finely chopped
1 pint (500 ml) grape or cherry tomatoes, halved
½ lemon
freshly ground pepper
⅓ cup (75 ml) Parmesan cheese shavings for garnish (optional)
2 tablespoons (30 ml) Fried Capers (see page 298) for garnish (optional)
handful of croutons (see page 127) for garnish (optional)

TO MAKE THE DRESSING

Coddle the egg by placing it in a small saucepan with enough cold water to cover and bringing the water to a simmer on medium heat. Do not bring water to a full boil. Remove pan from heat, cover, and let sit for 3 to 4 minutes. Run cold water over egg to stop the cooking process. The result should be an egg that is more lightly cooked than a soft-boiled egg. (Note that the size of an egg and its temperature will affect cooking time. An extra large egg taken directly from refrigerator will take longer to coddle than a medium egg at room temperature.)

Drop garlic through feed tube of a food processor while machine is running. Add anchovies and pulse until minced. Add coddled egg and remaining dressing ingredients (except oil and cheese) and process for 5 to 10 seconds. Add oil through feed tube and process for 15 to 20 seconds. Add cheese and pulse until just incorporated.

TO ASSEMBLE THE SALAD

Place lettuce, spinach, and kale in a large bowl; toss in tomatoes. Add desired amount of dressing and toss to combine.

Squeeze fresh lemon juice over salad and sprinkle with freshly ground black pepper. Garnish with Parmesan cheese shavings, fried capers, and croutons. Serve immediately.

Store remaining dressing in refrigerator.

kale peanut salad with peanut dressing

Touted as a nutritional powerhouse, kale has become all the rage, whether sautéed, juiced, or used in a salad. This recipe demonstrates just how scrumptious it can taste.

PEANUT DRESSING

¼ cup (60 ml) dry roasted peanuts
1 tablespoon (15 ml) packed brown sugar
¼ cup (60 ml) cider vinegar
3 tablespoons (45 ml) water
½ teaspoon (2 ml) salt
½ cup (125 ml) canola oil

SALAD

6 cups (1.5 L) finely chopped curly kale, centre ribs and stems discarded
1 cup (250 ml) assorted red and yellow bell peppers, diced small
1 large carrot, diced small
2 scallions, white and pale green parts only, thinly sliced
¼ cup (60 ml) raw sunflower seeds or toasted peanuts for garnish (optional)

Place all ingredients (except oil) for dressing in a blender and purée until smooth. Gradually add oil and blend until emulsified.

Toss salad ingredients in a large bowl. Just before serving, add desired amount of dressing and toss to combine. Store remaining dressing in refrigerator.

Sprinkle with peanuts and serve.

Serves 6 to 8 || **NUTRITION** (per serving): energy 109 kcal | total fat 9 g | saturated fat 1 g | carbohydrate 7 g | fibre 2 g | protein 2 g | sodium 42 mg | excellent source of vitamin A, vitamin C

SMART TIP

To trim kale leaves, fold the leaf in half lengthwise on a cutting board and use a sharp knife to slice away the coarse rib and stem.

To make a perfect julienne cut, use a sharp chef's knife and trim the rounded edges of the vegetable to make a block with four flat sides. Slice the vegetable lengthwise evenly. Stack the slices and cut lengthwise again into thin strips.

soba spinach edamame salad

A traditional part of Japanese cuisine, soba noodles are made from buckwheat flour. They adopt the flavour of any added sauce or dressing, making them quite versatile.

INGREDIENTS

6 ounces (175 g) soba noodles
2 cups (500 ml) frozen shelled edamame
12 cups (3 L) loosely packed fresh baby spinach, trimmed
1 carrot, peeled and julienned
2 scallions, white and pale-green parts only, thinly sliced
½ cup (125 ml) Sesame Miso Dressing (see page 111)

Bring a large pot of water to a boil and add a pinch of salt. Drop in noodles and cook 2 to 4 minutes until tender. Add the edamame for 15 to 20 seconds just to warm. Drain both in a colander; allow to cool and set aside.

Toss noodles, edamame, spinach, and carrots in a large bowl. Add scallions. Pour on desired amount of dressing and toss to combine.

Serves 8 to 10 ‖ NUTRITION (per serving): energy 172 kcal | total fat 6 g | saturated fat 0 g | carbohydrate 24 g | fibre 7 g | protein 9 g | sodium 201 mg | excellent source of vitamin A, vitamin C, potassium, calcium, folate | good source of iron, riboflavin, thiamin, vitamin B6, vitamin E, niacin

tricolour slaw with creamy yogurt dressing

Who doesn't like creamy coleslaw with its rich taste and crunchy texture? This cabbage-and-carrot slaw is dressed with a Middle Eastern–inspired blend of yogurt, lime juice, honey, and cumin. The no-mayonnaise approach makes for a lighter version with fewer calories from saturated fat.

SLAW

4 cups (1 L) very thinly sliced green or napa cabbage
1 cup (250 ml) very thinly sliced purple cabbage
2 cups (500 ml) very thinly sliced radicchio
2 large carrots, peeled and grated
1 Granny Smith apple, julienned and sprinkled with fresh lemon juice to prevent discoloration
2 scallions, white and green parts only, thinly sliced
4 radishes, thinly sliced
½ cup (125 ml) pomegranate seeds for garnish

CREAMY YOGURT DRESSING

½ cup (125 ml) low-fat plain Greek yogurt
¼ cup (60 ml) fresh lime juice
2 tablespoons (30 ml) honey
1 teaspoon (5 ml) ground cumin or chili powder
½ teaspoon (2 ml) kosher salt
¼ teaspoon (1 ml) freshly ground pepper
2 tablespoons (30 ml) canola oil

In a large bowl, combine cabbages, radicchio, carrots, apple, scallions, and radishes.

Place all dressing ingredients (except oil) in a blender and purée until smooth. Gradually add oil and blend until emulsified.

Pour dressing on top of cabbage mix; toss well and taste. Add salt and pepper if desired. Sprinkle pomegranate seeds on top and serve.

Store remaining dressing in refrigerator.

Serves 6 to 8 ‖ NUTRITION (per serving): energy 89 kcal | total fat 4 g | saturated fat 0 g | carbohydrate 14 g | fibre 2 g | protein 2 g | sodium 156 mg | good source of vitamin A, vitamin C, vitamin E

SMART TIP

To make this recipe in a quick and easy manner, substitute a bag of pre-shredded "slaw mix," available in most supermarkets, for the cabbage.

DR. JOE'S SMART FACT

Contrary to popular belief, the anti-cancer compound sulforaphane is not found in cabbage but, rather, forms from a precursor compound that is present when the vegetable is chopped, chewed, or cooked. Sulforaphane increases the production of enzymes that neutralize free radicals connected with aging and various diseases. Scientists at Stanford University discovered that sulforaphane boosts levels of these enzymes more than any other plant compound.

pesto zucchini "spaghetti"

This spaghetti recipe was inspired by a friend who can no longer eat gluten but loves pasta in all its forms. The "noodle" is replaced with a flavourful vegetable that can be used with any number of sauces.

INGREDIENTS

4 large zucchinis
kosher salt
½ cup (125 ml) Low-Fat Pesto (see page 302), plus more to taste
1 tablespoon (15 ml) fresh lemon juice
2 tablespoons (30 ml) chopped fresh parsley for garnish
¼ cup (60 ml) pine nuts, toasted, for garnish

Using a julienne cutter or a mandoline, cut zucchini into long spaghetti-like strands. Sprinkle with salt and transfer to a colander for 10 to 15 minutes to remove excess moisture.

Lightly toss zucchini with pesto. Drizzle lemon juice over zucchini and garnish with parsley and pine nuts.

Serves 6 ‖ NUTRITION (per serving): energy 64 kcal | total fat 3 g | saturated fat 1 g | carbohydrate 7 g | fibre 2 g | protein 3 g | sodium 59 mg | good source of vitamin A, riboflavin, iron, vitamin E, vitamin B12

grilled peach panzanella salad
with ciabatta croutons

This refined take on the classic Italian bread-and-tomato salad is a great way to use stale bread. Grilled peaches add a wonderful depth of flavour that delights the senses.

CIABATTA CROUTONS

½ small ciabatta loaf or ½ baguette, multi-grain or whole-wheat, cut into ½-inch (1 cm) cubes
olive oil or cooking spray

SALAD

4 firm peaches, pitted and halved
1 red onion, peeled and sliced into ¼-inch (5 mm) rounds
2 red bell peppers, each cut in half
olive oil or cooking spray
5 ounces (140 g) baby arugula
2 cups (500 ml) assorted-colour cherry tomatoes, halved
½ cup (125 ml) roughly chopped fresh basil leaves
4 ounces (115 g) feta cheese, crumbled (optional)
½ cup (125 ml) Maple Balsamic Vinaigrette (see page 109)
¼ cup (60 ml) coarsely chopped walnuts or soy nuts, toasted, for garnish
freshly ground pepper

Preheat grill or grill pan to medium heat. Brush grill rack with oil.

Place bread in a large, non-stick skillet or in grill pan. Drizzle or spray lightly with oil. Cook about 10 minutes on medium heat, stirring occasionally, until golden. Set aside.

Brush peaches, onion slices, and peppers with oil. Place them cut side down on grill, and cook for 2 minutes (with lid closed). Brush again very lightly with oil, turn over, and continue cooking another 4 minutes until softened. Remove from grill; transfer to cutting board and let rest 5 minutes. Cut peaches, onions, and peppers into bite-sized pieces.

Combine arugula, tomatoes, basil, feta cheese (if using), croutons, peaches, onions, and peppers into a large serving bowl.

Pour desired amount of vinaigrette over salad and toss. Let sit 5 to 10 minutes before serving.

Garnish with walnuts and freshly ground pepper. This salad may be served warm or at room temperature.

Serves 8 || NUTRITION (per serving): energy 135 kcal | total fat 5 g | saturated fat 1 g | carbohydrate 22 g | fibre 3 g | protein 4 g | sodium 173 mg | excellent source of vitamin C | good source of folate

SMART TIP

To toast walnuts, preheat oven to 425°F (220°C). Line a small cookie sheet with parchment paper. Place walnuts on prepared sheet and bake for about 4 minutes until fragrant.

avocado crab mesclun salad

The beauty of this salad lies not only in its simplicity but in its wide array of tastes and textures. From the crunch of the tart apple to the velvety smoothness of the rich avocado, the finished product is truly satisfying. Don't hesitate to serve this to the whole family as a light dinner. It might even become a weekly favourite.

INGREDIENTS

4 cups (1 L) loosely packed fresh baby spinach, trimmed
4 cups (1 L) loosely packed mesclun greens
1 Granny Smith apple, diced small and sprinkled with fresh lemon juice to prevent discoloration
1 cup (250 ml) snow peas, trimmed and cut diagonally
3 scallions, white and pale-green parts only, very thinly sliced
2 tablespoons (30 ml) slivered almonds, toasted
1 avocado, pitted and cubed
1½ cups (375 ml) lump crab meat
½ cup (125 ml) Asian Carrot Ginger Dressing (see page 109)
½ cup (125 ml) sunflower sprouts for garnish

In a large bowl, toss together all salad ingredients except avocado and crab meat.

Divide salad between six serving plates. Gently fold in avocado and crab meat. Drizzle with desired amount of dressing, garnish with sprouts, and serve.

Serves 4 to 6 ‖ **NUTRITION** (per serving): energy 185 kcal | total fat 11 g | saturated fat | carbohydrate 16 g | fibre 7 g | protein 10 g | sodium 329 mg | excellent source of vitamin A, vitamin C, folate | good source of potassium, calcium, iron, thiamin, vitamin B6

seared tuna seaweed salad

Wakame is an edible green seaweed with an understated salty-sweet taste. This salad, with its pungent and sweet accents, makes the perfect backdrop to a beautifully seared piece of tuna or salmon. Make certain the cooking surface is very hot so that the fish sears quickly.

SEAWEED SALAD

1 ounce (30 g) dried wakame seaweed
2 tablespoons (30 ml) low-sodium soy sauce
2 tablespoons (30 ml) seasoned rice vinegar
1 tablespoon (15 ml) sesame oil
1 teaspoon (5 ml) minced fresh ginger
½ teaspoon (2 ml) fresh lime juice
⅛ teaspoon (0.5 ml) Sriracha sauce, or more to taste
2 scallions, thinly sliced
¼ cup (60 ml) shredded carrot
2 tablespoons (30 ml) sesame seeds, toasted
2 tablespoons (30 ml) pomegranate seeds for garnish

TUNA

2 tuna steaks, 6 ounces (175 g) each, about 1 inch (2.5 cm) thick
kosher salt and freshly ground pepper
2 tablespoon (30 ml) seaweed salad liquid (from above)
1 tablespoon (15 ml) olive oil

Soak seaweed in enough warm water to cover for 5 minutes (not longer). Drain, rinse, and then squeeze out excess water. Cut seaweed into small pieces with kitchen shears. Stir soy sauce, vinegar, oil, ginger, lime juice, and Sriracha sauce together in a medium bowl. Add scallions, carrot, and sesame seeds, tossing until well combined. Set aside about half of the dressing to use as a marinade for fish. Add seaweed and stir until well coated.

Rinse tuna and pat dry. Brush both sides of tuna with reserved dressing and season with salt and pepper to taste. Let fish marinate for about 30 minutes before cooking.

Heat oil in large skillet on high heat. When the pan is very hot, sear tuna for 1 minute on each side (for rare) to form a slight crust, or up to 3 minutes (for medium).

Barbecue: Heat barbecue until hot and wipe the grate with oiled paper towels until the grate is black and glossy. Grill tuna without moving for 1 minute on each side (for rare) to form a slight crust, or up to 3 minutes (for medium).

Divide seaweed salad among serving plates.

Remove seared tuna to a cutting board, cut into ¼-inch slices, and fan tuna over salad. Garnish with pomegranate seeds and serve immediately.

Serves 2 as a main course, 4 as a side salad || NUTRITION (per serving): energy 372 kcal | total fat 20 g | saturated fat 4 g | carbohydrate 4 g | fibre 1 g | protein 41 g | sodium 477 mg | excellent source of vitamin A, vitamin D, vitamin E, vitamin B6, vitamin B12, thiamin, riboflavin, niacin | good source of iron

 DR. JOE'S SMART FACT

Nori, a red seaweed that turns black and green when dried, is great for snacking, as is kelp. Although the numerous health benefits associated with seaweed are based more on folklore than on scientific evidence, seaweed does contain a wide variety of vitamins and nutrients. A 2011 study published in the American Chemical Society's *Journal of Agricultural and Food Chemistry* reviewed 100 studies on the health benefits of seaweed and reported that some of the proteins in the plant could serve as better sources of bioactive peptides than those in milk products. These reduce blood pressure and boost heart health.

Explore the world of grains and legumes.

grains, legumes & more

perfect grains every time

Here's an at-a-glance guide to cooking grains and grain-like ingredients to perfection.

GRAIN (1 CUP)	COOKING LIQUID*	METHOD	YIELD
Barley (pearl)	2 cups	Rinse. Add barley to boiling liquid. Reduce heat. Cover. Simmer 35 minutes. Let stand 10 minutes.	3 cups
Bulgur	2 cups	Add bulgur to boiling liquid. Cover. Let stand 10 minutes.	2½ cups
Farro	1½ cups	Bring farro to boil in liquid. Reduce heat. Cover. Simmer 20 minutes. Drain. Return to pot. Let stand 10 minutes.	1¾ cups
Kasha (roasted buckwheat groats)	2 cups	Bring kasha to boil in liquid. Reduce heat. Cover. Simmer 12 to 15 minutes.	3 cups
Quinoa	1½ cups	Toast quinoa in dry pan 1 to 2 minutes. Add liquid. Bring to boil. Reduce heat. Cover. Simmer 15 minutes.	2½ cups
Rice—short- and medium-grain brown	1¾ cups	Rinse. Bring rice to boil in liquid. Reduce heat. Cover. Simmer 30 minutes. Let stand 10 minutes.	3 cups
Rice—long-grain brown basmati	1½ cups	Bring rice to boil in liquid. Reduce heat. Cover. Simmer 35 to 40 minutes. Let stand 10 minutes.	2½ cups
Rice—white basmati	1½ cups	Rinse. Bring rice to boil in liquid. Reduce heat. Cover. Simmer 15 minutes. Let stand 10 minutes.	3 cups
Wheat berries	5 cups	Bring wheat berries to boil in liquid. Reduce heat. Cover. Simmer 30 to 40 minutes. Drain.	2¼ cups
Wild rice	2 cups	Rinse. Add rice to boiling liquid. Bring back to boil. Reduce heat. Cover. Simmer 45 to 50 minutes. Let stand 10 minutes.	2½ cups

*Add ¼ to ½ teaspoon of salt to the cooking liquid. The amount of salt needed will depend on preference and the cooking liquid used. More salt will be needed for plain water than for vegetable broth.

perfect beans every time

Beans, both dry and canned, are an excellent source of protein and fibre. They also contain iron and vitamin B and are low in fat. There is a long-standing debate about the advantages of using dried versus canned beans. The "pros" for dried beans include lower cost, control over the presence of salt and preservatives, the reduction of wasteful packaging, and avoidance of bisphenol-A, which can be found in the lining of cans. Finally, soaking beans releases their nutrients and enhances their health benefits. Although preparing beans from the dry state is not difficult, it is time consuming. If the convenience of opening a can of cooked beans is more appealing, rinse them well under cold running water to remove added salt and preservatives.

Soaking beans before they are cooked allows them to absorb water, which begins the process of dissolving the starches that contribute to intestinal discomfort. We like the Quick Soak Method in preparing beans for our recipes. Alternatively, beans can be soaked in cold water for at least 8 hours.

QUICK-SOAK METHOD FOR DRY BEANS

1. Place beans in a colander, sort through to remove discolored ones and any debris, and rinse under cold water.
2. Place beans in a saucepan and cover with cold water. Bring to a boil over medium heat.
3. When water boils, remove pot from heat and let beans stand, covered, in the cooking water, for 1 to 2 hours.

HOW TO COOK BEANS AFTER SOAKING

1. Wash soaked beans thoroughly under cold water and drain well.
2. Place beans and water (consult table for amounts) in pot and bring to a boil.
3. Reduce heat to simmer and cook for required time, stirring occasionally. Add more water if needed and add any desired salt after the beans are cooked and nearly soft.
4. Cooking beans in an uncovered pot results in firmer beans that hold their shape. This technique is perfect for salads. Conversely, cooking beans in a pot with a partly covered lid results in beans that are softer and creamier, which is perfect for soups, sauces, and spreads.
5. Cooked beans stored in airtight containers will last up to 4 days refrigerated and up to 6 months in the freezer.

The cooking time depends on the type of bean and its age. It is best to check for doneness as they cook, starting after 30 to 45 minutes.

BEAN (1 CUP)	SOAK	COOKING LIQUID	COOKING TIME	YIELD
Black beans	Yes	4 cups	1½ to 2 hours	2½ cups
Chickpeas	Yes	4 cups	1½ hours	3 cups
Kidney beans	Yes	6 cups	1½ hours	2¼ cups
Lentils	No	3 cups	30 to 40 minutes	3 cups
Lima beans	Yes	3 cups	1 hour	2½ cups
Mung beans	Yes	3 cups	1¼ hour	3 cups
Navy beans (white beans)	Yes	4 cups	1½ hours	2½ cups
Pinto beans	Yes	3 cups	1½ hours	2¼ cups
Red beans	Yes	4 cups	1½ to 2 hours	2½ cups
Soybeans	Yes	4 cups	3 to 4 hours	2½ cups
Split peas	No	3 cups	30 to 40 minutes	3½ cups

farro and jerusalem artichoke salad

Farro, one of the oldest cultivated grains, has been a staple in the Middle East since Biblical times. Today, it is frequently used in Italian cuisine. This salad is wonderful the day after being assembled, when the flavours have had a chance to blend and mellow.

JERUSALEM ARTICHOKES

4 Jerusalem artichokes, scrubbed and thinly sliced
½ to 1 tablespoon (7 to 15 ml) olive oil
pinch of kosher salt

FARRO

1 cup (250 ml) dry farro, (option: toast in dry saucepan for 5 minutes over medium heat)
2½ cups (625 ml) Vegetable Stock (see page 80) or water
½ teaspoon (2 ml) kosher salt, to taste
¼ teaspoon (1 ml) freshly ground pepper, to taste

SALAD

2 cups (500 ml) baby peas, fresh or thawed from frozen
3 scallions, thinly sliced
1 cup (250 ml) finely chopped fresh flat-leaf parsley
½ cup (125 ml) finely chopped fresh mint
¼ cup (60 ml) coarsely chopped pistachios, toasted
grated zest and juice of 1 lemon
1 tablespoon (15 ml) extra-virgin olive oil
¼ cup (60 ml) pomegranate seeds for garnish

Preheat oven to 400°F (200°C). Line a baking sheet with crinkled aluminum foil.

Toss Jerusalem artichokes with oil and then spread in a single layer on prepared baking sheet. Roast about 15 to 20 minutes until golden brown. Remove from oven, sprinkle lightly with salt, and cool.

Bring farro and stock to a boil in a large saucepan over medium-high heat. Reduce heat to maintain a very gentle simmer, cover, and cook about 25 to 30 minutes until farro is tender. If any liquid remains, remove lid, increase heat, and stir until all liquid is absorbed. Scrape and incorporate any brown bits from bottom of pan. Transfer to a large bowl and cool. Add salt and pepper and stir.

Add peas, scallions, parsley, mint, and lemon zest to farro; mix until combined. Mix lemon juice and oil together and stir into salad until incorporated.

Just before serving, fold in pistachios and pomegranate seeds. Taste, adding more salt and pepper if necessary. Garnish with Jerusalem artichokes.

Serve warm or at room temperature.

Serves 6 to 8 ‖ NUTRITION (per serving): energy 173 kcal | total fat 6 g | saturated fat 1 g | carbohydrate 27 g | fibre 6 g | protein 7 g | sodium 140 mg | excellent source of vitamin C, iron, vitamin E | good source of thiamin

SMART TIP

To remove seeds from a pomegranate, roll the fruit on a counter to loosen seeds. Cut pomegranate in half. Holding one half in your hand with the seeds facing your palm, hit the back of the fruit with a wooden spoon. The seeds will release.

DR. JOE'S SMART FACT

People often state that eating mint makes the mouth feel cold. This is because menthol, a compound that occurs naturally in mint, tricks the brain into thinking that the mouth is cold when in fact no change in temperature has occurred.

wheat berries with cranberries and pecans

This chewy and nutty grain marries well with the sweetness of dried cranberries and onions to create a beautifully balanced side dish or salad. Ideal for the buffet table.

SMART TIP

To prevent grains from spoiling, store them in airtight containers in the freezer. This is especially important for whole grains such as wheat berries, which turn rancid with oxidation.

INGREDIENTS

1 cup (250 ml) dry hard wheat berries, rinsed and sorted
2 cups (500 ml) Vegetable Stock (see page 80)
1 tablespoon (15 ml) canola oil
½ Vidalia onion, diced small
½ cup (125 ml) Atoka dried cranberries
⅓ cup (75 ml) raw pecans, toasted
¼ cup (60 ml) chopped fresh chives
¼ cup (60 ml) chopped fresh flat-leaf parsley
2 tablespoons (30 ml) fresh lemon juice
½ teaspoon (2 ml) kosher salt, plus more for seasoning
¼ teaspoon (1 ml) freshly ground pepper, plus more for seasoning
2 tablespoons (30 ml) Not-So-Basic Vinaigrette (see page 109), optional

Place wheat berries in a large saucepan, add stock, and bring to a boil over medium-high heat. Reduce heat to maintain a very gentle simmer, cover, and cook about 45 to 60 minutes, stirring occasionally. Start checking for doneness at 45 minutes. Wheat berries are ready when chewy but not tough.

Meanwhile, heat oil in a large saucepan over medium heat. Add onion and sauté about 5 minutes until softened. Set aside.

In a large bowl, combine cooked wheat berries and onion with remaining ingredients. Taste, adding more salt and pepper if necessary. Serve warm or at room temperature.

Serves 4 to 6 ‖ NUTRITION (per serving): energy 202 kcal | total fat 6 g | saturated 1 g | carbohydrate 34 g | fibre 6 g | protein 5 g | sodium 171 mg | excellent source of vitamin E

freekeh blueberry salad

Freekeh (pronounced free-ka) is a high-protein grain laden with nutrients and fibre to keep you feeling full and satisfied. With its sweet, nutty flavour, this salad will truly delight the senses.

FREEKEH

1 teaspoon (5 ml) olive oil
1 cup (250 ml) whole-grain dry freekeh
2½ cups (625 ml) Vegetable Stock (see page 80) or water
½ teaspoon (2 ml) kosher salt, plus more for seasoning

SALAD

1 cup (250 ml) frozen shelled edamame beans
1 cup (250 ml) yellow and red cherry tomatoes, cut in quarters
1 cup (250 ml) fresh blueberries
8 radishes, diced small
1 jalapeño pepper, seeded and very finely chopped
⅓ cup (75 ml) finely chopped fresh parsley
⅓ cup (75 ml) finely chopped fresh mint
1 ripe avocado, halved, pit and peel removed, diced small
¼ teaspoon (1 ml) freshly ground pepper, plus more for seasoning
¼ to ½ cup (60 to 125 ml) Lime Vinaigrette (see page 110)

Heat oil in a medium saucepan over medium heat. Add freekeh, stir until fully coated with oil, and toast lightly for about 4 minutes. Add stock and bring to a boil over high heat. Lower heat to maintain a gentle simmer, cover, and cook for about 35 to 40 minutes until freekeh is tender and all liquid is absorbed. Remove from heat and let stand for 5 minutes. Add salt, fluff with a fork, and transfer to a bowl to cool.

Place edamame beans in a pot of boiling water on medium-high heat. Bring back to a boil and immediately drain in a colander. Refresh with cold water and let dry.

Combine remaining salad ingredients in a large bowl. Add cooled freekeh and edamame beans and mix well. Refrigerate for 30 minutes.

Pour 3 to 4 tablespoons of dressing over salad just before serving. Taste, adding more dressing, salt, and pepper if necessary. Serve at room temperature or chilled.

Serves 6 to 8 ‖ **NUTRITION** (per serving): energy 243 kcal | total fat 10 g | saturated fat 1 g | carbohydrate 30 g | fibre 7 g | protein 11 g | sodium 231 mg | good source of vitamin C, iron, thiamin, folate

SMART TIP

To prevent grains from sticking to the pot, coat the bottom and sides of the vessel with cooking spray before adding the grains.

couscous dried fruit medley

Warm or at room temperature, this adaptable grain dish can be served as a side or a main. For variety, bulgur and quinoa work equally well.

COUSCOUS

1 cup (250 ml) dry whole wheat couscous
1½ cups (375 ml) Vegetable Stock (see page 80)

SALAD

1 cup (250 ml) cooked chickpeas
½ cup (125 ml) seeded English cucumber, diced small
⅓ cup (75 ml) pitted and coarsely chopped dates or currants
⅓ cup (75 ml) coarsely chopped dried mango or apricot
½ cup (125 ml) slivered almonds, toasted
½ cup (125 ml) finely chopped fresh cilantro or parsley
½ cup (125 ml) finely chopped fresh mint
¼ cup (60 ml) finely chopped Vidalia onion
kosher salt and freshly ground pepper
¼ cup (60 ml) Sesame Miso Dressing (see page 111), plus
    additional if desired
¼ cup (60 ml) fresh cilantro or parsley, chopped, for garnish

Place couscous in a medium saucepan, add stock, and bring to a boil over medium-high heat. Stir for 30 seconds. Remove from heat, cover, let stand for 5 minutes, and then fluff with a fork. Transfer to a large bowl and cool.

In another large bowl, gently combine all salad ingredients (except dressing and garnish). Add cooled couscous.

Pour dressing over salad and toss to combine. Taste, adding more dressing, salt, and pepper if necessary.

Garnish with cilantro or parsley sprigs just before serving. Serve at room temperature or chilled.

Serves 8 || **NUTRITION** (per serving): energy 231 kcal | total fat 9 g | saturated fat 1 g | carbohydrate 37 g | fibre 5 g | protein 8 g | sodium 43 mg | excellent source of vitamin E, folate | good source of iron, niacin

DR. JOE'S SMART FACT

Interestingly, couscous is made from 100% durum wheat and is considered to be neither grain nor pasta.

quinoa with mushrooms and chickpeas

This protein-packed substitute for rice is made even more nutritious with the addition of sunflower seeds and chickpeas. Quinoa has a mild, nutty flavour that is sure to please.

INGREDIENTS

2 tablespoons (30 ml) canola oil
2 medium onions, chopped
8 ounces (225 g) cremini mushrooms, sliced
2 garlic cloves, minced
1 cup (250 ml) dry quinoa (black, red or white), rinsed and sorted
2 cups (500 ml) Vegetable or Chicken Stock (see page 80)
    or water
1 cup (250 ml) cooked chickpeas
½ cup (125 ml) chopped fresh parsley
1 teaspoon (5 ml) kosher salt, plus more for seasoning
½ teaspoon (2 ml) freshly ground pepper, plus more for seasoning
⅓ cup (75 ml) sunflower seeds, toasted, for garnish

Heat oil in a large, deep saucepan over medium-high heat. Add onions, mushrooms, and garlic and sauté about 6 to 7 minutes until softened and golden.

Stir in quinoa and cook for 2 minutes longer. Add stock and bring to a boil over medium-high heat. Reduce heat to maintain a gentle simmer, cover, and cook about 15 minutes or until all liquid is absorbed. Remove from heat and let stand for 5 minutes.

Add chickpeas, parsley, salt, and pepper and fluff with a fork. Taste, adding more salt and pepper if necessary.

Sprinkle with sunflower seeds. Serve immediately or at room temperature.

Serves 8 to 10 ‖ NUTRITION (per serving): energy 143 kcal | total fat 4 g | saturated fat 0 g | carbohydrate 22 g | fibre 3 g | protein 5 g | sodium 254 mg | good source of folate

SMART TIP

Quinoa has a natural coating of saponin, a bitter substance that protects the plant from insects and birds. Even though most of the saponin is removed during processing, it is a good idea to swish the quinoa in three or four changes of water until the water is clear.

DR. JOE'S SMART FACT

Although quinoa is often used as a grain, it is actually an ancient Peruvian seed. Quinoa, buckwheat, and millet are seeds, not grains. Quinoa is as versatile as rice but has a very different nutritional profile. Its protein content is superior to that of most grains because it contains all the essential amino acids. Quinoa is particularly high in lysine, an amino acid important for tissue growth and repair, and it also provides a host of helpful minerals.

A great time-saver is to cook up a big batch of a whole grain and let it cool completely. Spoon it into resealable plastic bags, press flat, and stack in the freezer.

toasted bulgur with cranberry beans

Bulgur is whole wheat that has been parboiled, dried, and cracked so that it cooks quickly. Cranberry beans—also known as Borlotti beans in Italy—are white with red speckles. They have a nutty flavour and make for a very colourful and palatable presentation.

INGREDIENTS

1 cup (250 ml) bulgur, rinsed and sorted
2 cups (500 ml) Vegetable Stock (see page 80)
1 tablespoon (15 ml) canola oil
2 or 3 shallots, diced small
2 teaspoons (10 ml) minced fresh ginger
½ cup (125 ml) coarsely chopped dried cherries
2 cups (500 ml) cooked cranberry beans or romano beans
2 tablespoons (30 ml) finely chopped fresh parsley
3 tablespoons (45 ml) fresh lemon juice
1 tablespoon (15 ml) extra-virgin olive oil
½ teaspoon (1 ml) ground cardamom or pinch of chili pepper
½ teaspoon (2 ml) kosher salt
¼ teaspoon (1 ml) freshly ground pepper
½ cup (125 ml) crumbled mild goat cheese for garnish (optional)
¼ cup (60 ml) coarsely chopped pecans or walnuts, toasted, for garnish (optional)

Place bulgur in a dry, medium saucepan on medium-high heat and toast about 2 to 3 minutes until grains begin to turn golden. Add stock and bring to a boil. Cover and reduce heat to low. Simmer about 15 minutes until all liquid is absorbed. Remove from heat and let stand for 5 minutes. Transfer to a large bowl and fluff with a fork.

Heat oil in a medium skillet over medium heat. Add shallots and ginger and sauté for 3 minutes. Add dried cherries, beans, and parsley and sauté for 1 to 2 minutes. Add to cooked bulgur.

In a small bowl, whisk together lemon juice, oil, cardamom, salt, and pepper. Pour onto cooked bulgur along with goat cheese and pecans (if using) and toss until well combined. Taste and adjust seasonings if necessary.

Serve warm or at room temperature.

Serves 6 to 8 ‖ NUTRITION (per serving): energy 197 kcal | total fat 4 g | saturated fat 1 g | carbohydrate 36 g | fibre 9 g | protein 7 g | sodium 135 mg | excellent source of folate | good source of thiamin

southwestern buckwheat salad

Loaded with beans, vegetables, and a hearty, chewy grain, this exceptional salad serves as a complete and satisfying meal.

BUCKWHEAT

1½ cups (375 ml) roasted buckwheat, rinsed and sorted
1 egg, beaten
2½ cups (625 ml) Vegetable Stock (see page 80)

SALAD

1 cup (250 ml) cooked black beans
1 cup (250 ml) corn kernels, fresh or thawed from frozen
1 small red onion, diced small
1 red bell pepper, diced small
1 jalapeño pepper, seeded and finely chopped
¼ cup (60 ml) finely chopped fresh cilantro
½ cup (125 ml) crumbled mild feta (optional)
½ teaspoon (2 ml) kosher salt, plus more for seasoning
¼ teaspoon (1 ml) freshly ground pepper, plus more for seasoning
¼ to ½ cup (60 to 125 ml) Lime Vinaigrette (see page 110)
tortilla strips (see Smart Tip), for garnish (optional)

In a small bowl, mix buckwheat with beaten egg until buckwheat is completely coated. Heat a large, non-stick saucepan over medium-high heat and add coated buckwheat. Cook, stirring, until egg dries. Add stock, bring to a boil, and then reduce heat to maintain a very gentle simmer. Cover and cook for 7 minutes. If any liquid remains, remove lid, increase heat, and stir until all liquid is absorbed. Scrape and incorporate any brown bits from bottom of pan. Remove from heat and cool.

In a large bowl, gently combine all salad ingredients (except vinaigrette and garnish). Add cooled buckwheat.

Pour 4 tablespoons of vinaigrette over salad and toss to combine. Taste, adding more dressing, salt, and pepper if necessary.

Garnish with tortilla strips just before serving. Serve at room temperature or chilled.

Serves 6 to 8 ‖ NUTRITION (per serving): energy 214 kcal | total fat 5 g | saturated fat 1 g | carbohydrate 38 g | fibre 4 g | protein 8 g | sodium 221 mg | good source of vitamin C

SMART TIP

Making your own tortilla strips is fast and easy. Preheat oven to 375°F (190°C). Lightly brush both sides of whole-wheat tortillas with canola oil. Make a stack of 4 tortillas. Using a pizza cutter or sharp knife, cut each tortilla in half and then into ¼-inch (5 mm) strips. Arrange on a baking pan and season with a little salt. Bake for 12 minutes.

SMART TIP

A sturdy, heavy-bottomed saucepan with a tight-fitting lid is a must for cooking any grain.

DR. JOE'S SMART FACT

The high protein and nutrient content in lentils is reason enough to incorporate them into our diet. The large dose of soluble fibre that lentils provide is of particular importance for people with diabetes, since it slows the digestion and absorption of carbohydrates and helps to reduce the risk of spikes in blood sugar levels.

lentil and barley citrus salad

This salad is a winner! Chock full of whole grains, it gains an unexpected sweetness from the oranges and figs.

INGREDIENTS

1 cup (250 ml) barley, rinsed and sorted
1 cup (250 ml) green lentils, rinsed and sorted
1 teaspoon (5 ml) salt, divided
2 navel oranges
½ cup (125 ml) roughly diced dried figs
½ cup (125 ml) finely chopped flat-leaf parsley or cilantro
¼ cup (50 ml) finely chopped fresh dill
½ cup (125 ml) roughly chopped shelled pistachio nuts, toasted
¼ to ½ cup (60 to 125 ml) Not-So-Basic Vinaigrette (see page 109)

In a large, high-sided saucepan, bring 3 cups of water and barley to boil over medium-high heat. Reduce heat to maintain a very gentle simmer, cover, and cook about 45 minutes or until tender and all liquid has been absorbed. Stir in ½ teaspoon of salt and fluff with a fork.

Bring 2 cups (500 ml) of water and lentils to boil over medium-high heat. Reduce heat to maintain a very gentle simmer and cook, uncovered, for 20 to 30 minutes or until tender. (Make sure lentils remain just covered by water, adding more if necessary.) Drain any excess water. Stir in remaining ½ teaspoon of salt and fluff with a fork.

Over a large serving bowl, zest the oranges with a fine grater. Remove and discard peel and membrane from oranges. Carefully remove orange segments and place in bowl.

Add in all remaining ingredients (except nuts) and lightly toss. Pour desired amount of vinaigrette over salad and toss to combine. Let salad sit for 2 hours before serving. Add nuts and season with additional vinaigrette as desired. Serve cold or at room temperature.

Serves 8 to 12 ‖ **NUTRITION** (per serving): energy 205 kcal | total fat 6 g | saturated 0 g | carbohydrate 31 g | fibre 6 g | protein 8 g | sodium 223 mg | excellent source of thiamin | good source of vitamin E, iron, folate

orecchiette with peas, edamame, ricotta, and lemon

You can almost feel the summer breeze when you eat this refreshing pasta. Young peas, chewy edamame, and sweet ricotta tossed with orecchiette make a perfect light meal any time of the year.

INGREDIENTS

2 cups (500 ml) shelled edamame beans
2 cups (500 ml) peas, fresh or thawed from frozen
½ pound (225 g) dry orecchiette noodles
1 cup (250 ml) ricotta cheese
½ cup (125 ml) grated Parmesan cheese
2 tablespoons (30 ml) finely grated lemon zest
¾ cup (175 ml) toasted walnuts, coarsely chopped
½ cup (125 ml) coarsely chopped fresh mint, basil, or dill
¼ teaspoon (2 ml) freshly ground pepper, plus more for seasoning
4 cups (1 L) lightly packed arugula leaves
3 tablespoons (45 ml) coarsely chopped fresh mint leaves for garnish
kosher salt and freshly ground pepper, to taste

Prepare an ice-water bath by filling a large bowl with 2 to 3 cups of ice and adding cold water. Set aside.

Bring a large pot of water to a boil over high heat. Place edamame and peas in sieve and lower into boiling water. Blanch for 1 to 2 minutes. Remove sieve from boiling water and lower into prepared ice bath. Transfer edamame and peas to a bowl lined with paper towels; allow to drain and set aside.

Discard blanching water, fill pot with fresh water, and bring to a boil. Add pasta and cook until *al dente*. Reserve 1 cup (250 ml) of pasta water; drain well.

In a large bowl or empty pasta pot, combine ricotta, Parmesan, lemon zest, walnuts, and chopped herbs. Add ½ cup (125 ml) of reserved pasta water to mixture and stir to combine. Add in drained pasta, edamame, peas, and arugula. Toss to combine. Add more pasta water if necessary. Taste and adjust seasonings with salt and pepper.

Sprinkle with mint leaves and serve.

Serves 6 to 8 ‖ **NUTRITION** (per serving): energy 360 kcal | total fat 19 g | saturated fat 5 g | carbohydrate 31 g | fibre 7 g | protein 21 g | sodium 254 mg | excellent source of calcium, iron, vitamin E, riboflavin, niacin, folate | good source of vitamin A, vitamin B12

SMART TIP

Use plenty of water to ensure pasta cooks evenly and has room to move and swell as it cooks. Don't add oil to the water, as it will coat the pasta and prevent sauce from clinging. Save the pasta cooking water; it can be used to bring the sauce to the right consistency.

DR. JOE'S SMART FACT

Edamame beans are immature soybeans. Many studies have linked soybean consumption with reduced cholesterol, but there has also been concern that the bean's isoflavones may have negative estrogen-like effects. On the other hand, there have been claims of reduced menopausal symptoms associated with soy consumption.

penne with roasted vegetables

Roasting vegetables intensifies their flavours; tossed with penne, they make for a colourful and deliciously satiating dish.

INGREDIENTS

1 tablespoon (15 ml) low-sodium soy sauce

2 tablespoons (30 ml) seasoned rice wine vinegar

1 tablespoon (15 ml) honey

1 red bell pepper, seeded and cut into 1½-inch (3.5 cm) squares

1 yellow bell pepper, seeded and cut into 1½-inch (3.5 cm) squares

1 orange bell pepper, seeded and cut into 1½-inch (3.5 cm) squares

12 ounces (325 g) asparagus spears, diagonally cut into 2-inch (5 cm) slices

8 ounces (225 g) portobello or cremini mushrooms, quartered

2 cups (500 ml) grape tomatoes, halved

8 ounces (225 g) whole-wheat or multi-grain dry penne pasta

1 tablespoon (15 ml) canola oil

2 shallots, thinly sliced

1 tablespoon (15 ml) minced fresh garlic

1 teaspoon (5 ml) Sriracha sauce or hot chili paste, to taste

2 tablespoons (30 ml) finely chopped fresh parsley

kosher salt and freshly ground pepper, to taste

¼ cup (60 ml) panko breadcrumbs for garnish (optional)

1 teaspoon (5 ml) canola oil

Mix soy sauce, vinegar, and honey together in a small bowl. Add peppers, asparagus, mushrooms, and tomatoes and toss until vegetables are coated. Let marinate for 1 hour. Transfer to a large rimmed baking sheet and spread vegetables out to form a single layer.

Preheat broiler. Broil vegetables for 10 to 15 minutes on one side; turn vegetables over and broil about 8 to 10 minutes until they are cooked through and beginning to char. Remove and set aside.

Bring a large pot of water to a boil over high heat, add pasta and cook until *al dente*. Reserve 1½ cups (375 ml) of pasta water; drain well.

Heat oil over medium heat and add shallots, garlic, and Sriracha sauce and sauté for 2 to 3 minutes. Add roasted vegetables and drained pasta and stir until combined. Add parsley and ½ cup (125 ml) reserved pasta water. Cook over medium-high heat, stirring gently, until combined and pasta water thickens slightly, about 2 minutes. If pasta is too dry, add more pasta water a little at a time until desired consistency is reached. Taste, adjusting seasoning with salt and pepper as desired.

Optional garnish: While the pasta cooks, heat 1 teaspoon of oil in a large saucepan over medium heat. Add panko and cook, stirring frequently, until crisp and golden, about 3 minutes. Set aside.

Place pasta in a large serving platter or divide among serving plates. Sprinkle on panko crumbs if using.

Serves 4 to 6 ‖ **NUTRITION** (per serving): energy 140 kcal | total fat 3 g | saturated fat 0 g | carbohydrate 26 g | fibre 4 g | protein 6 g | sodium 103 mg | excellent source of vitamin C, vitamin E | good source of iron, thiamin, niacin, folate, vitamin B6

vegetarian shepherd's pie

This vegetarian shepherd's pie is a healthy alternative to the classic meat-and-potatoes version. With the addition of beans, whole-grain brown rice, and assorted vegetables, it is high on flavour but low in fat.

VEGGIE FILLING

1 tablespoon (15 ml) olive oil
1 medium Vidalia onion, coarsely chopped
3 large garlic cloves, minced
1 large carrot, grated
1 teaspoon (5 ml) chili powder
1 teaspoon (5 ml) ground cumin
2 cups (500 ml) cooked red or black beans
1 cup (250 ml) cooked brown rice
2 tablespoons (30 ml) tomato paste
2 tablespoons (30 ml) Dijon or whole-grain mustard
1 tablespoon (15 ml) low-sodium soy sauce

LAYERS

1½ cups (375 ml) peas, fresh or thawed from frozen
2 cups (500 ml) Carrot and Butternut Squash Mash (see page 181)

TOPPING

1 teaspoon (5 ml) extra-virgin olive oil
¼ cup (60 ml) panko breadcrumbs

Heat oil in a large pot over medium heat. Add onions and garlic and sauté about 5 minutes until softened. Add remaining filling ingredients and cook, stirring, for 3 to 5 minutes. Remove from heat and roughly mash mixture with a large fork or potato masher.

Preheat oven to 450°F (230°C). Lightly grease an 8 × 10 inch (20 × 25 cm) casserole dish.

Spoon veggie mixture into casserole dish and lightly pack down. Layer peas over veggie mixture, followed by carrot and butternut squash mash; spread to edges of baking dish.

Wipe pot with paper towel. Heat oil over medium heat. Add panko and toss about 3 minutes until coated and toasted. Sprinkle casserole with panko topping and bake about 25 to 30 minutes until juices are bubbling and topping is golden brown.

Let sit 5 minutes before serving.

Serves 8 ‖ **NUTRITION** (per serving): energy 248 kcal | total fat 5 g | saturated fat 1 g | carbohydrate 35 g | fibre 8 g | protein 9 g | sodium 272 mg | excellent source of folate | good source of niacin, iron, thiamin, vitamin B6

DR. JOE'S SMART FACT

The indigestible fraction (IF), or what we more commonly refer to as "fibre," in black beans has recently been shown to be greater than the IF in both lentils and chickpeas. The fibre provides food for bacteria in the colon, allowing them to produce butyric acid, which helps maintain the health of cells that line the colon. Reports of lowered colon cancer risk associated with black bean intake in some research studies may be related to the high IF content of this legume.

eggplant roll-ups

Save on calories. Eggplant slices stand in for pasta, increasing the fibre and nutritional value. Tastes amazing.

Preheat oven to 375°F (190°C).

Brush eggplant on both sides with oil and season with salt and pepper. Brown in batches in a large skillet on medium-high heat. Transfer to paper towel to drain.

Cover bottom of baking dish with tomato sauce and set aside.

In a large bowl, combine spinach, ricotta, mozzarella, garlic, egg yolk, salt, and pepper. Spread mixture on eggplant slices. Roll up each slice and place, standing, in baking dish. Pour remaining tomato sauce around eggplant roll-ups and bake for 20 to 30 minutes.

Makes 8 roll-ups ‖ NUTRITION (per serving): energy 153 kcal | total fat 11 g | saturated fat 2 g | carbohydrate 8 g | fibre 3 g | protein 7 g | sodium 373 mg | good source of vitamin E, folate, calcium, vitamin B12

tangy tomato sauce

Beautifully seasoned with capers and anchovies, our tomato sauce can be used in many different recipes. Simply delicious!

INGREDIENTS

2 tablespoons (30 ml) olive oil
3 garlic cloves, minced
2 tablespoons (30 ml) capers, rinsed, drained, and chopped
3 bay leaves
½ tablespoon (7 ml) chopped fresh oregano
½ tablespoon (7 ml) chopped fresh thyme
1 teaspoon (5 ml) crushed red pepper flakes, to taste
4 ripe plum tomatoes, cut into large chunks
28-ounce (796 ml) can whole cherry tomatoes, with juice
6 anchovies, minced, or 2 tablespoons (30 ml) anchovy paste

Heat oil in a large deep saucepan over medium heat. Add garlic and capers and sauté about 2 minutes until softened.

Add bay leaves, seasonings, and plum tomatoes; sauté for 5 minutes or until tomatoes begin to lose their shape. Add canned tomatoes with juice and cook for 5 minutes, stirring and breaking up tomatoes with the back of a spoon.

Add anchovies or anchovy paste and simmer, stirring, for 10 to 15 minutes. Taste, adding more salt and pepper if necessary.

Remove bay leaves.

SMART TIP

To make the most of leftover fresh herbs, wrap a piece of string around the stems and hang upside down in a cool dry place. Leave to dry for 4 to 10 days. Once the herbs are dry and crisp, remove stems and store leaves in a tightly sealed spice jar.

Makes 4½ cups ‖ NUTRITION (per 1 cup): energy 127 kcal | total fat 8 g | saturated fat 1 g | carbohydrate 10 g | fibre 2 g | protein 6 g | sodium 864 mg

portobello veggie burgers

The veggie burger is all the rage today, but making one that tastes great can be quite a challenge. With this recipe you can build a meatless burger that is both moist and delicious.

In a large, high-sided saucepan, bring 2 cups of salted water and barley to a boil over medium-high heat. Reduce heat to maintain a very gentle simmer. Cover and cook for 30 to 35 minutes or until chewy. Drain and place half in food processor and other half in a large bowl.

In a medium-size saucepan, bring 2 cups (500 ml) of salted water and lentils to a boil over medium-high heat. Reduce heat to maintain a very gentle simmer. Cook, uncovered, for 15 to 20 minutes or until lentils begin to fall apart. Drain and place half in food processor and the remainder in the bowl with barley.

Preheat oven to 425°F (220°C).

Remove stems and gills from mushroom caps and set aside. Brush both sides of mushroom caps with oil, season with salt and pepper and set on baking sheet. Bake about 8 to 10 minutes until tender. Set aside until ready to serve.

Heat 1 tablespoon of oil in a sauté pan over medium heat. Chop the mushroom stems and add with gills along with sliced cremini mushrooms to pan. Cook for 8 to 10 minutes. Transfer half to food processor and place balance in bowl with barley and lentils.

In the same sauté pan, heat 1 tablespoon oil over medium heat. Add leeks and thyme and cook about 15 to 20 minutes until leeks are softened. Stir in garlic and tomato paste and cook 2 minutes longer. Transfer half to food processor and place other half in bowl with barley mixture.

Add cashews, eggs, salt, and pepper to mixture in food processor. Pulse 6 to 8 times until the mixture is blended but has some texture remaining. Transfer to bowl with other ingredients. Mix well. Add panko and stir until all ingredients are combined.

Shape mixture into 6 to 8 patties.

Lower oven temperature to 325°F (160°C).

Heat remaining tablespoon of oil in a large, non-stick, oven-proof skillet over medium-high heat. When hot, add patties and cook until browned (about 3 minutes per side). Transfer skillet to oven and bake 8 to 10 minutes until burgers are firm and cooked through.

Place patty on cooked mushroom cap and serve with a dollop of low-fat tzatziki.

Serves 6 to 8 ‖ **NUTRITION** (per serving): energy 255 kcal | total fat 12 g | saturated fat 2 g | carbohydrate 30 g | fibre 6 g | protein 10 g | sodium 213 mg | excellent source of thiamin, niacin, riboflavin, folate | good source of vitamin E, iron, vitamin B12, vitamin B6

❄

Shown with Low-Fat Tzatziki (see page 302)

INGREDIENTS

⅓ cup (75 ml) pearl barley, rinsed and sorted

⅓ cup (75 ml) red lentils, rinsed and sorted

3 tablespoons (45 ml) canola oil, divided, plus additional for brushing

6 to 8 portobello mushrooms

kosher salt and freshly ground pepper, to taste

8 cremini mushrooms, thinly sliced

3 leeks, white and pale green part only, finely chopped

1 tablespoon (15 ml) finely chopped fresh thyme or rosemary

3 garlic cloves, minced

2 tablespoons (30 ml) tomato paste

½ cup (125 ml) raw cashews, toasted

2 large eggs

½ teaspoon (2 ml) salt

¼ teaspoon (1 ml) freshly ground pepper

½ cup (125 ml) panko breadcrumbs, toasted

dr. joe's vegetarian goulash

This goulash recipe offers multiple layers of delicious flavours. Hats off to our co-editor for this wonderfully hearty and healthy meal!

GOULASH

2 tablespoons (30 ml) canola oil
2 medium onions, coarsely chopped
2 tomatoes, coarsely chopped
1 cup (250 ml) sliced green beans
3 bell peppers, red, green, and yellow, seeded and diced small
4 or 5 large garlic cloves, finely chopped
1 teaspoon (5 ml) salt, plus more for seasoning
2 tablespoons (30 ml) sweet Hungarian paprika
10 red baby potatoes, diced large
1 cup (250 ml) water
2 cups (500 ml) thinly sliced mushrooms
freshly ground black pepper

TOFU TOPPING

1 tablespoon (15 ml) canola oil
1 medium onion, coarsely chopped
1 large garlic clove, minced
1-pound (455 g) package firm tofu, diced small
pinch Hungarian paprika (sweet or hot)
½ red bell pepper, seeded and diced small
½ yellow bell pepper, seeded and diced small
¼ cup finely chopped fresh parsley for garnish

Heat oil in a large saucepan over medium-high heat. Add onions and sauté about 5 minutes until light brown and translucent. Add tomatoes, beans, and pepper; stir well. Cover pot; reduce heat and simmer 5 minutes. Add garlic, salt, and paprika; simmer 5 minutes. Add potatoes and water and stir well; simmer about 10 to 15 minutes until potatoes are soft. Add mushrooms and stir; simmer for 5 minutes. Taste, adding more salt and pepper if necessary.

In a separate skillet, prepare topping by heating oil over medium heat. Add onions and garlic and sauté about 5 minutes until light brown and translucent. Add tofu and cook until tofu starts to turn brown. Sprinkle with paprika and continue to cook. Add peppers and cook about 5 to 7 minutes until peppers are soft.

Place goulash in a serving dish and top with tofu mixture. Sprinkle with parsley. Serve warm.

Serves 6 ‖ **NUTRITION** (per serving): energy 404 kcal | total fat 12 g | saturated fat 1 g | carbohydrate 66 g | fibre 11 g | protein 18 g | sodium 428 mg | excellent source of potassium, vitamin C, iron, vitamin E, thiamin, riboflavin, niacin, folate, vitamin B6 | good source of vitamin A, calcium

Eat your vegetables: they are your health's best allies. Revitalize your diet with herbs and seasonings that give eating your veggies a whole new appeal.

sides & savoury fare

roasted brussels sprouts medley

Inspired by a wonderful restaurant in New York City named Ilili, this Brussels sprouts recipe is unparalleled. Its unusual combination of ingredients results in sublime tastes and textures.

MINT YOGURT SAUCE

¼ cup (60 ml) low-fat plain Greek yogurt
1 tablespoon (15 ml) very finely chopped fresh mint leaves

FIG PURÉE

¼ cup (60 ml) water
¼ cup (60 ml) fig jam

BRUSSELS SPROUTS

20 to 30 large Brussels sprouts, stems trimmed, sliced in half lengthwise, outer leaves removed
2 tablespoons (30 ml) extra-virgin olive oil
1 to 2 teaspoons (5 to 10 ml) sherry, balsamic, or rice vinegar, to taste
½ teaspoon (2 ml) salt
¼ cup (60 ml) coarsely chopped walnuts, toasted
½ cup (125 ml) blueberries
¼ cup (60 ml) finely chopped fresh mint leaves for garnish

Mix yogurt and mint leaves together. Let sit for 30 minutes.

Bring water and fig jam to a boil in a small saucepan over medium heat. Remove from heat and purée with an immersion blender; set aside.

Preheat oven to 450°F (230°C).

Toss Brussels sprouts and oil together in a large bowl. Transfer to rimmed baking sheet and roast about 10 or 15 minutes until tender but still green, with only the outer leaves browned.

Remove from oven and toss with vinegar and salt.

Transfer Brussels sprouts to a shallow serving bowl. Toss with 3 tablespoons of yogurt sauce. Drizzle with fig sauce and sprinkle with walnuts and blueberries. Just before serving, add mint and additional sauce if desired.

Serves 6 ‖ NUTRITION (per serving): energy 165 kcal | total fat 8 g | saturated fat 1 g | carbohydrate 21 g | fibre 5 g | protein 5 g | sodium 191 mg | excellent source of vitamin C, vitamin E | good source of folate, thiamin

DR. JOE'S SMART FACT

Like other cruciferous vegetables, Brussels sprouts are a source of sulforaphane, a chemical with anti-cancer properties. Roasting is better than boiling to retain this benefit.

grilled artichokes

Although most people are intimidated by the prospect of preparing fresh artichokes, this method is quite easy. Steaming the artichokes first and then finishing them on the grill amplifies their delicate flavour. This recipe makes a wonderful appetizer or side dish.

ARTICHOKES

1 lemon, cut in half
4 medium artichokes, 8 to 10 ounces (225 to 285 g) each

LEMON GARLIC DIPPING SAUCE

¼ cup (60 ml) olive oil
juice and finely grated zest of 1 lemon
1 garlic clove, minced
1 teaspoon (5 ml) kosher salt
¼ teaspoon (1 ml) freshly ground pepper

Fill a large bowl with cold water. Squeeze lemon juice into water and drop spent lemon halves into water.

Trim artichokes according to the SMART TIP at left.

Place a steamer rack in a large pot, add water to fill just below rack, and set artichokes on rack. Cover and bring water to a boil over medium-high heat. Reduce heat and simmer about 10 to 15 minutes until outer artichoke leaves are easily removed.

While artichokes are cooking, prepare dipping sauce by whisking all ingredients together in a medium bowl until thoroughly blended. Set aside.

Preheat grill or grill pan over medium heat.

Carefully remove artichokes from pot. Allow the water to drain off and then slice each artichoke in half lengthwise. Remove prickly choke. Brush with dipping sauce, reserving remaining sauce for serving.

Grill artichokes, cut side down, about 5 minutes until tender and charred in spots. Transfer to a platter and serve with remaining dipping sauce.

Serve warm or at room temperature.

Serves 4 ‖ **NUTRITION** (per serving): energy 100 kcal | total fat 4 g | saturated 0 g | carbohydrate 14 g | fibre 6 g | protein 4 g | sodium 72 mg | good source of folate

---

broccolini gremolata

Gremolata is a condiment made of lemon zest, garlic, parsley, and olive oil. This somewhat untraditional version can be used to enhance the taste of asparagus, broccoli, green beans, rapini, or any desired vegetable.

GREMOLATA

2 anchovies, minced, or 2 teaspoons (10 ml) anchovy paste
2 teaspoons (10 ml) minced fresh garlic
1 tablespoon (15 ml) finely grated lemon zest
3 tablespoons (45 ml) very finely chopped flat-leaf parsley
2 tablespoons (30 ml) very finely grated Parmesan cheese
1 tablespoon (15 ml) olive oil
kosher salt and freshly ground pepper to taste

2 heads broccolini, trimmed
¼ cup (60 ml) slivered almonds, toasted, for garnish

Mash anchovies and garlic in a small bowl or with a mortar and pestle. Add remaining gremolata ingredients, mash together to make a paste, and set aside for at least an hour to allow flavours to blend.

In a large, wide pot, bring about 3 cups of water to a boil. Place broccolini in a steamer basket and place steamer in pot, allowing to rest above the water. Steam broccolini about 4 or 5 minutes until tender but still crisp.

Remove from heat and toss with gremolata. Season with salt and pepper to taste.

Garnish with almonds and serve.

Serves 4 ‖ **NUTRITION** (per serving): energy 79 kcal | total fat 4 g | saturated fat 1 g | carbohydrate 6 g | fibre 1 g | protein 4 g | sodium 74 mg | excellent source of vitamin A, vitamin C

DR. JOE'S SMART FACT

A wide range of therapeutic properties are associated with broccoli and broccolini, one of which is the prevention of osteoarthritis. When chewed and digested, broccolini and broccoli release sulforaphane, a compound that has been shown to have anti-cancer properties in laboratory and animal studies.

grilled bok choy

Grilling bok choy adds a smoky subtlety, while seasonings embrace its authentic flavour. This sauce and cooking method work equally well with endives, radicchio, and Swiss chard.

MARINADE

3 tablespoons (45 ml) sesame oil
2 teaspoons (10 ml) low-sodium soy sauce
1 small Thai chili, seeded and finely chopped
2 garlic cloves, minced
1 tablespoon (15 ml) grated fresh ginger
kosher salt and freshly ground pepper, to taste

6 heads baby bok choy, cut in half lengthwise

Preheat grill or grill pan to medium-high heat.

In a small bowl, whisk marinade ingredients together. Arrange bok choy on a large tray in a single layer and brush with marinade. Let bok choy rest in marinade, turning occasionally, about 15 to 20 minutes.

Remove bok choy from marinade, letting any excess drip back into bowl. Place bok choy on grill, cut side down. Grill until slightly wilted and charred, about 4 to 6 minutes per side. Transfer bok choy to bowl with marinade and toss to coat. Taste, adding more salt and pepper if necessary. Rest in marinade, tossing one last time before serving.

Serve hot or at room temperature.

Serves 6 || **NUTRITION** (per serving): energy 70 kcal | total fat 7 g | saturated fat 1 g | carbohydrate 2 g | fibre 1 g | protein 1 g | sodium 83 mg | good source of vitamin C

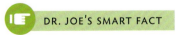

SMART TIP

To rid your hands of a garlic scent, rub your hands along a stainless steel sink or utensil and rinse under cool running water.

DR. JOE'S SMART FACT

Like all cruciferous vegetables, Asian greens such as bok choy, gai choy, and choy sum may be beneficial in reducing the risk of certain cancers, and their vitamin E content helps fight stress and fatigue.

chana masala

Garam masala, a main flavour component of this recipe, is a blend of dry-roasted spices commonly used in North Indian and other South Asian cuisines. The word *garam* refers to the intensity of the spices, which can add a real kick to almost any meat or vegetable recipe. Garam masala can be found in the international section of most large supermarkets. Serve this fragrant dish with yogurt on a bed of steamed brown rice, or scoop it up with naan bread.

INGREDIENTS

1 tablespoon (15 ml) vegetable oil
2 small onions, finely chopped
2 garlic cloves, minced
2 teaspoons (10 ml) ground cumin
pinch of cayenne pepper
1 teaspoon (5 ml) ground turmeric
1 ripe plum tomato, coarsely chopped
1 cup (250 ml) water
4 cups (1 L) cooked chickpeas
1 teaspoon (5 ml) garam masala
½ teaspoon (2 ml) kosher salt
1½ tablespoons (22 ml) fresh lemon juice
2 teaspoons (10 ml) grated fresh ginger
½ jalapeño pepper, seeded and very finely diced
¼ cup (60 ml) finely chopped fresh cilantro, with a sprig or two reserved for garnish

Heat oil in a large skillet over medium-high heat. Add onions and garlic and sauté about 5 minutes until softened and browned. If vegetables stick to the bottom, add a tablespoon or two of water.

Reduce heat to medium-low. Add cumin, cayenne, and turmeric and stir for a few seconds. Add tomatoes and cook about 10 minutes until lightly browned. Stir in chickpeas and water. Add remaining ingredients and cook, covered, for 10 minutes.

Garnish with the reserved sprigs of cilantro. Serve immediately or at room temperature.

Serves 6 to 8 ‖ **NUTRITION** (per serving): energy 163 kcal | total fat 4 g | saturated fat 1 g | carbohydrate 25 g | fibre 4 g | protein 8 g | sodium 128 mg | excellent source of folate | good source of iron

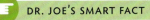 **DR. JOE'S SMART FACT**

Ground and whole cumin seeds are commonly used in cooking, and cumin oil is also used as a flavouring. It is believed that this spice may have antioxidant, anti-cancer, and antibacterial effects, but there is no clinical evidence to support these claims.

herbed sautéed kale

This healthy side dish derives lots of flavour from the kale, herbs, and spices, while the lemon adds a bright note. A wide variety of vegetables—such as Swiss chard, spinach, broccoli, and green beans—can be used in place of kale.

INGREDIENTS

1 tablespoon (15 ml) olive oil
1 yellow onion, finely chopped
1 garlic clove, finely chopped
1 head kale, centre ribs and stems discarded, leaves
    roughly chopped
¼ cup (60 ml) finely chopped fresh chives
¼ cup (60 ml) finely chopped fresh dill
1 cup (250 ml) Vegetable or Chicken Stock (see pages 80 and 81)
½ teaspoon (2 ml) kosher salt
½ teaspoon (2 ml) freshly ground pepper
½ teaspoon (2 ml) crushed red pepper flakes
juice and finely grated zest of ½ lemon
1 tablespoon (15 ml) pine nuts, lightly toasted, for
    garnish (optional)
¼ cup (60 ml) crumbled feta for garnish (optional)

Heat oil in a wide large saucepan over medium-high heat. Add onions and sauté for 5 minutes until softened. Add garlic and cook for 1 minute. Add kale, chives, dill, and stock. Lower heat and simmer for about 7 to 10 minutes until liquid is reduced.

Toss with salt, pepper, and red pepper flakes. Remove from heat.

Stir in lemon zest and juice, pine nuts, and feta (if using). Transfer to serving bowl and serve hot.

Serves 4 to 6 ‖ NUTRITION (per serving): energy 69 kcal | total fat 3 g | saturated fat 1 g | carbohydrate 9 g | fibre 2 g | protein 3 g | sodium 197 mg | excellent source of vitamin A, vitamin C

DR. JOE'S SMART FACT

There is some science behind the hype when it comes to kale. This cruciferous vegetable has the same benefits as cabbage and broccoli but is more versatile. It can be put in a smoothie, baked into chips, grilled, stewed, or simply enjoyed raw.

callaloo

Callaloo is a hearty soup or stew that originated in West Africa and is common in Caribbean cuisine. Its main ingredient, a leaf vegetable with local names such as *callaloo* and *bhaaj*, varies from region to region, which can make the soup taste quite different from one table to another. Outside the Caribbean, spinach is more commonly used. Freeze this soup in small portions and use to fortify weekday meals.

INGREDIENTS

1 cup (250 ml) whole grain rice
6 leeks, white and pale green parts only, trimmed and
    coarsely chopped
1½ cups (375 ml) water
2 pounds (900 g) fresh spinach leaves
10 okra, chopped
4 ounces (115 g) pumpkin, cubed
4 scallions, chopped
2 garlic cloves, minced
1 teaspoon (5 ml) kosher salt
½ teaspoon (2 ml) freshly ground pepper
6 sprigs fresh thyme
1 Scotch bonnet pepper, wrapped in cheesecloth
1 cup (250 ml) low-fat coconut milk
pinch of cayenne pepper, if desired

Prepare rice according to package directions and keep warm while you are making the callaloo.

Place all ingredients (except coconut milk and cayenne pepper) in a large pot over medium heat. Bring to a boil, lower heat, and simmer, covered, for 30 to 40 minutes until vegetables are very soft and okra seeds turn brown.

Turn off heat; remove and discard Scotch bonnet pepper. Stir in coconut milk. Pulse mixture briefly with an immersion blender, or pulse in batches using a food processor, allowing callaloo to remain as chunky as desired.

Adjust seasoning to taste with salt and cayenne pepper. Divide rice among serving dishes and spoon callaloo on top. Serve hot.

Serves 8 ‖ **NUTRITION** (per serving): energy 241 | total fat 9 g | saturated fat 7 g | carbohydrate 38 g | fibre 7 g | protein 8 g | sodium 409 mg | excellent source of potassium, vitamin A, vitamin C, iron, vitamin E, folate, vitamin B6 | good source of calcium, thiamin, riboflavin, niacin

asian eggplant

A popular and versatile vegetable, eggplant can be prepared in a variety of ways. This unique recipe delights the taste buds with pungent and sweet seasonings. Any of the cooking methods described below—baking, grilling, or microwaving—will result in one great dish!

INGREDIENTS

2 large eggplants
2 tablespoons (30 ml) brown sugar
2 tablespoons (30 ml) low-sodium soy sauce
1 tablespoon (15 ml) seasoned rice vinegar
1 tablespoon (15 ml) water
1 teaspoon (5 ml) canola oil
4 cloves garlic, minced
1 teaspoon (5 ml) minced fresh ginger
4 scallions, white and pale green parts only, thinly sliced
½ teaspoon (2 ml) hot chili paste
1 teaspoon (5 ml) sesame oil (optional)
2 tablespoons (30 ml) fresh cilantro or flat-leaf parsley, finely chopped, for garnish

Oven method: Preheat oven to 350°F (180°C). Pierce eggplant with a fork. Place on rimmed baking sheet and bake for 30 minutes. Turn and continue to bake for an additional 30 to 45 minutes until eggplant is very soft.

Barbecue method: Pierce eggplant with a fork. Place on a hot barbecue and grill on medium-high heat, covered, for 15 to 20 minutes. Turn and grill for an additional 15 minutes.

Microwave method: Pierce eggplant with a fork. Cook in microwave on high for 10 minutes.

Cool. Dice eggplant into large pieces.

In a small bowl, combine soy sauce, sugar, vinegar, and water.

Heat oil in a large skillet over high heat. Add garlic, ginger, scallions, and chili paste and cook about 30 seconds until fragrant. Add soy sauce mixture and cook, stirring, until sauce comes to a boil. Add eggplant and stir until well combined and heated through.

Remove from heat and stir in sesame oil, if using.

Transfer to serving bowl.

Let rest for at least an hour before serving to allow flavours to blend. Sprinkle with fresh herbs and serve either warm or cold.

Makes about 3 cups ‖ **NUTRITION** (per serving): energy 64 kcal | total fat 1 g | saturated fat 0 g | carbohydrate 14 g | fibre 6 g | protein 2 g | sodium 186 mg

crispy cauliflower

Roasting cauliflower at a high temperature brings out its sweetness and retains a crispy texture. Be creative and use roasted cauliflower in a salad or as a satisfying substitute for potatoes or rice.

INGREDIENTS

1 large head cauliflower, outer leaves and core removed, cut into 1-inch (2.5 cm) pieces
1 tablespoon (15 ml) extra-virgin olive oil
4 garlic cloves, very finely chopped
1 tablespoon (15 ml) finely chopped fresh dill
½ teaspoon (2 ml) kosher salt
¼ teaspoon (1 ml) freshly ground pepper
2 tablespoons (30 ml) slivered almonds, toasted, for garnish

Preheat oven to 400°F (200°C). Line a large rimmed baking sheet with aluminum foil.

Toss cauliflower and oil together in a large bowl. Add remaining ingredients and mix until cauliflower is well coated.

Transfer to prepared baking sheet and bake for 20 to 25 minutes, turning every 10 minutes, until cauliflower is brown and fragrant.

Arrange on serving platter, garnish with toasted almonds, and serve.

SMART TIP

Overcrowding your baking sheet will cause the cauliflower to steam; using two baking sheets and rotating them halfway through cooking will prevent this. Cut the florets small so they will turn golden and crisp.

Serves 4 ‖ **NUTRITION** (per serving): energy 88 kcal | total fat 4 g | saturated fat 1 g | carbohydrate 12 g | fibre 4 g | protein 4 g | sodium 301 mg | excellent source of vitamin C, folate | good source of vitamin B6

greek lima beans

Preheat oven to 350°F (180°C).

In a large casserole dish, combine tomatoes, onions, and parsley. Stir in cooked lima beans, garlic, oil, and water.

Bake for 2 hours, stirring every half hour. Add additional water if sauce becomes too thick.

Taste and adjust seasoning with salt and pepper as needed. Serve hot.

Serves 8 ‖ **NUTRITION** (per serving): energy 227 kcal | total fat 9 g | saturated fat 1 g | carbohydrate 28 g | fibre 9 g | protein 10 g | sodium 129 mg | excellent source of folate | good source of potassium, iron, thiamin, vitamin E

INGREDIENTS

2 large tomatoes, finely chopped

½ Spanish onion, coarsely chopped

½ bunch flat-leaf parsley, coarsely chopped

5 cups (1.25 L) cooked jumbo lima beans

1 garlic clove, minced

⅓ cup (75 ml) extra-virgin olive oil

½ cup (125 ml) water, plus more if necessary

½ teaspoon (2 ml) kosher salt

¼ teaspoon (1 ml) freshly ground pepper

celery root pear mash

INGREDIENTS

1 tablespoon (15 ml) extra-virgin olive oil
3 medium celery roots, peeled and coarsely chopped
3 firm Anjou or Bosc pears, peeled, cored,
    and coarsely chopped
½ teaspoon (2 ml) salt, plus additional to taste
pinch of freshly ground pepper,
    plus additional to taste
½ cup (125 ml) water
⅓ cup (75 ml) finely chopped
    fresh oregano
coarsely chopped fresh
    flat-leaf parsley for garnish

Heat oil in a large pot over
medium-high heat.

Add celery root, pears,
salt, and a pinch of pepper.

Cover and cook, stirring
occasionally, about 30 minutes
until almost tender (reduce heat
if mixture begins to brown).

Add water, cover, and
simmer about 30 minutes
until mixture is completely
tender and water has
evaporated.

Use an immersion blender
or potato masher to purée
mixture to desired consistency.

Add oregano and stir to combine.

Taste, adding more salt and pepper
if necessary. Garnish with parsley
and serve.

Makes 5 cups ‖ NUTRITION (per ½ cup):
energy 55 kcal | total fat 2 g | saturated fat 0 g |
carbohydrate 11 g | fibre 2 g | protein 1 g |
sodium 152 mg

cauliflower apple mash

INGREDIENTS

1 large head cauliflower, trimmed and coarsely chopped
2 large apples, peeled, cored, and coarsely chopped
1 tablespoon (15 ml) extra-virgin olive oil
½ teaspoon (2 ml) salt, plus additional to taste
pinch of freshly ground pepper plus additional to taste
⅓ cup (75 ml) coarsely chopped fresh dill, plus additional for garnish

Preheat oven to 425°F (220°C).

Toss cauliflower and apple with oil, salt, pepper, and dill. Transfer to a rimmed baking sheet and roast 40 to 45 minutes until brown and tender. Stir and rotate pan halfway through cooking.

Use an immersion blender or potato masher to achieve desired consistency.

Adjust seasoning to taste with salt and pepper. Garnish with dill sprig and serve.

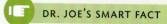

DR. JOE'S SMART FACT

Cauliflower is a source of indole-3-carbinol, a compound that fosters the repair of damaged DNA. One way to consume enough cauliflower to reap the benefits is to eat it mashed.

Makes 6 cups ‖ NUTRITION
(per ½ cup): energy 38 kcal | total fat 1 g | saturated fat 0 g | carbohydrate 6 g | fibre 2 g | protein 1 g | sodium 101 mg | excellent source of vitamin C

pea zucchini mash

Heat oil in a large pot over medium-high heat. Add peas, zucchini, salt, and a pinch of pepper.

Cover and cook, stirring occasionally, about 5 minutes until almost tender (reduce heat if mixture begins to brown).

Add water, cover, and simmer for another 5 minutes or so until vegetables are completely tender and water has evaporated.

Use an immersion blender or potato masher, purée mixture to desired consistency.

Add chives and stir to combine.

Adjust seasoning to taste with salt and pepper.

INGREDIENTS

1 tablespoon (15 ml) extra-virgin olive oil
7 cups (1.75 L) frozen peas
6 zucchini, coarsely chopped
½ teaspoon (2 ml) salt, plus additional to taste
pinch of freshly ground pepper, plus additional to taste
½ cup (125 ml) water
⅓ cup (75 ml) chopped fresh chives

Makes 7 cups ‖ **NUTRITION** (per ½ cup): energy 75 kcal | total fat 2 g | saturated fat 0 g | carbohydrate 12 g | fibre 4 g | protein 4 g | sodium 150 mg | good source of vitamin C, thiamin

carrot and butternut squash mash

INGREDIENTS

5 large carrots, peeled and coarsely chopped
1 small butternut squash, peeled, seeded, and cut into chunks
1 tablespoon (15 ml) extra-virgin olive oil
½ teaspoon (2 ml) salt, plus additional to taste
pinch of freshly ground pepper, plus additional to taste
⅓ cup (75 ml) coarsely chopped fresh thyme, plus additional for garnish

Preheat oven to 425°F (220°C).

Toss carrots and butternut squash with oil, salt, pepper, and thyme. Transfer to a rimmed baking sheet and roast for about 45 to 50 minutes until brown and tender. Stir vegetables and rotate pan halfway through cooking.

Use an immersion blender or potato masher to achieve desired consistency.

Adjust seasoning to taste with salt and pepper. Garnish with thyme leaves and serve.

SMART TIP

Keep your vegetable mash warm by placing it in a covered double boiler or a covered bowl set over a pan of barely simmering water.

Makes 6 cups ‖ **NUTRITION** (per ½ cup): energy 40 kcal | total fat 1 g | saturated fat 0 g | carbohydrate 7 g | fibre 1 g | protein 1 g | sodium 102 mg | excellent source of vitamin A

wild rice pilaf with scallion vinaigrette

Simply adding seeds, dried fruit, or herbs can turn something as simple as rice into a tantalizing dish. Cooked properly, wild rice is tender but chewy. This recipe makes a perfect side dish for Spinach Dill Stuffed Salmon.

INGREDIENTS

1 cup (250 ml) wild rice, rinsed well under cold water
3 cups (750 ml) water
½ teaspoon (2 ml) salt
½ cup (125 ml) long grain brown rice, rinsed well under cold water
½ teaspoon (2 ml) salt
1 cup (250 ml) water

SCALLION VINAIGRETTE

½ cup (125 ml) fresh orange juice
2 scallions, white and pale-green parts only, thinly sliced
¼ cup (60 ml) balsamic vinegar
½ tablespoon (7 ml) whole-grain mustard
1 large garlic clove, minced
½ teaspoon (2 ml) freshly ground pepper, plus more for seasoning
¼ cup (60 ml) extra-virgin olive oil

FLAVOURINGS

½ cup (125 ml) toasted raw pecans, coarsely chopped
½ cup (125 ml) pumpkin seeds
½ cup (125 ml) finely chopped fresh flat-leaf parsley
¼ cup (60 ml) finely chopped fresh mint
⅓ cup (75 ml) thinly sliced dried apricots
⅓ cup (75 ml) dried Atoka cranberries

Bring 3 cups water to a boil. Add wild rice and salt; return water to a boil. Cover, lower heat to maintain a gentle simmer, and cook about 45 minutes to 1 hour until rice is tender.

Put brown rice, salt, and water in a heavy-bottomed medium saucepan and bring to a boil over medium-high heat. Lower heat, cover pot, and simmer undisturbed for about 40 minutes until liquid is completely absorbed and rice is just tender. Remove from heat and let sit for 5 minutes. Uncover and fluff with a fork.

Meanwhile, combine vinaigrette ingredients (except oil) in a blender. With machine running, gradually add oil and blend until emulsified. Adjust seasoning to taste with salt and pepper.

In a large serving bowl, stir wild and brown rice together. Add flavourings; pour on desired amount of vinaigrette and toss.

Serve warm or at room temperature.

Serves 10 || **NUTRITION** (per serving): energy 233 kcal | total fat 14 g | saturated fat 2 g | carbohydrate 25 g | fibre 3 g | protein 6 g | sodium 247 mg | excellent source of vitamin E

smashed roasted potatoes

These crispy and golden potatoes will satisfy even the most avid French fry lover. They also make a great appetizer served with a dollop of Raita (see page 302).

INGREDIENTS

12 to 18 assorted red, yellow, and purple baby potatoes
extra-virgin olive oil
2 teaspoons (10 ml) finely chopped fresh thyme
2 teaspoons (10 ml) finely chopped fresh rosemary or chives
½ teaspoon (2 ml) kosher salt
½ teaspoon (2 ml) freshly ground pepper
1 tablespoon (15 ml) finely grated lemon zest

Rinse potatoes in cold water and drain well.

Transfer potatoes to a pot large enough to hold them without crowding. Add enough water to cover by 1½ inches. Partly cover pot and bring to a boil over high heat. Reduce heat to a simmer and cook potatoes for about 20 to 30 minutes until they are completely tender and can be pierced easily with a fork.

Gently drain potatoes in a large colander and carefully place in a single layer onto dishtowels to dry. Cool.

Preheat oven to 400°F (200°C). Line a large rimmed baking sheet with parchment paper or lightly greased aluminum foil.

Transfer potatoes to prepared baking sheet. With the palm of your hand, gently press down on each potato to flatten it to a ½-inch (1 cm) thick "pancake." Thinner pancakes will become crisper than thicker ones.

Brush potatoes with olive oil and roast for 15 minutes. Turn potatoes over, sprinkle with fresh herbs, salt, pepper, and lemon zest, and continue to roast another 15 minutes or so until crispy and golden.

Serve immediately.

Serves 4 to 6 ‖ **NUTRITION** (per serving): energy 80 kcal | total fat 1 g | saturated fat 0 g | carbohydrate 15 g | fibre 1 g | protein 2 g | sodium 292 mg

Shown with Raita (see page 302)

CRUST

¾ cup (175 ml) whole-wheat or
   multi-grain flour, plus additional
   for dusting pan
¾ cup (175 ml) spelt flour
½ teaspoon (2 ml) salt
2 tablespoons (30 ml) sesame seeds,
   toasted, plus additional for
   garnish
juice and finely grated zest of
   1 orange
¼ cup (60 ml) extra-virgin olive oil
⅓ cup (75 ml) water

FILLING

1 tablespoon (15 ml) olive oil
1 large onion, finely chopped
1 to 2 teaspoons (5 to 10 ml) hot chili
   paste or Sriracha sauce
2 garlic cloves, minced
1 green (unripe) papaya
3 large carrots, peeled
4 large eggs, divided
2 tablespoons (30 ml) whole-wheat
   flour
¾ cup (175 ml) finely chopped fresh
   herbs: dill, parsley, or cilantro
1½ teaspoons (7 ml) salt, plus more
   for seasoning
½ teaspoon (2 ml) freshly ground
   pepper, plus more for seasoning
½ cup (125 ml) milk (dairy, soy or
   almond)

⚡ SMART TIP

Pastry crusts turn out best when
the liquid used (in this case,
orange juice and water) is cold.

papaya quiche

Green (unripe) papaya is used to create this beautiful and unique side dish.
Serve this tarte-like quiche on special occasions: it's well worth the effort.

CRUST

Preheat oven to 350°F (180°C). Lightly grease the bottom and sides of a 10-inch (25 cm)
tart pan and then dust with flour.

Whisk flours, salt, sesame seeds, and orange zest together in large bowl. Stir in orange
juice, oil, and water, then knead until ball forms. Roll out dough into a 12-inch (30 cm)
round and fit into tart pan, bringing dough up sides of pan. Trim any excess length. Prick
bottom all over with fork and bake about 25 to 30 minutes until crust is golden brown
and crisp. Let cool on wire rack.

FILLING

While crust is baking, heat oil in a large pan over medium heat. Add onions and sauté
about 5 minutes until softened. Add hot chili paste and garlic. Continue to cook for
2 minutes. Remove from heat. Transfer to a large bowl.

Holding green papaya upright with thick end on work surface, peel and discard skin
with a vegetable peeler. Slice papaya flesh into thin ribbons with vegetable peeler
or mandoline. Add ribbons to bowl with sautéed onion mixture. Slice carrots into thin
ribbons with vegetable peeler or mandoline; add to bowl with onion mixture and
papaya ribbons.

Mix 2 eggs, flour, dill, salt, and pepper together in a small bowl. Add to papaya and
carrot ribbons and stir until just incorporated.

Holding papaya and carrot ribbons to the side, pour liquid from bowl into baked
crust. Form loose rolls with papaya and carrot ribbons and place in a neat pattern on
prepared crust.

In a small bowl, beat remaining 2 eggs, milk, and a pinch of salt and pepper. Pour evenly
to cover the quiche and bake for 30 to 40 minutes.

Garnish by sprinkling the quiche with toasted sesame seeds.

Serves 12 ‖ **NUTRITION** (per serving): energy 168 kcal | total fat 9 g | saturated fat 2 g | carbohydrate
18 g | fibre 3 g | protein 5 g | sodium 393 mg | good source of vitamin A, vitamin E

cauliflower onion cake

Luscious and elegant, this cake makes a great light meal or an impressive centrepiece at any brunch buffet. It is similar to traditional quiche but so much more tasty with its peppery citrus flavours.

INGREDIENTS

½ cup (125 ml) panko breadcrumbs, divided
1 large head cauliflower, outer leaves and core removed, cut into small pieces
2 tablespoons (30 ml) olive oil
2 large Vidalia onions, coarsely chopped
1 banana pepper, seeded and diced small
2 garlic cloves, finely chopped
2 tablespoons (30 ml) finely chopped fresh rosemary or thyme
1 teaspoon (5 ml) kosher salt
1 teaspoon (5 ml) freshly ground pepper
1 cup (250 ml) whole-wheat flour
2 teaspoons (10 ml) baking powder
1 teaspoon (5 ml) ground turmeric
¾ cup (175 ml) grated low-fat cheddar cheese
8 large eggs, lightly beaten
⅓ cup (75 ml) finely chopped fresh chives, plus 1 tablespoon (15 ml) for garnish

Preheat oven to 350°F (180°C). Generously grease a 10-inch (25 cm) springform pan. Press about ¼ cup of panko breadcrumbs into bottom of pan.

Cook cauliflower in a large pot of boiling salted water for about 7 minutes or steam until soft. Drain well; spread out on paper towels to cool and dry.

Heat oil in a large skillet over medium heat. Add onion, banana pepper, garlic, rosemary, ½ teaspoon salt, and ½ teaspoon pepper. Cover and cook about 8 minutes over medium-low heat, stirring occasionally, until softened. Remove from heat and let cool completely.

Meanwhile, in a large bowl, whisk together flour, baking powder, turmeric, and remaining salt and pepper. Stir in cheese.

Add eggs and chives to cooled onion mixture, and then add to flour mixture along with cooled cauliflower. Gently combine all ingredients. Transfer "batter" into prepared pan and sprinkle with remaining panko.

Bake until golden brown on top and set in centre, about 45 to 50 minutes.

Remove cake from oven and let cool in pan for 10 minutes.

To serve, sprinkle with chives and cut into wedges. Can be served warm or at room temperature.

Serves 12 ‖ **NUTRITION** (per serving): energy 168 kcal | total fat 7 g | saturated fat 2 g | carbohydrate 17 g | fibre 3 g | protein 9 g | sodium 387 mg | excellent source of vitamin B12 | good source of vitamin C, niacin, folate, thiamin, riboflavin

DR. JOE'S SMART FACT

Onions have a high concentration of quercetin, which has anti-inflammatory benefits, as well as chromium, which helps to balance blood sugar levels. Onions also contain the phytonutrient allyl propyl sulfoxide, the compound responsible for their smell and tearing of the eyes. Studies show that the stronger the smell, the more concentrated the nutrients.

fall vegetable pie

The word *beautiful* does not begin to describe this delectable nutrition-packed pie, which tastes as fabulous as it looks. Perfect to serve at a luncheon, it is sure to impress.

PIE

1 small sweet potato, peeled and diced medium
3 large shallots, peeled
3 small beets, peeled
2 carrots, peeled
1½ cups (375 ml) cooked chickpeas
⅓ cup (75 ml) finely chopped fresh dill or basil
½ cup (125 ml) whole-wheat flour
1 teaspoon (5 ml) salt
½ teaspoon (2 ml) freshly ground pepper
3 to 5 tablespoons (45–75 ml) extra-virgin olive oil, divided

TOPPING

3 cups (750 ml) lightly packed fresh spinach leaves
1½ to 2 tablespoons (22–30 ml) extra-virgin olive oil
1 tablespoon (15 ml) fresh lemon juice
¼ cup (60 ml) crumbled goat cheese

Place diced sweet potato in a steam basket in a medium pot and fill with 2 cups (500 ml) of water. Bring to a boil, reduce heat, and simmer. Cover and steam about 10 to 15 minutes until tender. Remove from heat and drain.

Coarsely grate shallots in a food processor or with a box grater; set aside.

Grate beets and carrots and transfer to a large bowl. Stir in cooked sweet potato and remaining pie ingredients (except shallots and oil). Mash sweet potato chunks slightly to hold pie together.

Heat 1 tablespoon of oil in a large, non-stick skillet over medium heat. Add shallots and sauté about 3 to 5 minutes until softened. Add to beet mixture and stir until combined.

Heat 1 to 2 tablespoons of oil in the same skillet over medium heat, add beet mixture, and firmly press into pan using a spatula. Cook undisturbed for 15 to 20 minutes.

Remove pan from heat. Invert onto a large plate. Heat remaining 2 tablespoons of oil in skillet, then slide pie back into pan. Cook 12 to 15 minutes until crisp and brown around edges. Slide onto serving platter.

In a large bowl, toss spinach with oil and lemon juice; season with salt and pepper. Top pie with spinach and goat cheese mixture, cut into wedges and serve warm.

Serves 8 ‖ NUTRITION (per serving): energy 204 kcal | total fat 10 g | saturated fat 2 g | carbohydrate 24 g | fibre 4 g | protein 6 g | sodium 365 mg | excellent source of vitamin A, folate | good source of iron, vitamin E

spinach arugula pear strudel

Sweet and savoury, this wonderful strudel recipe uses prepared phyllo dough to create a light flaky crust.

SPINACH ARUGULA MIXTURE

2 tablespoons (30 ml) olive oil
1 large onion, diced small
4 scallions, white and pale green parts only, diced small
8 ounces (225 g) fresh baby spinach leaves, trimmed
8 ounces (255 g) arugula

CHEESE MIXTURE

2 large eggs, lightly beaten
½ cup (125 ml) ricotta
½ cup (125 ml) crumbled feta
3 tablespoons (45 ml) finely chopped fresh flat-leaf parsley
3 tablespoons (45 ml) finely chopped fresh mint
2 tablespoons (30 ml) finely chopped fresh dill
1 pear, diced small
1 teaspoon (5 ml) finely grated orange zest
½ teaspoon (2 ml) salt
¼ teaspoon (1 ml) freshly ground pepper

PASTRY

6 sheets phyllo dough
olive oil for brushing
2 tablespoons (30 ml) panko breadcrumbs

Preheat oven to 400°F (200°C). Line a large rimmed baking sheet with parchment paper.

Heat oil in a large skillet over medium heat. Add onion and scallions and sauté about 5 minutes until softened. Add spinach and arugula and continue cooking for 2 to 3 minutes until leaves are wilted. Remove from heat and transfer to a colander to allow excess water to drain; cool.

In a large bowl, stir the cheese mixture ingredients together until well combined. Squeeze out as much water as possible from the spinach-arugula mixture and add to cheese mixture; mix well.

Place one sheet of phyllo dough on a damp tea towel. Cover remaining sheets with a moistened tea towel so that phyllo does not dry out. Lightly brush phyllo with oil and sprinkle with 2 teaspoons of panko. Layer remaining phyllo sheets on top one by one, brushing every second layer with a light coat of oil and a sprinkling of panko crumbs.

About 2 inches (5 cm) from one long edge of phyllo, spoon filling lengthwise in a 3-inch (7.5 cm) wide strip, leaving 2 inches (5 cm) on each short end. Using the tea towel as an aid, fold long edge over filling; roll to create a log, folding in short ends as you roll. Place strudel, seam side down, on prepared baking sheet. Brush lightly with oil.

Bake 30 to 35 minutes until golden and crisp. Transfer to rack or serving platter and serve warm or at room temperature.

SMART TIP

If you must substitute dried herbs for fresh, use half the amount called for in any recipe.

DR. JOE'S SMART FACT

Peppermint calms the muscles of the stomach and improves the flow of bile, which the body uses to digest fats. As a result, food passes through the stomach more quickly. Now you know why many restaurants provide peppermints with the bill.

Serves 10 ‖ NUTRITION (per serving): energy 161 kcal | total fat 9 g | saturated fat 3 g | carbohydrate 15 g | fibre 2 g | protein 7 g | sodium 306 mg | excellent source of folate | good source of vitamin A, riboflavin, iron, vitamin E, vitamin B12

Fish contains omega-3 fatty acid, an essential fat that protects the heart.

fish

fish: flavour intensity

An overwhelming amount of research has shown that eating fish twice a week can have a positive effect on your health. Fish is a great source of essential vitamins, minerals, and fatty acids that can lower the risk of heart disease and stroke.

Women who are trying to become pregnant or are pregnant, nursing mothers, and young children are advised to avoid fish that are high in mercury, such as king mackerel, marlin, shark, swordfish, and tilefish. Grouper, halibut, lobster, orange roughy, sablefish, striped bass, and tuna have mid-range mercury levels and it is advised to limit consumption of these species to once a week.

When buying fish, it is best to pick what the fishmonger recommends, and our recipes work equally well with a wide variety. We have categorized fish from those with a mild flavour to those with a strong flavour. Expand your base and enjoy these wonderful varieties of fish!

Mild flavour: Black sea bass, branzino, flounder, fluke, Mediterranean sea bass, perch, porgy, sole, wild striped bass

Medium flavour: Arctic char, black fish, cod, grouper, haddock, halibut, monkfish, red snapper, sablefish (black cod), trout

Strong flavour: Anchovies, bluefish, mahi-mahi, salmon, sardines, swordfish, tuna, wild salmon

braised snapper with cherry tomatoes

So simple to make yet bursting with flavour, this recipe has a pleasant aroma of garlic and tomatoes that will bring a touch of the Mediterranean into your home. It also works well with other light to medium-firm fish, such as grouper, Arctic char, and cod. Having your fishmonger prep the fish makes cooking this recipe easier than you might think.

INGREDIENTS

one 2-pound (1 kg) whole snapper, cleaned and scaled
kosher salt and freshly ground pepper
2 tablespoons (30 ml) extra-virgin olive oil
3 garlic cloves, thinly sliced
1 teaspoon (5 ml) crushed red pepper flakes
1 cup (250 ml) cherry tomatoes, halved
¼ cup (60 ml) pitted green olives, halved
1 cup (250 ml) water or white wine
Herbed Sautéed Kale (see page 172)

Preheat oven to 375°F (190°C).

Rinse fish and pat dry. Season flesh with salt and pepper, and set aside.

Heat 2 tablespoons of oil in a large ovenproof saucepan over medium-high heat. Add garlic and red pepper flakes and sauté until garlic is browned, about 2 to 3 minutes. Add tomatoes and olives and sauté for 2 to 3 minutes. Place fish in pan and add water or white wine. Bake fish in preheated oven for about 20 minutes until fish reaches an internal temperature of 135°F to 140°F (57°C to 60°C).

While fish is cooking, prepare Herbed Sautéed Kale (optional).

Divide sautéed kale, tomatoes, and olives among dinner plates. Fillet snapper, place over sautéed kale, and serve immediately.

Serves 4 || **NUTRITION** (per serving): energy 333 kcal | total fat 12 g | saturated fat 2 g | carbohydrate 3 g | fibre 1 g | protein 52 g | sodium 247 mg | excellent source of vitamin D, niacin, vitamin B6, vitamin B12, vitamin E | good source of potassium

Shown with Herbed Sautéed Kale (see page 172)

DR. JOE'S SMART FACT

Vitamin D is produced in the skin upon exposure to sunlight but it also has dietary sources. People living in northern climates, where the hours of sunlight are limited in the winter, are more likely to have vitamin D deficiency than those living in southern climes. To counter this problem, the food industry in Canada and the United States fortifies dairy products and some cereals with the vitamin. Fish and fish oils also provide rich sources of vitamin D and should be a regular part of the diet. In fact, it was cod oil, in combination with exposure to sunlight, that was found to cure rickets, a disease characterized by bow-leggedness caused by softening of the bones.

halibut with grilled pepper anchovy relish and israeli couscous

The anchovies and herbs in the delightful relish used in this dish amplify the mild flavour of the halibut. The relish can be used to accompany any fish of your choosing.

GRILLED PEPPER ANCHOVY RELISH

2 red bell peppers, stems and seeds removed, sliced in half

2 yellow bell peppers, stems and seeds removed, sliced in half

2 garlic cloves, minced

8 white anchovies, finely chopped

3 tablespoons (45 ml) red wine vinegar

¼ cup (60 ml) finely chopped fresh flat-leaf parsley

1 tablespoon (15 ml) finely chopped fresh oregano, plus additional for garnish

⅓ cup (75 ml) olive oil

ISRAELI COUSCOUS

½ tablespoon (7 ml) olive oil

2 shallots, finely chopped

1 tablespoon (15 ml) minced fresh ginger

¾ cup (175 ml) Israeli couscous

1 cup (250 ml) water

1 ripe plum tomato, seeded and diced small

¼ cup (60 ml) finely chopped fresh flat-leaf parsley

kosher salt and freshly ground pepper, to taste

FISH

four 6-ounce (175 g) halibut fillets, skin on, bones removed

olive oil

½ lemon

kosher salt and freshly ground pepper

RELISH

Oven method: Preheat oven to broil. Line a large baking sheet with lightly greased aluminum foil.

Broil peppers, skin side up, until skins are browned and blistered, about 20 minutes.

Barbecue method: Pre-heat barbecue. Grill peppers, skin side down, about 15 to 20 minutes until skins are browned and blistered.

Place broiled or grilled peppers in a bowl, cover with plastic wrap and cool for at least 10 minutes until peppers can be handled. (This step allows the peppers to sweat in the trapped steam, making it easier to remove the skin.)

Remove skins and dice peppers into ½-inch (1 cm) pieces.

Combine all relish ingredients (except oil) in a large bowl and mix well. Whisk in oil and let relish rest for 30 minutes before using.

ISRAELI COUSCOUS

Heat oil in a large saucepan over medium heat. Add shallots and sauté about 3 to 4 minutes until softened. Add ginger and stir for about 1 minute. Add couscous, stir until all ingredients are combined, and toast for 3 to 4 minutes. Stir in water, cover pan, and lower heat to simmer. Cook couscous for 8 to 10 minutes. Remove cover, add tomato and parsley, and stir until combined. Adjust seasoning with salt and pepper to taste.

FISH

Rinse halibut and pat dry. Brush both sides with oil; squeeze lemon juice over fish and season with salt and pepper to taste.

Stove-top method: Heat oil in large skillet over high heat. Sear halibut, skin side up, about 4 minutes until lightly browned and firm on the bottom. Carefully flip and cook an additional 2 minutes.

Barbecue method: Heat barbecue until hot and wipe the grate with oiled paper towels until the grate is black and glossy. Grill fish, skin side down and without moving it in the pan, for about 4 minutes until lightly browned and firm on bottom. Carefully flip and cook the second side about 2 minutes longer.

Place a bed of couscous on each plate. Lay a piece of fish on top of couscous and garnish with a spoonful of relish.

Serves 4 || **NUTRITION** (per serving of fish): energy 416 kcal | total fat 23 g | saturated fat 3 g | carbohydrate 13 g | fibre 3 g | protein 41 g | sodium 39 mg | excellent source of potassium, vitamin C, vitamin D, vitamin E, niacin, vitamin B6, vitamin B12 | good source of vitamin A, iron, thiamin, riboflavin, folate

NUTRITION (per serving of Israeli Couscous): energy 155 kcal | total fat 3 g | saturated fat 0 g | sodium 5 mg | carbohydrate 28 g | protein 4 g

buckwheat-coated black cod

Imagine the taste of Southern fried fish made with the goodness of healthy grains and without all the fat. Absolutely addictive!

INGREDIENTS

four 6-ounce (175 g) black cod fillets, skin and bones removed
½ lemon
kosher salt and freshly ground pepper
2 tablespoons (30 ml) Dijon mustard or Hot Mustard (see page 299)
1 tablespoon (15 ml) finely chopped fresh tarragon or flat-leaf parsley
½ cup (125 ml) roasted buckwheat

Preheat oven to 350°F (180°C). Lightly grease a large baking sheet.

Rinse fish and pat dry. Squeeze lemon over fish and lightly season with salt and pepper. Set aside.

Mix mustard and tarragon together in a small bowl. Brush both sides of cod with mustard tarragon mixture. Lightly dredge in buckwheat and transfer to prepared baking sheet.

Bake for 8 to 10 minutes and then preheat oven to broil. Broil fish 1 to 2 minutes until buckwheat is well toasted.

Serve immediately.

Serves 4 ‖ NUTRITION (per serving): energy 366 kcal | total fat 27 g | saturated fat 6 g | carbohydrate 6 g | fibre 1 g | protein 25 g | sodium 129 mg | excellent source of niacin, vitamin B6, vitamin B12 | good source of vitamin A, thiamin, riboflavin

Shown with Broccolini Gremolata (see page 168)

DR. JOE'S SMART FACT

Turmeric has been shown to be one of the most effective anti-inflammatories.

tandoori fish

This recipe was inspired by a fabulous dish eaten at a traditional Indian restaurant in London, England. A tandoor is a clay oven, often used when preparing Indian cuisine, that allows food to grill and roast at the same time. You can get a similar effect at home by cooking at a high temperature on the upper rack of your oven.

Rinse fish and pat dry. Transfer to a broiling pan or baking dish.

In a small bowl, mix all ingredients together. Brush marinade on both sides of fish to coat well. Cover with plastic wrap; marinate for 1 hour.

Preheat oven to 400°F (200°C). Position rack to top of oven.

Cook fish for 10 to 15 minutes. Broil fish for last 2 minutes of cooking.

INGREDIENTS

1½ pounds (680 g) grouper fillet (or any firm white fish or salmon), cut into 4
¼ cup (60 ml) low-fat plain Greek yogurt
1 tablespoon (15 ml) tomato paste
1 teaspoon (5 ml) canola oil
½ teaspoon (2 ml) grated fresh ginger
½ teaspoon (2 ml) garam masala
½ teaspoon (2 ml) ground turmeric
pinch of cayenne pepper
pinch of kosher salt

Shown with Chana Masala (see page 171)

Serves 4 ‖ **NUTRITION** (per serving): energy 193 kcal | total fat 3 g | saturated fat 1 g | carbohydrate 5 g | fibre 1 g | protein 35 g | sodium 260 mg | excellent source of niacin, vitamin B6, vitamin B12 | good source of riboflavin

arctic char parcels

This fish is steamed in a bath of its own juices with the subtle influence of herbs and seasonal vegetables. The best part about this dish—besides the taste, of course—is its beautiful presentation. Everyone receives a parcel and takes delight in opening it up at the table. Oh, and did we mention that clean-up is a breeze?

INGREDIENTS

four 6-ounce (175 g) Arctic char fillets, skin and bones removed
finely grated zest and juice of 1 lemon, plus a second lemon cut into wedges for serving
kosher salt and freshly ground pepper
8 ounces (225 g) shiitake mushrooms, trimmed and thinly sliced
8 ounces (225 g) asparagus, trimmed and halved lengthwise
1 carrot, julienned
2 scallions, thinly sliced
2 tablespoons (30 ml) finely chopped fresh dill or cilantro
2 tablespoons (30 ml) toasted coarsely chopped pecans or soy nuts (for nut free),
    for garnish (optional)

Preheat oven 400°F (200°C). Cut four pieces of parchment paper measuring 12 × 17 inches (30 × 43 cm).

Rinse fish and pat dry. Sprinkle lemon juice over fish and season with salt and pepper.

Lay each fillet on a piece of parchment paper. Place mushrooms, asparagus, and carrots on top of each fillet, then sprinkle with lemon zest, scallions, dill, pecans (if using), salt, and pepper. To close, fold the parchment paper over fish and seal tightly to prevent steam from escaping.

Transfer packages to a baking sheet and bake about 10 to 15 minutes until fish is cooked through.

Carefully open packets and transfer to serving plates. Serve with lemon wedges.

Serves 4 ‖ **NUTRITION** (per serving): energy 342 kcal | total fat 12 g | saturated fat 6 g | carbohydrate 10 g | fibre 4 g | protein 38 g | sodium 146 mg | good source of vitamin A, vitamin C, riboflavin

DR. JOE'S SMART FACT

Fish has a well-deserved reputation as a healthy food. Some studies have shown that eating fish twice a week can reduce the risk of potentially deadly heart rhythm disturbances. Consuming fish also lowers blood pressure and heart rate, improves blood vessel function, and can lower blood triglycerides. These benefits are thought to derive from the presence of specific omega-3 fatty acids found in fish.

ginger steamed fish

Steaming fish enhances its flavour while maintaining its velvety texture. The method outlined below will prove to be easier than you think. Any light and flaky white fish such as sea bass or sole steams well.

INGREDIENTS

four 6-ounce (175 g) white fish fillets, skin and bones removed
½ lemon
kosher salt and freshly ground pepper, to taste
½ teaspoon (2 ml) crushed red pepper flakes
1 tablespoon (15 ml) finely grated fresh ginger
2 garlic cloves, minced
1 tablespoon (15 ml) finely grated orange zest
2 tablespoons (30 ml) chopped fresh chives for garnish
banana leaf for serving (optional)
Pea Zucchini Mash (see page 181)

Rinse fish and pat dry. Place fillets in steamer lined with parchment paper (see SMART TIP for alternative methods).

Squeeze lemon over fish and season with salt, pepper, and crushed red pepper flakes.

In a small bowl, mix ginger, garlic, and orange zest and spread evenly over fish.

Fill steamer with 2 inches of water and bring to a boil over high heat (do not let water touch fish). Cover tightly and steam about 5 to 7 minutes until fish is opaque throughout. Carefully remove the fish, pouring out excess liquid.

Cut a banana leaf into 4 pieces and place in middle of serving plates. Arrange Pea Zucchini Mash on banana leaf and nestle fish into mash. Sprinkle with chives. Serve immediately.

Serves 4 ‖ NUTRITION (per serving): energy 161 kcal | total fat 2 g | saturated fat 1 g | carbohydrate 2 g | fibre 1 g | protein 32 g | sodium 140 mg | excellent source of niacin, vitamin B6, vitamin B12

Shown with Pea Zucchini Mash (see page 181)

sesame ginger salmon

This easy yet show-stopping whole fillet combines sweet and salty accents. The recipe can be prepared ahead of time and served at room temperature. Relaxed entertaining at its best!

INGREDIENTS

1 salmon fillet, about 3 pounds (1.5 kg), skin on and bones removed
1 lime
kosher salt and freshly ground pepper

GINGER SESAME MARINADE

⅓ cup (75 ml) mirin
3 tablespoons (45 ml) low-sodium soy sauce
1 tablespoon (15 ml) honey mustard
3 tablespoons (45 ml) sesame seeds
2 tablespoons (30 ml) sesame oil
2 tablespoons (30 ml) minced fresh ginger
1 tablespoon (15 ml) minced fresh garlic
6 scallions, thinly sliced, reserving 1 to 2 tablespoons (15 to 30 ml) for garnish
zest of 1 lime for garnish
a few fresh coriander or flat-leaf parsley leaves for garnish

Rinse fish and pat dry. Squeeze juice from lime over fish and lightly season with salt and pepper. Place fillet skin-side down in a shallow 12 × 17 inch (30 × 45 cm) roasting pan.

Prepare marinade by mixing all ingredients together. Spoon over the salmon and allow to marinate at room temperature for 1 hour.

Adjust broiler tray in oven so that it is 4 inches from heat source. Place second rack in middle of oven. Preheat oven to broil.

Broil salmon for 10 minutes until it has almost cooked through. (If salmon is very thick, broil for up to 12 minutes. For medium-rare, broil for 8 to 10 minutes)

Reduce oven temperature to 450°F (230°C). Transfer salmon to middle rack and bake for an additional 5 minutes, checking frequently to ensure that juices are not burning. (If juices evaporate too quickly, add a bit more mirin.)

Remove salmon fillet from roasting pan. Place on serving platter. Garnish with scallions and lime zest. Pour fish juices accumulated in roasting pan over the fillet.

Serve hot or at room temperature.

Serves 8 ‖ NUTRITION (per serving): energy 405 kcal | total fat 26 g | saturated fat 5 g | carbohydrate 2 g | fibre 1 g | protein 39 g | sodium 333 mg | excellent source of vitamin D, thiamin, niacin, riboflavin, vitamin B6, vitamin B12 | good source of folate

Shown with Grilled Bok Choy (see page 169) and Wild Rice Pilaf with Scallion Vinaigrette (see page 182)

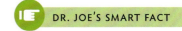

SMART TIP

The easiest and best way to remove the skin from ginger is to scrape the ginger with the side of a spoon or fork. The skin lifts right off, leaving all the aromatic flesh behind. Store unused pieces of ginger in the freezer.

DR. JOE'S SMART FACT

Ginger, in various forms, such as non-alcoholic beer, pills, and candied ginger root, has been used to counter nausea and vomiting from motion sickness. One study found that ginger was as effective as the prescription drug scopolamine in preventing motion sickness and, unlike the drug, did not cause drowsiness.

spinach dill stuffed salmon

HONEY DIJON MUSTARD SAUCE

2 tablespoons (30 ml) low-fat plain Greek yogurt
1 tablespoon (15 ml) Dijon mustard
1 tablespoon (15 ml) honey mustard
1 tablespoon (15 ml) finely chopped fresh dill
½ teaspoon (2 ml) ground cumin (optional)

FISH

1 tablespoon (15 ml) olive oil
1 pound (455 g) lightly packed baby spinach leaves
2 garlic cloves, minced
½ lemon
kosher salt and freshly ground pepper
four 6-ounce (175 g) salmon fillets, skin and bones removed
½ cup (125 ml) finely chopped fresh dill, plus additional for garnish
½ teaspoon (2 ml) freshly ground pepper, divided
1 lemon, thinly sliced, reserving enough for garnish

This divine recipe will certainly satisfy and impress family and dinner guests alike. Delicious sautéed spinach is sandwiched between two pieces of wonderfully marinated salmon. Modify the stuffing using Swiss chard instead of spinach and a blood orange instead of the lemon. For heat, add a pinch of chili flakes.

Mix yogurt, mustards, dill, and cumin (if using) in a small bowl. Let rest 10 to 15 minutes to allow flavours to blend.

Heat 1 tablespoon of oil in a large saucepan over medium-high heat. Add garlic and sauté for 1 minute; add spinach and cook, stirring 1 to 2 minutes until wilted. Sprinkle with salt and pepper. Remove from heat and set aside.

Preheat oven to 400°F (200°C).

Rinse salmon and pat dry. Place each fillet on a cutting board and, using a very sharp knife, slice each fillet in half horizontally. Squeeze with lemon and sprinkle with salt and pepper.

Place bottom half of each fillet on a baking sheet and spread a spoonful of mustard sauce evenly over top.

Place a thin layer of cooked spinach on top of mustard-covered fillet, reserving remaining spinach for serving. Place some dill sprigs on top of spinach. Cover each fillet half with its other half. Lightly brush mustard sauce over top fillet. Layer lemon slices on top.

Roast in oven for 12 to 15 minutes until fish is cooked and top is lightly browned.

Divide reserved spinach among 4 serving plates. Carefully remove salmon from oven and place on top of greens.

Garnish with additional lemon slices and dill sprigs.

Serves 4 ‖ **NUTRITION** (per serving): energy 391 kcal | total fat 24 g | saturated fat 5 g | carbohydrate 6 g | fibre 3 g | protein 39 g | sodium 243 mg | excellent source of iron, potassium, vitamin A, vitamin D, vitamin C, vitamin E, thiamin, riboflavin, niacin, folate, vitamin B6, vitamin B12

salmon burgers

Bursting with flavour, these burgers are simple and satisfying. Substitute salmon with any fish such as tuna, whitefish, or northern trout. If you prefer a curry flavour, simply use curry powder instead of Dijon, or create an Asian version by using soy sauce and cilantro instead of Dijon and dill. The possibilities are endless!

SALMON

1½ pounds (680 g) salmon fillet, skin and bones removed, coarsely chopped
2 teaspoons (10 ml) Dijon mustard
1 shallot, finely diced
1 tablespoon (15 ml) minced fresh ginger
1 tablespoon (15 ml) finely chopped fresh dill
½ cup (125 ml) panko breadcrumbs
½ teaspoon (2 ml) kosher salt
¼ teaspoon (1 ml) freshly ground pepper

1 tablespoon (15 ml) olive oil for skillet or grill

6 whole-wheat or multi-grain buns or pita pockets
sliced avocado and lettuce leaves for garnish

Coarsely grind about one quarter of salmon and mustard in a food processor until it forms a paste. Add remaining salmon and shallot. Pulse until salmon is roughly chopped. Do not over-process, or the salmon will turn to mush! Mix in remaining ingredients by hand.

Shape salmon mixture to form 6 patties, each about 1 inch (2.5 cm) thick. Refrigerate at least 20 minutes before cooking. (The patties may be prepared up to 6 hours in advance, wrapped in plastic and refrigerated.)

In a large, heavy skillet or grill pan, heat oil over medium-high heat. Add salmon patties and cook about 2 or 3 minutes until golden brown on one side. Turn and cook about 2 minutes longer until opaque and golden brown on the other side. The burgers may also be prepared by barbecuing for 2 to 3 minutes per side on a greased hot barbecue.

Serve salmon burgers on toasted buns or in pita pockets topped with a dollop of Low-Fat Tzatziki (see page 302), slices of avocado, and lettuce.

Serves 6 ‖ **NUTRITION** (per 1 burger, without bun): energy 260 kcal | total fat 14 g | saturated fat 3 g | carbohydrate 8 g | fibre 1 g | protein 25 g | sodium 209 mg | excellent source of vitamin D, thiamin, niacin, vitamin B6, vitamin B12 | good source of riboflavin

Shown with Low-Fat Tzatziki (see page 302)

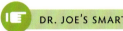

SMART TIP

To dice a shallot, trim the stem end of bulb using a sharp paring knife. Remove peel and slice in half lengthwise. Lay flat side down and at small, even intervals, slice horizontally almost to the root end and then slice vertically. The small-diced pieces will fall away.

DR. JOE'S SMART FACT

Concerns have been raised about the mercury content of some fish. As far as salmon goes, no need to worry. Both canned and fresh salmon are very low in mercury.

baja fish tacos

FISH

1 pound (455 g) mahi-mahi or any
   flaky fish (whitefish, sable fish,
   or haddock), skin and bones
   removed, cut into 4 pieces
½ lemon
kosher salt and freshly
   ground pepper

TACO MARINADE

3 tablespoons (45 ml) canola oil
2 tablespoons (30 ml) honey
½ tablespoon (7 ml) chili powder
½ tablespoon (7 ml) dried oregano
½ teaspoon (2 ml) dried thyme
½ teaspoon (2 ml) smoked sweet
   paprika
¼ cup (60 ml) lightly packed finely
   chopped fresh cilantro leaves,
   plus additional for garnish
1 jalapeño or habanero chili
   pepper, seeded, membrane
   removed, and finely diced
   (depending on desired heat)
kosher salt and freshly ground
   pepper

8 fresh soft corn or whole-wheat
   flour tortillas
1½ cups (375 ml) Tricolour Slaw (see
   page 123)
1½ cups (375 ml) Apple
   Pomegranate Guacamole (see
   page 64)
1½ cups (375 ml) Tomato Corn Salsa
   (see page 300)

Making a taco dinner can be a fun-filled activity in which everyone participates. When all the elements are ready, simply place warm tortillas on a serving platter covered with damp paper towels and surround with all the accompaniments, including the delectable fish. Serve buffet-style for an assemble-it-yourself dinner.

Rinse fish and pat dry. Squeeze lemon over fish and season with salt and pepper.

In a small bowl, mix all marinade ingredients together. Gently place fish and marinade in a resealable bag. Seal bag, pressing out air, and massage fish until well coated with marinade. Let sit for 20 minutes.

Heat a non-stick sauté pan over medium-high heat. Remove fish from marinade and place in hot pan. Cook fish for 4 minutes, undisturbed, then turn over and cook another 2 minutes. Remove pan from heat and flake fish in pan with a fork; mix in all marinade that has stuck to bottom of pan.

Transfer fish to a serving platter, pour remaining sauce into a small serving bowl, and keep warm.

Place tortillas on a plate and sandwich them between slightly dampened sheets of paper towel. Microwave on high for 1 minute. Transfer to a serving plate and cover to keep warm.

If serving buffet-style, arrange slaw, guacamole, salsa, and sauce in serving bowls and bring to table along with fish, fish sauce, and tortillas.

To assemble tacos, place a heaping tablespoon of slaw, guacamole, and salsa on tortilla. Layer a heaping tablespoon of flaked fish in centre of wrapper and drizzle with fish sauce. Bring up sides of tortilla and enjoy!

Makes 8 tacos ‖ **NUTRITION** (per 1 fish taco without toppings): energy 127 kcal | total fat 6 g | saturated fat 1 g | carbohydrate 7 g | fibre 1 g | protein 11 g | sodium 47 mg | excellent source of vitamin E, vitamin B12 | good source of niacin

DR. JOE'S SMART FACT

The heat of the jalapeño pepper resides in the stem, seeds, and membrane. Removing these will reduce the heat.

Shown with Tricolour Slaw (see page 123)

cilantro lime shrimp

A divine appetizer for any occasion, these shrimps are best when served on a platter accompanied by our dipping sauce. This can easily be turned into a hearty meal by serving over rice or grains and drizzled with sauce.

CILANTRO LIME SAUCE

2 garlic cloves, minced
⅓ cup (75 ml) apricot preserves or jam
½ cup (125 ml) fresh lime juice
½ cup (125 ml) fresh cilantro, finely chopped
2 tablespoons (30 ml) olive oil
½ teaspoon (2 ml) crushed red pepper flakes
1 tablespoon (15 ml) low-sodium soy sauce

SHRIMP

2 pounds (1 kg) extra jumbo shrimp (size 16/20), peeled and deveined
1 tablespoon (15 ml) olive oil if pan-cooking

In a small bowl, mix sauce ingredients together. Reserve one third of sauce for serving.

Place shrimp and remaining cilantro lime sauce in a resealable bag and marinate in fridge for at least one hour.

Drain shrimp from marinade and discard marinade.

Preheat barbecue to medium-high. Skewer shrimp and barbecue until light pink, about 1½ to 2 minutes per side. Or, heat oil in a large saucepan on medium-high heat and sauté shrimp 1½ to 2 minutes per side. Do not overcook.

Serve with reserved sauce.

Serves 10 as an appetizer, 4 as a main course ‖ NUTRITION (per main course serving): energy 124 kcal | total fat 3 g | saturated fat 1 g | carbohydrate 5 g | fibre 0 g | protein 19 g | sodium 241 g | excellent source of niacin, vitamin B12 | good source of iron, vitamin D, vitamin E

asian noodles with shrimp

¼ cup (60 ml) Vegetable Stock (see page 80)

2 tablespoons (30 ml) low-sodium soy sauce

2 tablespoons (30 ml) mirin

1 tablespoon (15 ml) sesame oil

1 teaspoon (5 ml) hot chili paste

½ teaspoon (2 ml) freshly ground pepper

3 scallions, thinly sliced

SHRIMP

1 pound (455 g) jumbo shrimp (size 21/25), peeled and deveined

2 tablespoons (30 ml) fresh lemon juice

1 teaspoon (5 ml) minced fresh garlic

ASIAN NOODLES

4 dried or fresh shiitake mushrooms

6 ounces (170 g) sweet potato noodles, cellophane noodles, or rice vermicelli

3 tablespoons (45 ml) canola oil, separated

2 eggs, lightly beaten

1 Spanish onion, thinly sliced

1 tablespoon (15 ml) minced fresh ginger

4 garlic cloves, minced

½ teaspoon (2 ml) freshly ground pepper

2 Thai or jalapeño chilis, seeded, membrane removed, and finely diced (depending on desired heat)

1 red and 1 yellow bell pepper, thinly sliced

2 medium carrots, peeled and julienned

2 scallions, thinly sliced, plus 1 scallion, thinly sliced, for garnish

8 ounces (255 g) baby spinach leaves, coarsely chopped

1½ cups (375 ml) snow peas, trimmed and sliced on diagonal

½ tablespoon (7 ml) sesame seeds for garnish

2 tablespoons (30 ml) finely chopped fresh cilantro or flat-leaf parsley for garnish

This Asian-inspired favourite is chock full of vegetables. Sweet potato noodles complement the exquisitely seasoned sauce. This recipe works well with tofu or chicken.

Mix all ingredients for "special" sauce together and set aside.

Mix shrimp with lemon juice and garlic and set aside.

If using dried shiitakes, soak them in hot water for about 30 minutes until softened. Drain well. For dried and fresh mushrooms, remove and discard stems. Slice caps thinly.

Cook noodles as per package directions; drain well. Cut noodles into shorter lengths with kitchen shears. Loosen and spread on a dishtowel; set aside.

Heat ½ tablespoon of oil in a large wok or saucepan over medium-high heat. Cook shrimp in 2 single-layer batches, about 1½ minutes on each side until opaque. Do not overcook. Remove each batch from pan and set aside.

Heat ½ tablespoon of oil in a large wok or saucepan over medium heat. Add eggs and swirl until they form a thin coat on bottom of pan. Leave undisturbed until cooked around edges; push any uncooked egg toward sides of pan. When cooked, remove from pan; slice into strips and set aside.

Heat 2 tablespoons of oil in same pan. Add onions and stir-fry about 10 to 15 minutes until caramelized. Add ginger, garlic, and pepper and stir-fry for 2 or 3 minutes. Add mushrooms, chilis, red and yellow peppers, carrots, and scallions and stir-fry 4 to 5 minutes until peppers are softened but still crunchy. Add spinach and snow peas for last 2 minutes of cooking.

Add all reserved components to wok, pour in sauce, and stir until well incorporated. Taste and add salt as needed.

Garnish with reserved scallions, sesame seeds, and fresh herbs.

Serves 6 ‖ **NUTRITION** (per serving): energy 346 kcal | total fat 13 g | saturated fat 2 g | carbohydrate 31 g | fibre 4 g | protein 26 g | sodium 477 mg | excellent source of vitamin A, vitamin C, vitamin E, iron, folate, niacin, vitamin B12, vitamin B6 | good source of potassium, riboflavin, thiamin

cioppino

Cioppino is an Italian-American fish soup that originated in San Francisco. Not unlike bouillabaisse from Provence or cataplana from Portugal, this fragrant seafood dish is a true delicacy.

INGREDIENTS

¼ cup (60 ml) olive oil
1 medium onion, thinly sliced
3 garlic cloves, finely minced
3 bay leaves
½ teaspoon (2 ml) crushed red pepper flakes
4 sprigs fresh thyme leaves, coarsely chopped, plus a few sprigs for garnish
1 medium red pepper, seeded, halved and thinly sliced
1 teaspoon (5 ml) saffron threads, dissolved in 1 tablespoon (15 ml) of water
19-fluid-ounce (540 ml) can whole plum tomatoes with juice
1 cup (250 ml) dry white wine
salt and freshly ground pepper, to taste
3 cups (750 ml) water
1 dozen littleneck clams, scrubbed and washed
½ pound (225 g) salmon fillet, skin and bones removed, cut into 6
½ pound (225 g) cod or halibut fillet, skin and bones removed, cut into 6
10 ounces (285 g) mussels, scrubbed and debearded
3 cleaned squid, cut into ½-inch (1 cm) rings
¼ cup (60 ml) finely chopped fresh flat-leaf parsley
3 tablespoons (45 ml) finely chopped fresh basil

Heat oil in a large soup pot over medium heat. Add onion and sauté about 5 minutes until softened. Add garlic, bay leaves, red pepper flakes, and thyme and sauté, stirring frequently, about 5 minutes until softened. Stir in red pepper and diluted saffron and sauté 1 minute.

Add tomatoes (with juice), wine, and water and simmer, covered, for 30 minutes. Taste and season with salt and pepper as necessary. The cioppino can be made ahead to this point.

Add clams and simmer, covered, for 5 to 10 minutes until clams just open, checking every minute after 5 minutes and transferring opened clams to a bowl. (Discard any unopened clams after 10 minutes.)

Add fish, mussels, and squid and simmer, covered, about 5 minutes until just cooked through. Discard bay leaves, return clams to pot, and gently stir in parsley and basil.

Serve immediately in large soup bowls.

Serves 6 ‖ **NUTRITION** (per serving): energy 352 kcal | total fat 16 g | saturated fat 3 g | carbohydrate 12 g | fibre 2 g | protein 30 g | sodium 328 mg | excellent source of vitamin C, iron, folate, vitamin D, vitamin E, thiamin, riboflavin, niacin, vitamin B6, vitamin B12 | good source of potassium, vitamin A

DR. JOE'S SMART FACT

Although there is no scientific evidence to support the medicinal use of saffron, the spice is often used in holistic and Ayurvedic medicine. It is commonly added to foods to impart a rich yellow colour (think ballpark mustard) and can be used for the same purpose in textiles.

Poultry and red meat are loaded with protein. Think "lean" and "moderation."

poultry & meat

rosemary mustard cornish hens

Cornish hens are simply small, young, male or female chickens with an abundance of breast meat. Cooking them whole with the skin on ensures that the meat underneath remains moist and tender. Spreading seasoning under the skin gives the meat such a delicious flavour that you might happily leave the fat-laden skin aside. This dish is fancy enough for a special occasion but easy enough for a simple family dinner.

Preheat oven to 375°F (190°C).

Rinse hens and pat dry with paper towel. Rub all over (including cavity) with lemon wedge.

Lay onions in bottom of roasting pan.

In a small bowl, combine paste ingredients. Carefully lift skin from breasts and thighs and spread paste between meat and skin as much as possible. Rub remaining paste inside cavity and all over hens.

Place hens, breast side down, on top of onions. Pour half of orange juice and chicken stock around hens.

Roast hens for about 60 minutes. Hens are done when a meat thermometer placed between the thigh and breast shows 165°F (70°C), or until hens are golden and juices run clear. Baste with pan juices every 15 minutes, adding remaining half-cup of juice and stock, or more as needed.

Remove hens to platter, tent with aluminum foil to keep warm, and let stand 15 minutes before carving.

In the meantime, ladle onions and pan juices plus additional stock (if desired) into a bowl. Refrigerate for at least 15 minutes, allowing fat to rise to surface. Skim fat, reheat gravy, and transfer to serving dish.

Serve hens with gravy, warm or at room temperature.

Serves 4 to 8 ‖ NUTRITION (per serving): energy 328 kcal | total fat 11 g | saturated fat 2 g | carbohydrate 8 g | fibre 1 g | protein 50 g | sodium 304 mg | excellent source of protein, thiamin, riboflavin, niacin, vitamin B6, vitamin B12 | good source of potassium, vitamin A

INGREDIENTS

four 1¼-pound (795-g) Cornish game hens
1 lemon, quartered
2 large onions, sliced into wedges
1 cup (250 ml) fresh orange juice
1 cup (250 ml) Chicken Stock (see page 81), plus more to taste

MUSTARD ROSEMARY PASTE

2 tablespoons (30 ml) mustard powder
¼ cup (60 ml) fresh orange juice
2 tablespoons (30 ml) balsamic vinegar
1 tablespoon (15 ml) finely chopped fresh rosemary
2 garlic cloves, minced
½ teaspoon (2 ml) coarse salt
½ teaspoon (2 ml) freshly ground pepper

DR. JOE'S SMART FACT

Kosher salt, like conventional salt, is composed of sodium chloride, but since it has a larger grain the volume of equal weights is not the same. A teaspoon of kosher salt is roughly equivalent to half a teaspoon of regular salt. So, when it comes to kosher salt, less is more.

MARINATING TIPS

- If a dipping sauce is required, set some of the marinade aside before combining the remainder with the raw meat.
- Heavy-duty resealable plastic bags as well as glass or stainless steel bowls work well as vessels for marinating.
- Rub the marinade into the meat and turn frequently to help the marinating process.
- Refrigerate meat while it marinates. Never let it sit out at room temperature for more than an hour.
- After marinating, remove meat from container and let juice drip off meat. Discard remainder of marinade.
- Wipe off excess marinade, as it can cause flare-ups while cooking.

DR. JOE'S SMART FACT

The amino acid tryptophan is said to induce sleep because it is the body's precursor for serotonin, a neurotransmitter associated with calmness. This is more or less a myth, given that chicken and ground beef contain the same amount per weight of tryptophan as turkey, and so do pork and Swiss cheese.

piri piri spatchcocked chicken

Spatchcocking is a method of preparing poultry in which the backbone is removed and the bird flattened, allowing for faster cooking. Piri piri is a traditional Portuguese sauce that derives its name from the African bird's-eye chili used in the recipe. The result is a dish with extraordinary flavour.

PIRI PIRI MARINADE

3 tablespoons (45 ml) fresh lemon juice
3 tablespoons (45 ml) olive oil
3 tablespoons (45 ml) white vinegar
1 Thai chili or 2 jalapeño peppers, seeded and coarsely chopped
4 large garlic cloves
2 teaspoons (10 ml) paprika
2 teaspoons (10 ml) cayenne pepper
½ teaspoon (2 ml) salt

3½ pounds (1.75 kg) spatchcocked chicken

Combine all ingredients for piri piri marinade in a blender. Let stand for an hour to allow flavours to meld. Reserve 2 tablespoons of sauce for serving.

Rinse chicken and pat dry. Score chicken with a knife a few times. Place chicken in a resealable plastic bag. Pour in piri piri sauce, seal bag, and rub marinade into chicken. Marinate, refrigerated, for at least 6 hours or overnight.

Preheat oven to 400°F (200°C). Arrange a metal rack on a baking sheet lined with aluminum foil.

Remove chicken from marinade, allowing excess to drip off, and place on prepared rack; discard marinade. Bake for 45 minutes. Turn heat to broil; broil chicken for 5 minutes, watching carefully to ensure it does not burn.

Serve chicken with reserved piri piri sauce.

Serves 6 ‖ **NUTRITION** (per serving): energy 245 kcal | total fat 13 g | saturated fat 3 g | carbohydrate 2 g | fibre 0 g | protein 30 g | sodium 195 mg | excellent source of niacin, vitamin B6 | good source of riboflavin, vitamin B12

sweet 'n savoury crunchy chicken

Baked instead of fried, these sweet and savoury chicken cutlets have just the right amount of crunch. For variety, try using different types of cereal and mustards. Deliciously satisfying!

INGREDIENTS

3 boneless and skinless chicken breasts
6 boneless and skinless chicken thighs
1 teaspoon (5 ml) cayenne pepper
1 teaspoon (5 ml) curry powder
1 teaspoon (5 ml) kosher salt
½ teaspoon (2 ml) freshly ground pepper
¼ cup (60 ml) finely chopped fresh basil leaves
2 teaspoons (10 ml) fresh garlic, minced
1 tablespoon (15 ml) honey mustard
½ cup (125 ml) apricot preserves or jam
2 cups (500 ml) multi-grain, whole-grain, or gluten-free flake-style cereal, crushed
½ cup (125 ml) walnuts, finely chopped

Rinse chicken and pat dry with paper towels. Place chicken on a platter and season with cayenne pepper, curry powder, salt, and pepper. Combine basil, garlic, mustard, and preserves in a small bowl. Brush both sides of chicken with preserve mixture.

Marinate in the refrigerator for at least 3 hours or overnight.

Preheat oven to 375°F (190°C). Line a large baking sheet with well greased crumpled aluminum foil.

Toss cereal and walnuts in a shallow dish. Remove chicken from marinade, allowing excess to drip off. Working with one piece at a time, coat chicken with cereal-nut mixture, pressing gently so that the crumbs adhere.

Arrange coated chicken pieces in a single layer on prepared pan.

Bake for 30 minutes or until golden brown, turning chicken gently halfway through baking.

Serves 6 ‖ **NUTRITION** (per serving): energy 380 kcal | total fat 13 g | saturated fat 2 g | carbohydrate 28 g | fibre 2 g | protein 38 g | sodium 305 mg | excellent source of thiamin, niacin, vitamin B6 | good source of iron, folate, vitamin B12

DR. JOE'S SMART FACT

To maximize the health benefits of garlic, let it sit for 5 to 10 minutes after chopping or pressing before you cook or eat it. This has to do with alliin and the enzyme alliinase, which are separated in the cell structure when the garlic is whole. Chopping or pressing the garlic ruptures the cells, releasing the alliin and alliinase and thus allowing them to combine to form a powerful new compound called allicin. Allicin, a phytonutrient, is responsible for both the strong smell of garlic and its health-promoting benefits. The finer the chopping, mincing, pressing, or dicing, the more allicin may be produced.

greek-style kabobs

This splendid marinade of yogurt, lemon, garlic, thyme, and oregano is also excellent when used with lamb.

MARINADE

⅓ cup (75 ml) extra-virgin olive oil
¼ cup (60 ml) each finely chopped fresh mint, oregano and dill
1 tablespoon (15 ml) minced fresh garlic
finely grated zest and juice of 1 lemon
½ teaspoon (2 ml) kosher salt
¼ teaspoon (1 ml) freshly ground pepper
1 pound (455 g) boneless, skinless, chicken breasts or thighs, trimmed and cut into
   1½-inch (3.5 cm) chunks

VEGETABLES

½ pineapple, peeled, cored, and cut into large cubes
1 large zucchini, cut into 8 pieces
1 large red onion, cut into 8 wedges
1 large yellow or red pepper, seeded and cut into 8 pieces
2 tablespoons (30 ml) extra-virgin olive oil
¼ teaspoon (1 ml) kosher salt
pinch of freshly ground pepper
1 cup (250 ml) Low-Fat Tzatziki (see page 302)

Whisk marinade ingredients together in a medium bowl. Transfer ¼ cup (60 ml) of marinade to a small bowl, cover, and set aside in the refrigerator.

Place chicken in a resealable plastic bag. Pour in remaining marinade, seal bag, and rub marinade into chicken. Marinate, refrigerated, for at least 3 hours or overnight.

Preheat barbecue or grill until hot. Lightly grease cooking grate.

Toss pineapple and vegetables with oil and seasonings and set aside.

Remove chicken from marinade, allowing excess to drip off. Discard marinade.

Using eight pre-soaked 12-inch (30 cm) skewers, thread each skewer with chicken, pineapple, and a variety of vegetables.

Grill uncovered for about 12 to 15 minutes, giving each kebab a quarter-turn every 3 minutes until the chicken is fully cooked and juices run clear.

Pour reserved marinade over chicken and serve with Low-Fat Tzatziki.

Serves 4 ‖ **NUTRITION** (per serving): energy 257 kcal | total fat 6 g | saturated fat 1 g | carbohydrate 20 g | fibre 4 g | protein 34 g | sodium 239 mg | excellent source of vitamin C, thiamin, niacin, riboflavin, vitamin B6, vitamin B12 | good source of potassium, calcium, folate

SMART TIP

If you are using wooden skewers, soak them in water for at least one hour before using to prevent them from burning.

chicken burgers

Simplicity at its best, these tasty burgers are far from ordinary. Pairing them with salsa adds a fresh burst of flavour.

BURGERS

½ cup (125 ml) panko breadcrumbs
2 tablespoons (30 ml) finely chopped fresh rosemary
1 jalapeño pepper, seeded and very finely diced
2 garlic cloves, minced
2 teaspoons (10 ml) low-sodium soy sauce
1 tablespoon (15 ml) whole-grain or Dijon mustard
1 tablespoon (15 ml) Worcestershire sauce
1 teaspoon (5 ml) crushed red pepper flakes
½ teaspoon (2 ml) freshly ground pepper
2 pounds (900 g) ground chicken

TOPPINGS

whole-wheat or multi-grain English muffins
lettuce leaves

In a large bowl, mix all burger ingredients together except ground chicken. Add ground chicken and combine.

Shape mixture into 6 patties. Chill burgers in refrigerator for at least 20 minutes before cooking.

Preheat barbecue or broiler to medium-high. Lightly grease grill rack.

Grill burgers, covered, about 6 to 8 minutes per side until cooked through. Grill English muffins about 2 minutes until golden.

Place burger on English muffin and top with Avocado Mango Red Onion Salsa (see page 300). Cover with lettuce leaf.

Serves 6 || **NUTRITION** (per burger, without bun): energy 278 kcal | total fat 16 g | saturated fat 5 g | carbohydrate 9 g | fibre 1 g | protein 28 g | sodium 272 mg | excellent source of riboflavin, niacin, vitamin B6, vitamin B12 | good source of iron, thiamin

SMART TIP

Because meat shrinks as it cooks, form patties ½-inch (2.5 cm) larger than the size of the bun so that the cooked burger and the bun will be the same size. Handle the ground chicken as little as possible and don't compress the meat too much, as this will result in a tougher burger.

Shown with Avocado Mango Red Onion Salsa (see page 300)

veal burgers

A perfect balance of sweetness and spice transforms this everyday food into a gourmet delight.

BURGERS

1 tablespoon (15 ml) canola oil
3 tablespoons (45 ml) finely chopped red onion
1 celery stalk, finely chopped
1 Granny Smith apple, peel left on, grated
⅓ cup (75 ml) toasted hazelnuts, finely chopped
2 pounds (900 g) lean ground veal
½ teaspoon (2 ml) Sriracha sauce or chili
    paste (optional)
½ teaspoon (2 ml) kosher salt, plus more
    for seasoning
½ teaspoon (2 ml) freshly ground pepper,
    plus more for seasoning
1 tablespoon (15 ml) finely chopped fresh dill
1 teaspoon (5 ml) finely grated lemon zest
1 large egg, beaten

TOPPINGS

6 multi-grain thin-crust buns or pita breads
lettuce, tomato, avocado, and red onion, sliced

Heat oil in a large skillet over medium heat. Add onions, celery, apple, and nuts. Sauté for 5 minutes.

Transfer to a large bowl, add remaining ingredients, and combine thoroughly.

Shape mixture into 6 patties. Chill burgers in refrigerator for at least 30 minutes.

Preheat barbecue or broiler to medium-high. Lightly grease grill rack.

Grill burgers about 5 to 7 minutes per side for medium-rare.

Place each burger in a thin-crust bun or pita pocket and add a dollop of mustard. Top with lettuce, tomato, avocado, and red onion.

Serves 6 ‖ **NUTRITION** (per burger, without bun): energy 302 kcal | total fat 17 g | saturated fat 5 g | carbohydrate 5 g | fibre 1 g | protein 31 g | sodium 298 mg | excellent source of vitamin E, thiamin, riboflavin, niacin, vitamin B6, vitamin B12

Shown with Tahini Mustard Sauce (see page 299)

SMART TIP

To clean a barbecue grate, slice a large onion in half. Holding the onion with tongs, wipe the hot grate with the onion. To grease the grate, coat the other half of the onion with oil and use it to wipe the oil on the grate in the same manner.

contemporary shepherd's pie

Celery root and pear add a tier of flavour to this modernized classic, which is equally delicious when made with minced chicken or ground beef instead of turkey.

TURKEY FILLING

1 tablespoon (15 ml) canola oil
1½ pounds (680 g) ground turkey
1 medium onion, diced small
8 ounces (225 g) cremini mushrooms, coarsely chopped
2 large garlic cloves, minced
5½ ounces (156 ml) tomato paste
1½ tablespoons (22 ml) Worcestershire sauce
1 teaspoon (5 ml) chili powder, or more to taste
1 cup (250 ml) water
salt and freshly ground pepper
2 ripe plum tomatoes, sliced
1½ to 2 cups (375 to 500 ml) corn niblets, fresh or thawed from frozen
1 recipe of Celery Root Pear Mash (see page 178)
pinch of paprika

 **DR. JOE'S SMART FACT**

The comfort food we call shepherd's pie was probably originally made by the shepherd's wife, not the shepherd. The idea was to extend leftover meat by lining a pan with mashed potatoes and covering the meat with the same. When corn was available, that was mixed in as well. Mrs. Lovett, Sweeney Todd's accomplice, made the most authentic shepherd's pie using … well, real shepherd.

Heat oil in a large skillet over high heat. Add turkey and cook for about 5 minutes until brown, breaking up turkey with a wooden spoon or spatula. Transfer meat to a bowl using a slotted spoon, leaving as much cooking liquid in the pot as possible.

Reduce heat to medium, add onion, and cook about 5 minutes until the onions are translucent. Add mushrooms and cook about 8 to 10 minutes more, stirring occasionally, until mushrooms are soft. Add garlic and cook, stirring, about 1 minute.

Return meat and collected juices to pan and stir in tomato paste, Worcestershire sauce, and chili powder. Cook, stirring, about 2 minutes. Add the water and bring to a boil. Reduce heat and simmer about 5 to 7 minutes until liquid is thickened. Adjust seasoning to taste with salt and pepper.

Preheat oven to 400°F (200°C). Set eight 16-ounce (450 ml) glasses or ramekins in a roasting pan.

Divide meat mixture evenly into glasses. Layer sliced tomato over meat. Spoon corn over tomatoes and distribute into an even layer. Cover with Celery Root Pear Mash. Instead of individual serving dishes, a 10-inch (25 cm) round or square baking dish may be used.

Sprinkle with paprika and bake about 30 (individual glasses) to 45 minutes (baking dish) until juices are bubbling and topping is golden brown.

Let sit 5 minutes before serving.

Serves 8 || **NUTRITION** (per serving): energy 264 kcal | total fat 10 g | saturated fat 2 g | carbohydrate 29 g | fibre 5 g | protein 20 g | sodium 296 mg | excellent source of riboflavin, niacin, vitamin B12 | good source of vitamin E, vitamin B6

barbecue sesame veal stir-fry

STIR-FRY BARBECUE SAUCE

2 tablespoons (30 ml) tomato paste

2 tablespoons (30 ml) red
  wine vinegar

1 tablespoon (15 ml) honey

1 tablespoon (15 ml) low-sodium
  soy sauce

2 teaspoons (10 ml) Sriracha sauce
  or hot chili paste, more or less
  to taste

1 tablespoon (15 ml) sesame seeds,
  toasted, plus additional for
  garnish

1 teaspoon (5 ml) sesame oil

1 large garlic clove, minced

AROMATICS

2 large garlic cloves, minced

1 teaspoon (5 ml) minced
  fresh ginger

1 teaspoon (5 ml) sesame oil

MEAT

4 teaspoons (20 ml) canola oil,
  divided

1 pound (455 g) veal fillet, trimmed,
  cut into cubes or thin strips

VEGETABLES

½ tablespoon (7 ml) canola oil

2 pounds (1 kg) assorted vegetables
  (broccoli, green beans, shiitake
  mushrooms, snow peas, bell
  peppers, etc.), cut into bite-
  sized pieces

3 scallions, white and pale-green
  parts only, thinly sliced

Stir-frying is a quick cooking method with endless possibilities. Any preference can be indulged, be it savoury, sweet, pungent, or spicy, by adding different seasonings and ingredients. Getting organized is the key to a successful stir-fry, so prepare all the vegetables and the sauce ahead of time.

Whisk sauce ingredients together in a small bowl.

Combine the aromatic ingredients in another small bowl and set aside.

Heat 2 teaspoons of oil in a wok or large frying pan over medium-high heat. Add half the veal in a single layer. Cook until golden brown on one side; turn and brown the other side. Transfer to a bowl and set aside. Repeat with the remaining oil and veal.

Heat ½ tablespoon of oil in wok until it just begins to smoke. Add broccoli and green beans and stir-fry for 1 minute. Add mushrooms and stir-fry for about 3 minutes until they are lightly browned and softened. Add snow peas and scallions; move vegetables to side of wok and add aromatics. Cook and mash aromatics for about 30 seconds until fragrant and then stir with vegetables for about 30 seconds until incorporated and beans are crisp.

Return veal to wok, whisk barbecue sauce to recombine, and then add to wok. Reduce heat to medium and cook for about 30 seconds, stirring constantly, until sauce is thickened and veal is cooked through.

Transfer to serving platter and sprinkle with additional sesame seeds.

Serves 6 as a main dish ‖ NUTRITION (per serving): energy 314 kcal | total fat 8 g | saturated fat 1 g | carbohydrate 41 g | fibre 7 g | protein 22 g | sodium 304 mg | excellent source of potassium, vitamin C, vitamin E, riboflavin, niacin, folate, vitamin B6, vitamin B12 | good source of iron, thiamin

veal and bulgur stuffed acorn squash

As fall arrives, so does the bountiful harvest of hearty vegetables. Special among them is the highly nutritious acorn squash, which is used as both the vessel and as part of the scrumptious filling. Makes a show-stopping presentation!

INGREDIENTS

2 medium acorn squash, about 1 pound (455 g) each, halved and seeded

VEAL STUFFING

2 tablespoons (30 ml) canola oil, divided
½ pound (225 g) lean ground veal
¼ teaspoon (1 ml) salt, plus more for seasoning
¼ teaspoon (1 ml) freshly ground pepper, plus more for seasoning
1 medium onion, diced small
1 large garlic clove, minced
¾ cup (175 ml) dry bulgur
2 cups (500 ml) Chicken Stock (see page 81)
1 cup (250 ml) sliced cremini mushrooms
2 plum tomatoes, seeded and diced medium
2 tablespoons (30 ml) coarsely chopped almond slivers, toasted
2 tablespoons (30 ml) chopped fresh basil

Preheat oven to 400°F (200°C).

Place squash, cut side down, in a 9 × 13 inch (23 × 33 cm) baking dish. Bake 35 to 40 minutes until tender.

Meanwhile, heat 1 tablespoon of oil in a large skillet with a tight-fitting lid over medium-high heat. Add veal, salt, and pepper and brown for 5 to 10 minutes, uncovered, breaking up veal with back of a spoon. Transfer veal to a bowl using a slotted spoon and set aside.

Heat remaining tablespoon of oil in skillet, add onion, and cook about 3 to 5 minutes until softened and translucent. Stir in all other stuffing ingredients except almonds and basil. Reduce heat to medium-low, cover, and cook for 15 minutes. Remove from heat and let stand, covered, for 5 minutes. Fluff with fork and add reserved veal, almonds, and basil.

Scrape out baked squashes, forming ¼-inch (5 mm) thick bowls, and fold flesh into veal mixture.

Sprinkle inside of squash "bowls" with salt and pepper. Divide veal mixture evenly among squash halves and return to oven. Bake until warmed through and tops are browned, 10 to 15 minutes.

Serves 4 ‖ **NUTRITION** (per serving): energy 368 kcal | total fat 14 g | saturated fat 3 g | carbohydrate 50 g | fibre 10 g | protein 18 g | sodium 178 mg | excellent source of potassium, fibre, vitamin E, vitamin C, thiamin, niacin, vitamin B6, vitamin B12 | good source of iron, riboflavin, folate

SMART TIP

Squash is easier to cut if microwaved on high for 1 to 2 minutes. Pierce the rind in a few places before heating. Let stand for 3 minutes before cutting.

DR. JOE'S SMART FACT

Some consumers are concerned about the use of hormones in the raising of cattle. Although hormones can be used in beef cattle, growth-promoting hormonal products are not approved in Canada in any form for use in milk-fed, grain-fed, or grass-fed calves intended for veal production. Dairy cattle are not given any hormones.

grilled peaches and pork chops

The sweetness of peaches highlights the grilled meat. Veal or lamb chops work equally well.

INGREDIENTS

four 6-ounce (175 g) bone-in pork chops, 1½ inches (3.5 cm) thick
kosher salt and freshly ground pepper
2 peaches, pitted and halved or quartered

MARINADE

⅓ cup (75 ml) orange marmalade
1 tablespoon (15 ml) Dijon mustard
1 teaspoon (5 ml) Worcestershire sauce
2 tablespoons (30 ml) fresh thyme leaves

Preheat barbecue or grill to medium-high.

Place pork chops on baking sheet and season with salt and pepper. Place peaches on separate plate.

Mix marinade ingredients in a small bowl until well combined. Brush marinade on peaches, and then on both sides of chops until entirely and generously coated.

Grill chops over indirect heat about 4 to 6 minutes per side until cooked through. At the same time, grill peaches, flesh side down, until softened, also about 4 to 6 minutes.

Place peaches alongside chops and serve.

Serves 4 ‖ **NUTRITION** (per serving): energy 242 kcal | total fat 10 g | saturated fat 4 g | carbohydrate 8 g | fibre 1 g | protein 29 g | sodium 121 mg | excellent source of thiamin, riboflavin, niacin, vitamin B6, vitamin B12

braised lamb shanks with figs and orzo

Searing meat at a high temperature and finishing the cooking slowly in liquid in a covered vessel is called braising. The result is a tender piece of meat infused with delicious flavour. Enriched by figs and orzo, this comfort food can be served directly from oven to table.

LAMB

4 lamb shanks, 1 to 1½ pounds (455 to 680 g) each
kosher salt and freshly ground pepper
2 tablespoons (30 ml) canola oil
2 large yellow onions, coarsely chopped
3 cups (750 ml) Chicken Stock (see page 81)
1 cup (250 ml) dry red wine
1 cup (250 ml) water
28-ounce (796 ml) can diced tomatoes, with juice
1 large bulb of garlic, peeled
2 tablespoons (30 ml) finely chopped fresh rosemary
2 carrots, peeled and diced large
2 parsnips, peeled and diced large

ORZO

1 to 2 cups (250 to 500 ml) Chicken Stock (see page 81) or water, if needed
12 dried Mission or Calimyrna figs
3 tablespoons (45 ml) balsamic glaze or fig balsamic vinegar
2 bay leaves
1½ cups (375 ml) orzo

Preheat oven to 325°F (160°C).

Rinse lamb, pat dry, and season with salt and pepper.

Heat 1 tablespoon of oil over medium-high heat in a deep, ovenproof casserole or Dutch oven large enough to hold lamb and liquid. Sear lamb on all sides for about 10 to 12 minutes in total. Transfer to platter and set aside.

In the same pan, heat remaining tablespoon of oil over medium heat. Add onion and sauté about 5 minutes until softened. Add remaining ingredients to pot and bring to a simmer. Return lamb to pot and submerge in liquid. Cover and cook in oven for 4 hours, basting halfway through. Lamb should be tender and falling off the bone. Carefully transfer lamb to a platter.

Add ingredients for orzo to casserole or Dutch oven and stir. Add 1 to 2 cups (250 to 500 ml) of stock if sauce is thick. Return lamb to pot, cover, and cook in oven for 20 to 30 minutes until orzo is cooked. Discard bay leaves, taste, and adjust seasoning. Serve immediately.

Serves 8 ‖ NUTRITION (per serving): energy 442 kcal | total fat 15 g | saturated fat 5 g | carbohydrate 44 g | fibre 5 g | protein 29 g | sodium 150 mg | excellent source of iron, vitamin C, vitamin E, thiamin, riboflavin, niacin, folate, vitamin B6, vitamin B12 | good source of potassium, vitamin A

⭐ SMART TIP

To remove outer skins from a whole bulb of garlic, firmly press down on the bulb, loosening skins, and place in mixing bowl. Cover with a bowl of the same size and shake vigorously for 10 seconds. It really works!

flank steak with chimichurri sauce

INGREDIENTS

2 pounds (1 kg) flank steak, trimmed

MARINADE

¼ teaspoon (1 ml) salt, plus more for seasoning

¼ teaspoon (1 ml) freshly ground pepper, plus more for seasoning

½ cup (125 ml) finely chopped shallots

½ cup (125 ml) white wine

⅓ cup (75 ml) Dijon or whole-grain mustard

3 tablespoons (45 ml) extra-virgin olive oil

2 teaspoons (10 ml) Worcestershire sauce

1 tablespoon (15 ml) minced fresh garlic

CHIMICHURRI SAUCE

2 large garlic cloves

1 jalapeño pepper, seeded and coarsely chopped

1 bunch fresh flat-leaf parsley

1 bunch fresh cilantro leaves

2 tablespoons (30 ml) fresh oregano leaves

½ cup (125 ml) canola oil

3 tablespoons (45 ml) red wine vinegar

1 teaspoon (5 ml) kosher salt

½ teaspoon (2 ml) freshly ground pepper

½ teaspoon (2 ml) red pepper flakes

An Argentinian specialty, chimichurri sauce is similar to both pistou and pesto. Often served with grilled steak because of its bold seasonings, it can also accompany chicken or fish and tastes wonderful on grilled vegetables.

Place steak on a cutting board and lightly score (cut) top diagonally in a large criss-cross pattern. Season with salt and pepper.

Whisk all marinade ingredients in a medium bowl. Transfer meat to a large resealable plastic bag and pour marinade on top. Marinate meat in refrigerator for at least 4 hours or overnight.

Make chimichurri sauce by pulsing garlic and jalapeño pepper in a food processor or blender until chopped. Add parsley, cilantro, and oregano and pulse briefly until finely chopped. Transfer to a small bowl.

Process oil, vinegar, salt, pepper, and red pepper flakes until blended. Add to parsley mixture and set aside. (Adding liquids separately from herbs results in a chimichurri sauce that is finely chopped rather than puréed.)

Remove steak from refrigerator a half hour before cooking and discard marinade.

Preheat barbecue or broiler. Lightly grease grill rack or broiling pan.

Brush chimichurri sauce on both sides of steak and place on grill or broiling pan. Grill steak until medium-rare, about 5 minutes per side, or broil 3 to 4 minutes per side.

Transfer steak to cutting board, loosely tent with foil, and let stand for about 5 minutes. Thinly slice steak diagonally across the grain. Serve with remaining chimichurri sauce.

Serves 4 ‖ **NUTRITION** (per serving): energy 376 kcal | total fat 25 g | saturated fat 5 g | carbohydrate 3 g | fibre 1 g | protein 33 g | sodium 471 mg | excellent source of vitamin B6, vitamin B12, niacin, vitamin E | good source of folate, iron

SMART TIP

In general, meat should stand between 5 to 10 minutes after cooking, tented by foil, to allow the juices to retreat back into the meat. This way, less juice will ooze out when the meat is cut.

pecan-crusted beef tenderloin

Tenderloin is one of the leanest cuts of meat. The pecan rub in this recipe blankets the beef with a crunchy and tasty exterior while the sauce adds an amazing depth of flavour.

INGREDIENTS

1 beef tenderloin, about 4 pounds (1.8 kg)
kosher salt and freshly ground pepper

PECAN RUB

1½ cups (375 ml) very finely chopped raw pecans
3 tablespoons (45 ml) olive oil
½ cup (125 ml) loosely packed finely chopped flat-leaf parsley
2 garlic cloves, minced
1 teaspoon (5 ml) kosher salt, plus more for seasoning
½ teaspoon (2 ml) freshly ground pepper, plus more for seasoning
½ teaspoon (2 ml) crushed red pepper flakes

8 shallots, peeled and sliced in half
2 tablespoons (30 ml) balsamic vinegar
1 cup (250 ml) low-sodium beef stock or Chicken Stock (see page 81)
1 tablespoon (15 ml) Dijon mustard
1 tablespoon (15 ml) whole-grain mustard

Adjust oven rack to upper-middle position and heat oven to 425°F (220°C).

Place tenderloin on a piece of plastic wrap and rub with salt and pepper. Combine all ingredients for pecan rub in a bowl and toss well. Coat meat evenly on all sides with mixture, pressing mixture firmly onto beef so that it will stick. Lift the sides of the plastic wrap and press any rub that has fallen onto the plastic back on the meat.

Carefully transfer beef to a shallow roasting pan; add shallots. Roast about 30 to 40 minutes until an instant-read thermometer inserted into centre of beef reads 125°F (52°C). Remove beef from pan and let meat rest on a cutting board for about 10 minutes.

Place the pan with shallots on stove over medium-high heat and deglaze by adding balsamic vinegar and scraping up any browned bits from the bottom with a wooden spoon. Add stock and simmer 2 to 3 minutes until slightly reduced. Reduce heat to low and stir in mustards. Keep sauce warm until serving.

Cut beef into slices; top with sauce, if desired, and serve.

Serves 10 ‖ NUTRITION (per serving): energy 360 kcal | total fat 26 g | saturated fat 5 g | carbohydrate 6 g | fibre 2 g | protein 27 g | sodium 334 mg | excellent source of iron, vitamin E, thiamin, riboflavin, niacin, vitamin B6, vitamin B12

Shown with Smashed Roasted Potatoes (see page 185)

Shallots are milder than onions. They have purple-tinged white flesh and can be used instead of onions in most recipes.

Ask your butcher to cut your tenderloin from the thick end so that the meat will cook evenly.

DR. JOE'S SMART FACT

People say that chewing on parsley can help get rid of halitosis, a claim attributed to the chlorophyll content found in the herb. Although there is no actual evidence that chlorophyll is effective in this regard, it has been found that some of the natural oils in parsley can mask disturbing smells. Remember that the goat that reeks on yonder hill has dined all day on chlorophyll.

Sweets are treats!

sweets & treats

honey cake

Tina loves allspice. Gail not so much. Either way, this cake is delicious!

DRY INGREDIENTS

1½ cups (375 ml) whole-wheat flour
1 tablespoon (15 ml) cocoa powder
2 teaspoons (10 ml) baking powder
2 teaspoons (10 ml) ground cinnamon
pinch of cloves and allspice, to taste (optional)

WET INGREDIENTS

2 large eggs
½ cup (125 ml) packed brown sugar
½ cup (125 ml) canola oil
½ cup (125 ml) honey
½ cup (125 ml) chai tea, cooled
½ cup (125 ml) fresh orange juice

Preheat oven to 350°F (180°C). Line a large 9 × 5 × 3 inch (23 × 13 × 8 cm) or a sectioned loaf pan with four 6 × 3 × 2 inch (15 × 8 × 5 cm) compartments with parchment paper, leaving an overhang on the long sides. Grease lightly.

In a medium bowl, mix dry ingredients together.

In a large bowl, whisk eggs and sugar. Add oil and honey, whisking after each addition.

Add flour mixture, tea, and orange juice and mix until just combined. Batter will be thin.

Pour batter into prepared pan and bake for 20 minutes. Rotate pan and continue to bake about 15 to 20 minutes longer until cake is deep brown and fragrant and a toothpick inserted in centre comes out clean. For mini honey cakes reduce baking time to 25 minutes.

Cool on a wire rack for 10 minutes. Gently run knife around edges and lift out of pan with overhanging parchment paper.

Store wrapped in plastic in the refrigerator or freezer.

Serves 20 ‖ **NUTRITION** (per serving): energy 116 kcal | total fat 4 g | saturated fat 1 g | carbohydrate 18 g | fibre 1 g | protein 2 g | sodium 40 mg

SMART TIP

Eggs used for baking cakes should be at room temperature. To quickly warm refrigerated eggs, place them in a bowl of warm (not hot) water for 5 to 10 minutes.

DR. JOE'S SMART FACT

Honey is a concentrated sugar solution with small amounts of chemicals that have antioxidant and antiseptic properties. The exact composition of honey depends on what type of flowers the bees have visited.

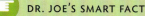
zucchini cake

Good-bye carrot, hello zucchini! Everything plays very well together in this amazing reinvention of the "tired" carrot cake. Loaded with many delicious ingredients, the texture and taste are just divine.

WET INGREDIENTS

2 eggs
1 tablespoon (15 ml) pure vanilla extract
⅓ cup (75 ml) honey
¼ cup (60 ml) pure maple syrup
3 tablespoons (45 ml) unsweetened applesauce

DRY INGREDIENTS

2 cups (500 ml) whole-wheat flour, plus 1 teaspoon (5 ml)
1½ teaspoons (7 ml) baking soda
1½ teaspoons (7 ml) baking powder
1 tablespoon (15 ml) ground cinnamon
2 teaspoons (10 ml) ground cardamom
½ teaspoon (2 ml) salt (optional)

FLAVOURINGS

½ cup (125 ml) coarsely chopped dried cranberries or cherries
½ cup (125 ml) dark chocolate chips (optional)
½ cup (125 ml) pistachios, toasted, plus 3 tablespoons (45 ml) finely chopped pistachios
   for garnish (optional)
2 large zucchini, shredded, about 4 cups (1 L)

Preheat oven to 325°F (160°C). Lightly grease a 9-inch (23 cm) Bundt pan.

In a medium bowl, mix wet ingredients together.

Sift dry ingredients into a large bowl.

Pour wet ingredients into dry ingredients and mix until combined.

Toss cherries, chocolate chips and pistachios with 1 teaspoon of flour. Add to batter.

Add zucchini to batter and mix until incorporated.

Pour batter into prepared pan and bake for 40 to 45 minutes until top springs back when touched or a toothpick inserted into centre comes out clean. Remove from oven and set on a wire rack to cool.

Garnish with chopped pistachios.

Serves 20 ‖ **NUTRITION** (per serving): energy 120 kcal | total fat 3 g | saturated fat 0 g | carbohydrate 21 g | fibre 2 g | protein 4 g | sodium 122 mg

biscotti thins

Simply irresistible, these thin and crispy biscuits just don't get any better. They provide the perfect ending to any meal.

WET INGREDIENTS

4 large eggs
½ cup (125 ml) granulated sugar
1 teaspoon (5 ml) finely grated orange zest
1 teaspoon (5 ml) pure vanilla extract

DRY INGREDIENTS

1½ cups (375 ml) whole-wheat flour
1 cup (250 ml) sliced almonds
¾ cup (175 ml) raisins
¾ cup (175 ml) shelled pistachios
¾ cup (175 ml) coarsely chopped dried cranberries
¾ cup (175 ml) coarsely chopped dried apricots

Preheat oven to 350°F (180°C). Line a 9 × 5 × 3 inch (23 × 13 × 8 cm) loaf pan with parchment paper, leaving an overhang on the long sides. Grease unlined sides very lightly.

Line a large cookie sheet with parchment paper (this is for the second baking).

Using an electric mixer, beat wet ingredients together until light and smooth.

Add flour and mix until just combined. Add remaining dry ingredients, stirring until combined.

Pour batter into prepared pan and bake for 45 to 50 minutes. Remove from oven and place on a wire rack to cool for 10 minutes. Lift loaf from pan using the parchment paper. Loaf should still be warm, but cool enough to handle. If not, wait 5 more minutes.

Raise oven temperature to 400°F (200°C).

Using a cutting board and a very sharp serrated knife, cut loaf into ⅛-inch (3 mm) slices. Carefully transfer slices to prepared cookie sheet.

Bake for 4 minutes; remove from oven and flip each biscotti over. Return to oven and bake for an additional 4 or 5 minutes.

Store in an airtight container in refrigerator or freezer.

Makes 40 biscotti ‖ NUTRITION (per biscotti): energy 86 kcal | total fat 3 g | saturated fat 0 g | carbohydrate 13 g | fibre 1 g | protein 3 g | sodium 8 mg

SMART TIP

To produce the most flavour, always add the citrus zest at the same time as the sugar so that the citrus oils are well incorporated.

seed jumble cookies

Bursting with protein-rich seeds and hearty oats, these cookies provide a sweet and satisfying boost any time of the day.

SMART TIP

Because of their high fat content, sunflower and pepita seeds should be stored in an airtight container in the refrigerator or freezer. Raw seeds can be refrigerated for 6 months and frozen for up to 12 months.

DRY INGREDIENTS

1¼ cups (310 ml) rolled oats
¼ cup (60 ml) spelt flour
¼ cup (60 ml) finely ground flax seeds
½ cup (125 ml) raw sunflower seeds
½ cup (125 ml) raw pumpkin seeds
⅔ cup (150 ml) dark chocolate chips
¼ cup (60 ml) sesame seeds

WET INGREDIENTS

¼ cup (60 ml) pure maple syrup
¼ cup (60 ml) honey
2 teaspoons (10 ml) pure vanilla extract
3 tablespoons (45 ml) Sunflower Seed Butter (page 297)
¼ cup (60 ml) tahini
1 large egg, lightly beaten

Preheat oven to 350°F (180°C). Line 2 large cookie sheets with parchment paper.

Mix dry ingredients in large mixing bowl.

In a medium bowl, mix wet ingredients together until smooth. Pour wet ingredients into dry and stir to combine well.

Using a tablespoon, drop batter on prepared cookie sheet, leaving 1 inch (2.5 cm) between cookies. Slightly flatten each cookie with a fork. (If fork sticks to dough, dip in a glass of water.)

Bake about 12 to 14 minutes until edges begin to brown.

Remove from oven and cool on a wire rack before removing cookies.

Store in an airtight container.

Makes 32 cookies ‖ NUTRITION (per cookie): energy 98 kcal | total fat 6 g | saturated fat 1 g | carbohydrate 11 g | fibre 2 g | protein 3 g | sodium 6 mg

cinnamon cashew crunches

Beware! These are highly addictive and you will not be able to stop at just one.

INGREDIENTS

3 cups (750 ml) roughly chopped raw cashews
¼ cup (60 ml) granulated sugar
2 large egg whites
½ teaspoon (2 ml) ground cinnamon

Preheat oven to 350°F (180°C). Line a large baking sheet with parchment paper.

Mix all ingredients together in a large bowl until cashews are well coated.

Place a small amount of batter onto one teaspoon and push it off with another teaspoon to form little mounds on prepared pan. Leave an inch between clusters.

Bake about 15 to 17 minutes until lightly browned.

Transfer tray to wire rack and let cool for 10 minutes before lifting cookies.

Store in an airtight container.

Makes 36 cookies || NUTRITION (per cookie): energy 66 kcal | total fat 5 g | saturated fat 1 g | carbohydrate 5 g | fibre 0 g | protein 2 g | sodium 4 mg

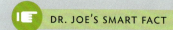

SMART TIP	DR. JOE'S SMART FACT
Most foods stick together when frozen, so use the flash-freeze method to eliminate the problem. Spread food on a cookie sheet, freeze it, and then transfer to an airtight container and return to the freezer.	The cashew is not technically a nut, but the seed of a fruit called the cashew apple. Although cashews are high in fat (and in calories), they are low in saturated fats.

chocolate mountains

Delectably satisfying without being a health hazard, these crunchy treasures can be eaten straight out of the freezer when that sweet tooth comes calling. Use any of your favourite multi-grain or gluten-free cereals.

INGREDIENTS

2 cups (500 ml) dark chocolate chips
5 to 6 cups (1.25 to 1.5 L) multi-grain flakes (or any whole-grain cereal flakes)
1 cup (250 ml) coarsely chopped dried cherries or cranberries
1 cup (250 ml) assorted seeds and/or nuts
½ cup (125 ml) unsweetened shredded coconut

Line a large baking sheet with parchment paper.

Melt chocolate in a large metal bowl set in a pan of simmering water. Remove from heat; add cereal and mix until well covered. Add remaining ingredients and stir until well combined.

Scoop coated cereal using a teaspoon or your hands, keeping mixture in a mound, and transfer to a prepared baking sheet.

Refrigerate or freeze until hardened.

Store in an airtight container in the fridge or freezer.

Makes 50 cookies ||
NUTRITION (per cookie):
energy 79 kcal | total fat 4 g |
saturated fat 2 g | carbohydrate
10 g | fibre 2 g | protein 1 g |
sodium 30 mg

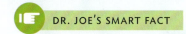
SMART TIP

Make this delicious treat gluten-free by using any gluten-free cereal as the base.

DR. JOE'S SMART FACT

Chocolate actually contains over 300 compounds with imposing names like furfuryl alcohol, dimethyl sulfide, phenylacetic acid, and phenylethylamine, which has been alluringly labelled the "chemical of love."

blueberry oatmeal cookies

This cookie will bring back memories of Grandma's delicious baking. Packed with dried fruit, they have just the right amount of sweetness. Consider making a double batch, as they will disappear before your eyes.

DRY INGREDIENTS

3 cups (750 ml) rolled oats
1½ cups (375 ml) spelt (or multi-grain) flour
1 teaspoon (5 ml) ground cinnamon
½ teaspoon (2 ml) baking soda
½ teaspoon (2 ml) baking powder
pinch of salt

WET INGREDIENTS

⅔ cup (150 ml) lightly packed brown sugar
⅓ cup (75 ml) canola oil
2 large eggs
3 tablespoons (45 ml) milk (dairy, soy or almond)
2 teaspoons (10 ml) pure vanilla extract
1 cup (250 ml) dried blueberries (or raisins, dried cherries, or cranberries)

Preheat oven to 350°F (180°C). Line 2 large cookie sheets with parchment paper.

Mix dry ingredients in large bowl.

Using an electric mixer, beat sugar and oil until creamy. Add eggs, one at a time, then add milk and vanilla; beat until creamy.

Add dry ingredients and mix until incorporated.

Fold in blueberries until just combined.

Using a tablespoon, place mounds of mixture on prepared cookie sheet, leaving 1 inch (2.5 cm) between cookies. Gently flatten each mound with a fork. (If dough sticks to fork, dip fork in a glass of water.)

Bake about 8 to 10 minutes until golden.

Remove from oven and cool on a wire rack before removing cookies.

Store in an airtight container.

Makes 45 cookies || **NUTRITION** (per cookie): energy 76 kcal | total fat 3 g | saturated fat 0 g | carbohydrate 11 g | fibre 1 g | protein 2 g | sodium 19 mg

SMART TIP

Always preheat the oven for 10 to 15 minutes before beginning to bake. To allow for variances in oven temperature and altitude, prevent over-baking by checking cookies a few minutes before the minimum baking time.

almond coconut chocolate chip cookies

These flourless cookies are sure to satisfy all the coconut lovers out there.
Just a few minutes to heaven!

DRY INGREDIENTS

1¼ cups (310 g) ground almond flour
½ cup (125 ml) unsweetened
    shredded coconut
½ teaspoon (2 ml) baking powder
¼ teaspoon (1 ml) salt
¼ cup (60 ml) granulated sugar
¼ cup (60 ml) dark chocolate chips

WET INGREDIENTS

1 egg
3 tablespoons (45 ml) coconut
    oil, melted
½ teaspoon (2 ml) pure
    vanilla extract

SMART TIP

To prevent cookies from spreading too much while baking, refrigerate the dough on the baking sheet for 30 minutes before baking.

Mix dry ingredients in large bowl.

In a separate bowl, beat egg. Whisk in oil and vanilla.

Pour wet ingredients into dry ingredients and mix until just combined.

Dampen hands to prevent dough from sticking and roll dough into 1-inch (2.5 cm) balls. Place on prepared cookie sheet, leaving an inch between cookies.

Gently flatten the top of each ball with a wet fork. Refrigerate for 30 minutes.

Preheat oven to 375°F (190°C). Line cookie sheet with parchment paper.

Bake about 10 to 12 minutes until edges begin to brown.

Remove from oven and cool on a wire rack before removing cookies.

Store in an airtight container in the fridge or freezer.

Makes 24 cookies ‖ **NUTRITION** (per cookie): energy 76 kcal | total fat 6 g | saturated fat 3 g | carbohydrate 5 g | fibre 1 g | protein 2 g | sodium 28 mg

orange almond chocolate bark

Nothing complements chocolate better than the flavour of orange. This is our version of paradise. A no-fuss chocolate treat that is simply divine.

INGREDIENTS

1 cup (250 ml) coarsely chopped
    raw almonds, toasted
½ cup (125 ml) coarsely chopped
    dried apricots, cranberries, or
    dates
zest of 1 small orange, cut into
    slivers, all pith removed (see
    SMART TIP, below)
1 pound (455 g) 70% cocoa dark
    chocolate, coarsely chopped

SMART TIP

For fine zest, use a zester and apply light pressure to avoid removing the bitter white pith. For larger zest, use a vegetable peeler to remove the rinds, then cut into slivers with a pair of kitchen shears.

Line a large baking sheet with parchment paper.

Mix almonds, dried fruit, and orange zest in a small bowl.

Very slowly, melt chocolate in a double boiler or bowl set over barely simmering water. Remove from heat and stir in half of almond-fruit mixture.

Scrape into prepared pan smoothing top into an even layer. Sprinkle evenly with remaining almond-fruit mixture.

Refrigerate until set, about one hour.

Break chocolate into jagged, varied-size pieces and serve.

Store in an airtight container in a dark, cool place.

Makes about 40 pieces ‖ **NUTRITION** (per piece): energy 98 kcal | total fat 7 g | saturated fat 3 g | carbohydrate 8 g | fibre 2 g | protein 2 g | sodium 3 mg | good source of vitamin E

berry squares

Overflowing with assorted berries, these moist squares impart a delightfully sweet and tart sensation. Dress up with Lemon Yogurt Sauce (see page 288). Berry, berry good!

CRUST AND TOPPING

¾ cup (175 ml) whole-wheat flour
¾ cup (175 ml) coarsely chopped raw walnuts
⅓ cup (75 ml) lightly packed brown sugar
½ teaspoon (2 ml) salt
½ teaspoon (2 ml) ground cardamom or ground cinnamon
1 cup (250 ml) rolled oats
¼ cup (60 ml) cold unsalted butter, sliced, or coconut oil

FILLING

6 cups (1.5 l) mix of raspberries, blueberries, blackberries, or chopped strawberries, fresh or thawed from frozen
3 tablespoons (45 ml) honey
finely grated zest of 1 lemon
2 tablespoons (30 ml) whole-wheat flour

Preheat oven to 350°F (180°C). Line a 9-inch (23 cm) square baking pan with parchment paper, leaving an overhang on two parallel sides. Grease the parchment paper and pan.

Combine crust and topping ingredients in bowl of electric mixer fitted with paddle attachment. Mix on low speed for about 1 to 2 minutes until mixture is coarsely crumbled.

Reserve ¼ cup (60 ml) of mixture for topping and set aside. Pour balance of mixture into prepared pan and press down to form an even layer of crust on bottom of pan.

Bake for 12 to 15 minutes until golden. Remove from oven and let cool on wire rack.

Place berries in a large bowl; add remaining filling ingredients and gently stir until well combined.

Spread filling evenly on top of cooled crust. Sprinkle reserved topping mixture evenly on top of filling.

Bake for 50 minutes.

Transfer to a wire rack to cool completely, then cut into squares and serve.

Store in an airtight container in refrigerator or freezer.

Makes 36 squares ‖ NUTRITION (per square): energy 70 kcal | total fat 3 g | saturated fat 1 g | carbohydrate 10 g | fibre 2 g | protein 1 g | sodium 27 g

DR. JOE'S SMART FACT

Although the benefits of blueberries are usually attributed to the antioxidant properties of anthocyanins, the pigments responsible for their blue colour, the berries contain a host of other potentially beneficial compounds, such as hydroxycinnamic acids, hydroxybenzoic acids, flavonols, and even resveratrol, the famous compound found in red wine.

Indulge responsibly!

the grand finale

hazelnut fudge pie

A chocolate lover's dream come true, this rich and decadent pie has the perfect amount of crunch. For those who prefer a fudge-like consistency, it can be enjoyed straight out of the freezer.

CRUST

1½ cups (375 ml) almond flour
¼ cup (60 ml) canola or coconut oil (melted)
1 tablespoon (15 ml) granulated sugar
1 teaspoon (5 ml) pure vanilla extract

FILLING

1 cup (250 ml) raw cashews, soaked 3 hours or overnight in cold water
½ teaspoon (2 ml) pure vanilla extract
12 ounces (340 g) 70% cocoa dark chocolate
¼ cup (60 ml) canola or coconut oil (melted)
½ cup (125 ml) coarsely chopped raw hazelnuts, roasted, plus additional for garnish
¼ teaspoon (1 ml) salt
Roasted Coconut (see page 298) for garnish

Preheat oven to 350°F (180°C). Using softened butter, lightly grease a 9-inch (23 cm) removable-bottom tart pan.

Prepare crust by combining all crust ingredients in a medium bowl. Transfer to prepared pan and pat crumbs down evenly on bottom and sides of pan. Prick bottom all over with a fork and bake for 12 to 15 minutes until slightly golden. Remove from oven and set aside to cool.

Drain and rinse soaked cashews. Add cashews and about ½ cup (125 ml) of water to blender or food processor. Purée for several minutes until smooth and thick. Add vanilla and blend until incorporated; set aside.

Melt chocolate in a bowl set over a pan of simmering water. Remove from heat. Add oil, hazelnuts, and salt; stir to blend. Add cashew cream and mix well. Pour chocolate mixture into cooled crust and smooth top with spatula. Let pie set in refrigerator for 3 hours, or freeze for 1½ hours. Keep refrigerated until served.

Garnish with roasted hazelnuts and coconut.

Serves 20 ‖ NUTRITION (per serving): energy 240 kcal | total fat 20 g | saturated fat 5 g | carbohydrate 13 g | fibre 3 g | protein 4 g | sodium 28 mg | excellent source of vitamin E

SMART TIP

For a golden and stick-free crust, brush pan with softened butter (not cooking spray) and then lightly dust with flour before adding batter.

DR. JOE'S SMART FACT

Plant phenols in dark chocolate can help lower blood pressure. Milk chocolate does not have the same effect.

apple cashew tartlets

Cashew cream gives these elegant dairy-free tartlets a wonderfully light and silky filling. Bake them for any occasion, as they will never fail to impress.

ALMOND FILLING

1¼ cups (310 ml) almond flour
¼ cup (60 ml) granulated sugar
1 large egg
½ teaspoon (2 ml) pure vanilla extract
pinch of salt
⅓ cup (75 ml) cashew, almond, or soy cream (see SMART TIP for recipe)

TART

5 sheets of phyllo dough
2 to 3 tablespoons (30 to 45 ml) canola oil
1 tablespoon (15 ml) granulated sugar
4 medium sweet apples, preferably Gala
¼ cup (60 ml) apple jelly
2 teaspoons (10 ml) water
1 teaspoon (5 ml) ground cinnamon for garnish

Preheat oven to 400°F (200°C). Line a large baking sheet with parchment paper.

Mix almond flour and sugar together in a small bowl.

Beat egg, vanilla, and salt in a large bowl until well combined.

Add almond mixture to egg mixture and stir until thoroughly combined. Add cashew cream and stir until incorporated.

Prepare tartlets by placing one sheet of phyllo dough on prepared pan. Lightly brush with oil and sprinkle lightly with sugar. Repeat 4 more times, using all sheets of phyllo dough. Using a sharp knife or pizza cutter, divide phyllo dough into 12 equal rectangles.

Spread almond filling onto phyllo rectangles in an even layer. Leave a small border around edges. Cover lightly with plastic wrap and set aside.

Peel, core, and cut apples into very thin and even slices. Arrange in a fanned-out fashion in rows on top of almond filling.

Bake for 10 to 15 minutes until apples are soft and filling is set. Remove from oven and cool on a wire rack.

Meanwhile, bring apple jelly and water to a boil in a small saucepan on medium heat. Brush over entire tart.

Sprinkle a pinch of cinnamon on the centre of each tartlet. Serve warm or at room temperature.

Serves 12 ‖ NUTRITION (per serving): energy 264 kcal | total fat 16 g | saturated fat 2 g | carbohydrate 27 g | fibre 4 g | protein 7 g | sodium 68 mg | excellent source of vitamin E | good source of riboflavin

---

SMART TIP

To make your own cashew cream, soak ½ cup (125 ml) raw cashews in cold water for 3 hours. Drain and rinse. Add cashews and about ¼ cup (60 ml) of water to blender or food processor. Purée for several minutes until smooth and thick. Add ¼ teaspoon (1 ml) vanilla and blend until incorporated; set aside.

date chocolate "ice cream" tart

The uniqueness of dates in the crust provides a delicious sweetness to this dairy-free frozen tart. A real crowd pleaser!

CRUST

1½ cups (375 ml) pitted Medjool dates
½ cup (125 ml) raw sunflower seeds, ground
⅓ cup (75 ml) whole flax seeds, ground
3 tablespoons (45 ml) cacao powder

FILLING

1 cup (250 ml) pitted Medjool dates
3 frozen bananas, thawed for 15 minutes
2 cups (500 ml) raw cashews
2 tablespoons (30 ml) Almond or Cashew Butter (see page 296)
2 tablespoons (30 ml) coconut oil
1 cup (250 ml) almond milk, or more as needed

Lightly grease a 9 × 3 inch (23 × 8 cm) springform pan.

Purée dates in a food processor for about 2 minutes. Transfer to a bowl. Process ground sunflower seeds, ground flax seeds, and cacao powder until well blended. Return dates to mixture and process until a sticky paste is formed. Press into bottom and up sides of pan. Refrigerate.

Process dates in a food processor until finely chopped. Add bananas, cashews, nut butter, and coconut oil and process until smooth. Add almond milk as needed to make filling creamy. Spread mixture evenly into crust.

Place cake in freezer about 4 hours until frozen. Remove about 30 minutes before serving.

Serves 12 ‖ **NUTRITION** (per serving): energy 405 kcal | total fat 17 g | saturated fat 4 g | carbohydrate 64 g | fibre 7 g | protein 8 g | sodium 13 mg | good source of potassium, vitamin B6, vitamin E, thiamin, niacin, iron

 SMART TIP

Save overripe bananas by peeling them, cutting them into chunks, and freezing them individually in freezer bags. Ready to use any time!

fabulous fruit flan

This exquisite flan tastes as good as it looks. The filling accentuates the sweetness of the gem-like berries that sparkle on its surface.

FILLING

Drain yogurt in a cheesecloth-lined colander in the refrigerator for 2 hours or overnight. Transfer drained yogurt to a large mixing bowl and whisk in sugar, zest, and juice.

CRUST

Place phyllo dough on a damp tea towel and cover. Mix panko, sugar, and cinnamon in a small bowl. Lightly brush a 10-inch (25 cm) round, rectangle, or square tart pan with removable sides with oil.

Preheat oven to 400°F (200°C).

Lay a sheet of phyllo in the pan. Lightly brush phyllo with oil and sprinkle with a spoonful of crumb mixture. Place another sheet of phyllo on top, lightly brush with oil, and sprinkle with crumbs. Repeat until all 5 sheets of phyllo are used. Fold any overhanging pastry back into the crust to obtain neat edges. If tart pan is rectangular, trim overhanging edges. Line crust with foil and fill it with pastry weights or dried beans. (This will hold the crust's shape as it bakes.)

Bake crust for 6 to 8 minutes or until edges are lightly browned. Remove foil and weights and continue baking for 3 to 4 minutes or until the entire crust is golden brown. Transfer to a wire rack to cool.

TOPPING

Melt fruit preserve in a small saucepan over medium heat. Add orange juice if needed to obtain a pourable glaze.

Just before serving, assemble the tart by transferring yogurt mixture into a pastry or plastic bag (see SMART TIP). Squeeze filling out of bag to form even rows in the tart crust.

Arrange berries on top in neat rows or circular pattern. Brush tops of berries with glaze and sprinkle with pistachio nuts.

With sides of tart pan removed, place on serving platter. Garnish with pistachios and serve immediately to avoid crust from becoming soggy.

Serves 8 to 10 ‖ **NUTRITION** (per serving): energy 172 kcal | total fat 5 g | saturated fat 1 g | carbohydrate 26 g | fibre 2 g | protein 6 g | sodium 90 mg | good source of vitamin E

FILLING

1 pound (455 g) low-fat plain Greek yogurt
3 tablespoons (45 ml) granulated sugar
1 tablespoon (15 ml) finely grated lemon zest
2 teaspoons (10 ml) fresh orange juice

CRUST

5 sheets phyllo dough
¼ cup (60 ml) panko breadcrumbs, toasted for 5 to 7 minutes in a 350°F (180°C) oven
1 tablespoon (15 ml) granulated sugar
¼ teaspoon (1 ml) cinnamon
3 tablespoons (45 ml) canola oil

TOPPING

¼ cup (60 ml) fruit preserve
1 tablespoon (15 ml) orange juice or water if needed
4 cups (1 L) fresh berries (blueberries, raspberries, or strawberries, alone or in combination)
1 tablespoon (15 ml) chopped toasted pistachios for garnish

SMART TIP

To make your own pastry bag, transfer your filling to a large plastic resealable bag. Snip off one bottom corner and you are ready to go!

DR. JOE'S SMART FACT

One cup of strawberries delivers more than a day's worth of vitamin C and is a good source of fibre, folate, potassium, and manganese, a mineral that helps to maintain healthy bones and to regulate blood sugar.

berry mousse

Sweet and tart, this mousse turns ordinary ingredients into something extraordinary.

INGREDIENTS

3 egg whites, room temperature
1 tablespoon (15 ml) fresh lemon juice
¼ cup (60 ml) granulated sugar
4 cups (1 L) frozen berries, partly thawed
⅓ cup (75 ml) dark chocolate shavings for garnish

Beat egg whites and lemon juice together with an electric mixer. Gradually add sugar and beat until stiff peaks form. Fold in berries. Beat continuously at high speed about 5 minutes until double in volume. Cover and freeze.

Remove from freezer and place in refrigerator an hour before serving.

Spoon mousse into fancy glasses and garnish with chocolate shavings.

Serves 12 ‖ **NUTRITION** (per serving): energy 38 kcal | total fat 0 g | saturated fat 0 g | carbohydrate 9 g | fibre 1 g | protein 1 g | sodium 9 mg

SMART TIP

When you separate eggs to make beaten egg whites, crack one at a time, pouring each white into a small bowl before transferring it to the mixing bowl. If a speck of yolk gets into the whites, use the corner tip of a paper towel to blot it up. Even a drop of yolk will prevent beaten egg whites from reaching their full volume.

DR JOE'S SMART FACT

Eggs provide protein and vitamins. Mixing egg whites into a recipe is an easy way to increase the protein without adding fat.

baked imperial apples

Pretty enough to serve at any dinner party, these apples are far from standard. The tops are reserved and used as crowns. Full on flavour, this recipe makes a nice change from traditional apple crisp.

Preheat oven to 375°F (190°C).

Peel, core, and dice one apple into ¼-inch (5 mm) pieces.

Combine diced apple, fruit preserve, pecans, raisins, oats, and spices in a mixing bowl and set aside.

Cut a thin slice off the bottom of remaining apples so that they stand upright. Cut half an inch off the top of each apple and reserve. Using a melon baller or apple corer, dig out the core of each apple, leaving the bottom intact. Place apples in an 8-inch (20 cm) square baking pan.

Divide filling among apples. Cover with reserved apple tops. Add orange juice and water to baking dish and bake about 35 to 40 minutes until tender, basting every 10 minutes with pan juices. Add additional orange juice or water if necessary.

Transfer apples to serving plates. Ladle pan juice over apples and serve.

Serves 4 ‖ **NUTRITION** (per serving): energy 202 kcal | total fat 6 g | saturated fat 1 g | carbohydrate 40 g | fibre 5 g | protein 2 g | sodium 3 g | good source of vitamin E

INGREDIENTS

5 large baking apples
¼ cup (60 ml) fruit preserve
¼ cup (60 ml) coarsely chopped
  raw pecans
¼ cup (60 ml) currants or raisins
¼ cup (60 ml) rolled oats
1 teaspoon (5 ml) ground cinnamon
  or ground cardamom
¼ cup (60 ml) fresh orange juice
¼ cup (60 ml) water

DR JOE'S SMART FACT

Although apples do not literally keep the doctor away, it really is a good idea to eat an apple a day. The *British Medical Journal* reports that regular consumption of apples reduces the risk of type 2 diabetes. Apples also contain pectin, a type of fibre that lowers cholesterol, and recent studies have shown that apple peel extracts can significantly reduce the proliferation of a variety of cancer cells, including those isolated from breast, prostate, and liver tumors.

pear mango pineapple compote

This compote is delicious on pancakes, mixed with plain Greek yogurt, or enjoyed as a healthy snack any time of day. As a condiment for grilled fish, try adding some chopped onions and fresh chopped mint.

INGREDIENTS

3 fresh Anjou pears
2 fresh mangoes, skin and stone removed, cut into chunks
1 pineapple, skin and core removed, cut into chunks
¼ cup (60 ml) water

If using a food mill, leave skin on pears; otherwise, peel, core, and cut into large chunks.

Place all ingredients in a medium saucepan over medium heat. Cover and bring to a boil.

Reduce heat to low; simmer covered about 30 minutes, stirring periodically until the pears have broken down and mango and pineapple have softened. If mixture gets too thick, add a little more water.

Remove from heat and pass through a food mill, or use an immersion blender to achieve desired consistency.

Serve warm, at room temperature, or chilled.

Makes about 8 cups ‖ **NUTRITION** (per ½ cup): energy 50 kcal | total fat 0 g | saturated fat 0 g | carbohydrate 13 g | fibre 2 g | protein 0 g | sodium 1 mg | good source of vitamin C, niacin

rhubarb strawberry raspberry compote

"Spring" and "rhubarb" are synonymous. This versatile compote makes an amazing pie filling. Double the recipe, freeze, and have a little springtime all year round.

Place rhubarb and water in a large saucepan over high heat. Cover and bring to a boil. Add honey and juices; reduce heat to low and simmer, covered, stirring occasionally, for 15 to 20 minutes until the rhubarb is tender.

Add strawberries and cook for about 10 minutes until softened. Remove from heat and mash with the back of a spoon or a potato masher to achieve desired consistency. Add raspberries and stir until warmed through.

Serve warm, at room temperature, or chilled.

INGREDIENTS

3 cups (750 ml) fresh rhubarb, cut into ½-inch (1 cm) chunks
2 tablespoons (30 ml) water
3 tablespoons (45 ml) honey
2 tablespoons (30 ml) fresh orange juice
2 cups (500 ml) hulled and sliced strawberries
2 cups (500 ml) raspberries

Makes about 6 cups ‖ **NUTRITION** (per ½ cup): energy 36 kcal | total fat 0 g | saturated fat 0 g | carbohydrate 9 g | fibre 2 g | protein 1 g | sodium 2 mg | good source of vitamin C

Greek yogurt is made by straining regular yogurt, thereby removing much of the liquid whey and the lactose and other sugars dissolved in it. For the same amount of calories, Greek yogurt has roughly double the protein and half the sugar of other yogurts.

gemstone fruit rolls

Rice paper serves as the canvas for these beautiful gemstone-coloured dessert rolls, highlighted by an exquisite sauce.

MINT MAPLE YOGURT SAUCE

½ cup (125 ml) plain low-fat Greek yogurt
1 tablespoon (15 ml) pure maple syrup
1 tablespoon (15 ml) finely chopped fresh mint

FRUIT ROLLS

1 mango, skin and stone removed, julienned
½ papaya, skin and seeds removed, julienned
1 cup (250 ml) fresh blackberries, reserving a few for garnish
1 cup (250 ml) fresh strawberries, sliced lengthwise, reserving a few for garnish
3 tablespoons (45 ml) finely chopped fresh mint, plus a few leaves for garnish
eight 8½-inch (22 cm) sheets of culinary rice paper

Combine all ingredients for yogurt sauce in a small bowl. Let sit for at least 15 to 20 minutes to allow flavours to blend.

Working with one sheet at a time, soak rice paper in warm water for 15 to 20 seconds and transfer to work surface.

About ½ inch (1 cm) from one long edge, place a row of mango and papaya slices on rice paper, leaving about ½ inch (1 cm) on each short end. Spread about 2 tablespoons of blackberries and strawberries on top of mango and papaya, and then sprinkle chopped mint on top of berries. Fold long edge over filling; roll to create a log, folding in short ends as you roll. Repeat with remaining rice papers.

Cover with plastic wrap until ready to serve. (Rolls are best served within a couple of hours, or the wrappers will dry out.)

Place a fruit roll on individual serving plate with a dollop of yogurt sauce. Garnish with mint and berries.

Serves 8 ‖ **NUTRITION** (per serving): energy 148 kcal | total fat 1 g | saturated fat 0 g | carbohydrate 31 g | fibre 3 g | protein 5 g | sodium 197 mg | good source of vitamin C, thiamin, riboflavin, folate

dessert soup

The vibrant layers of this refreshing dessert create a beautiful presentation. Choose a colour palette according to your preferences. A light choice after a not-so-light meal.

Purée kiwi and lime juice in a blender until smooth. Pour evenly into serving glasses. Rinse blender.

Purée strawberries and honey in blender until smooth. If desired, stir through a sieve to filter seeds. Slowly pour strawberry mixture on top of kiwi mixture. Rinse blender.

Purée mango and sparkling water in blender until smooth. Slowly pour mango mixture on top of strawberry mixture.

Garnish with pomegranate seeds or sliced kiwi.

INGREDIENTS

6 kiwis, peeled, 4 slices reserved for garnish (optional)

1 tablespoon (15 ml) fresh lime juice

10 ounces (285 g) strawberries or blueberries, fresh or thawed from frozen

1 tablespoon (15 ml) honey

2 mangoes, skin and stone removed, roughly chopped

6 ounces (175 ml) sparkling water

2 tablespoons (30 ml) pomegranate seeds for garnish (optional)

Serves 4 ‖ **NUTRITION** (per serving): energy 179 kcal | total fat 1 g | saturated fat 0 g | carbohydrate 45 g | fibre 6 g | protein 2 g | sodium 8 mg | excellent source of vitamin C | good source of vitamin E

vanilla-and-tea-scented melon

Simple yet sophisticated, the tea infuses the melon with subtle sweetness and the aroma of jasmine. Any fragrant tea works well.

INGREDIENTS

2 jasmine green tea bags
1½ cups (375 ml) boiling water
1 vanilla bean, sliced in half lengthwise
2 tablespoons (30 ml) honey
1 cup (250 ml) cantaloupe melon balls
1 cup (250 ml) watermelon balls
1 cup (250 ml) honey dew melon balls
½ cup (125 ml) coarsely chopped fresh mint leaves for garnish

Steep tea bags in boiling water for 5 minutes. Remove tea bags. Scrape vanilla seeds from pod into tea, add honey, and stir. Cool.

Arrange melon in a large bowl. Pour cooled tea syrup over top. Cover and refrigerate for 45 minutes, stirring halfway through.

Garnish with mint leaves and serve.

DR. JOE'S SMART FACT

Jasmine tea is typically a blend of green tea and jasmine petals. A small study conducted in 2005 showed that the aroma from this particular tea has a sedative and calming effect. As a result, jasmine tea is widely used in aromatherapy as a stress reliever.

Serves 6 || NUTRITION (per serving): energy 56 kcal | total fat 0 g | saturated fat 0 g | carbohydrate 14 g | fibre 1 g | protein 1 g | sodium 15 mg | good source of vitamin C

coconut rice pudding

This is a revival of an old standby, but with a unique twist. If coconut is not tops on your list, add 2 teaspoons (10 ml) of cinnamon and increase the milk to 2 cups (500 ml) instead. Delicious either way!

INGREDIENTS

1¼ cups (310 ml) water
½ cup (125 ml) brown rice
about 8 cups (2 L) of boiling water for *bain-marie*
3 large eggs
¼ cup (60 ml) granulated sugar
1 teaspoon (5 ml) pure vanilla extract
1 cup (250 ml) milk (dairy, soy, or almond)
1 cup (250 ml) unsweetened coconut milk
¼ teaspoon (1 ml) salt
1 cup (250 ml) fresh berries, divided
2 tablespoons (30 ml) Roasted Coconut (see page 298) for garnish

Bring water and rice to a boil over high heat in a small pot with a tight-fitting lid. Lower heat and cook, covered, for about 20 minutes until the rice grains are tender but still a little chewy. Remove pot from heat. Let rice steam, covered, for 10 minutes.

Preheat oven to 325°F (160°C). Prepare a *bain-marie* by placing six 6-ounce (175 ml) glass jars or ramekins in a roasting pan or large casserole dish. (See SMART TIP.)

In a large bowl, whisk together eggs, sugar, vanilla, milk, coconut milk, salt, and cooked rice. Divide mixture among prepared jars. Add enough boiling water to roasting pan to reach halfway up sides of jars.

Bake for 20 minutes. Remove from oven.

Add a few raspberries to each pudding and stir each pudding to distribute rice and raspberries evenly. Return to oven and bake 18 to 22 minutes more until puddings are set and no longer wobbly. Not all puddings will be ready at the same time.

Carefully remove pudding when ready and let cool slightly (about 15 minutes).

Garnish with remaining berries and roasted coconut. Serve warm.

Serves 6 ‖ NUTRITION (per serving): energy 235 kcal | total fat 11 g | saturated fat 8 g | carbohydrate 27 g | fibre 4 g | protein 7 g | sodium 146 mg | excellent source of vitamin B12 | good source of riboflavin

---

SMART TIP

A *bain-marie* is a hot-water bath that cooks food by providing a uniform heat. The water creates a barrier between the food and the direct heat of the oven, helping the food cook slowly and evenly. Use a roasting pan or a casserole dish large enough to hold your jars or ramekins and place the filled jars inside the pan. Bring a large pot of water to a boil and then pour the water into the roasting pan around the jars. (This step can be done with the roasting pan in the oven, thus avoiding having to transfer the water-filled pan.) The water should come about halfway up the sides of the jars. Check the *bain-marie* occasionally (the water should be barely simmering) and adjust the oven temperature as necessary. If the water evaporates before the dish is cooked, add hot tap water.

peach cranberry crisp with lemon yogurt sauce

Light and refreshing, this is always a great way to end any meal. Any fruit works well with this recipe.

PEACH FILLING

8 to 12 ripe and firm peaches
1 cup (250 ml) cranberries, fresh or thawed from frozen, or ½ cup (125 ml) dried
2 tablespoons (30 ml) whole-wheat flour
2 tablespoons (30 ml) pure maple syrup
½ tablespoon (7 ml) finely grated fresh ginger
1 tablespoon (15 ml) fresh lemon juice

CRISP TOPPING

1 cup (250 ml) whole-wheat flour
1 cup (250 ml) coarsely chopped raw walnuts
⅓ cup (75 ml) packed brown sugar
1 teaspoon (5 ml) salt
½ teaspoon (2 ml) ground cardamom or ground cinnamon
1¼ cups (310 ml) rolled oats
⅓ cup (75 g) cold unsalted butter, sliced, or coconut oil

LEMON YOGURT SAUCE

½ cup (125 ml) low-fat Greek yogurt
2 tablespoons (30 ml) fresh lemon juice
1 tablespoon (15 ml) honey

Preheat oven to 350°F (180°C). Lightly grease a 9-inch (23 cm) pie plate or cake pan.

Immerse peaches in boiling water for 1 minute. Peel immediately and place in cold water. Slice into half-inch wedges and place in a large bowl. Add remaining filling ingredients and toss to blend. Pour into prepared pan.

Combine crisp topping ingredients in bowl of electric mixer fitted with paddle attachment. Mix on low speed for 1 to 2 minutes until mixture forms large crumbles. Sprinkle topping evenly over filling.

Bake for 40 to 50 minutes or until topping is golden. Let cool for 10 minutes.

Meanwhile, prepare lemon yogurt sauce by combining yogurt, lemon juice, and honey in a small bowl. Let sit for at least 15 minutes to allow flavours to blend. Transfer to a small serving vessel.

Divide crisp onto serving plates and spoon yogurt around crisp. Serve warm or cold.

Serves 10 to 12 ‖ NUTRITION (per serving): energy 234 kcal | total fat 14 g | saturated fat 4 g | carbohydrate 36 g | fibre 5 g | protein 8 g | sodium 201 mg | excellent source of vitamin E

banana in a blanket

Banana and chocolate are a match made in heaven! The tangy sauce highlights the sweetness of the bananas.

INGREDIENTS

2 sheets phyllo dough
1 tablespoon (15 ml) canola oil
¼ cup (60 ml) panko breadcrumbs
2 ripe but firm bananas, peeled
2 ounces (55 g) 70% cocoa dark chocolate, finely chopped
1 large egg
1 teaspoon (5 ml) water
pinch of ground cinnamon for garnish

Preheat oven to 400°F (200°C). Lightly grease a small baking sheet.

Lie each sheet of phyllo dough on work surface with short side nearest you. Lightly brush each sheet with oil and sprinkle with 1 tablespoon of panko.

Arrange each banana horizontally on lower third of phyllo sheet. (Straighten any curved part of banana as much as possible.) Sprinkle chocolate over each banana.

Working with one sheet at a time, loosely roll phyllo lengthwise over banana, fold in sides, and then finish rolling. Place wrapped bananas, seam side down, on prepared baking sheet.

Mix egg with 1 teaspoon of water. Lightly brush top of strudel with egg mixture. Gently cut steam vents along top of strudel with a sharp knife.

Bake for 12 to 15 minutes or until golden brown.

Let strudel cool slightly and then serve with a dollop of yogurt sauce, some chocolate shavings, and a sprinkling of cinnamon.

Serves 4 to 6 ‖ **NUTRITION** (per serving): energy 160 kcal | total fat 8 g | saturated fat 3 g | carbohydrate 20 g | fibre 2 g | protein 3 g | sodium 77 mg | good source of vitamin E

Shown with Lemon Yogurt Sauce (see page 288).

mini mango cheesecakes

This reduced-fat adaptation of classic cheesecake has a wonderful flavour profile with a velvety crunchy texture. Customize the topping by using granola or a mix of chopped nuts. Truly satisfying!

CHEESECAKE

4 ounces (115 g) partly skimmed ricotta cheese
4 ounces (115 g) low-fat cream cheese
2 tablespoons (30 ml) low-fat sour cream
⅓ cup (75 ml) granulated sugar
2 large eggs
1 tablespoon (15 ml) fresh lemon juice
2 teaspoons (10 ml) finely grated lemon zest

About 8 (2 L) cups boiling water for *bain-marie*

TOPPING

½ cup (125 ml) finely chopped graham crackers or crushed gluten-free cereal

FILLING

2 ripe mangoes, skin and stone removed, or 1 cup (250 ml) raspberries, blueberries, or strawberries, fresh or thawed from frozen

Preheat oven to 325°F (160°C). Prepare a *bain-marie* by placing eight 6-ounce (175 ml) glasses, jars, or ramekins or an 8-inch (20 cm) square baking pan in a roasting pan or large casserole dish.

Beat ricotta, cream cheese, and sour cream with an electric mixer on medium speed until smooth. Add sugar and beat for 3 minutes more. Reduce speed to low and add eggs one at a time, beating well after each addition. Raise speed to medium and add lemon juice and zest. Beat for 3 minutes more.

Divide cheese mixture among glasses or jars, filling each about two-thirds full, or pour into baking pan. Add enough boiling water to roasting pan to reach halfway up sides of glasses, jars, or pan. Cover tightly with foil; cut 6 to 8 slits in top of foil to vent.

Bake about 25 minutes (40 to 45 minutes for 8-inch baking pan) until set. Transfer to a wire rack to cool. Refrigerate overnight to set completely.

When you are ready to assemble the cheesecakes, purée the mango with an immersion blender or fork until smooth. Top each cheesecake with a heaping tablespoon of puréed mango. Spread evenly with back of a spoon. Sprinkle a heaping tablespoon of graham cracker topping over mango.

Cheesecakes can be refrigerated for up to 4 days.

Serves 8 ‖ **NUTRITION** (per serving): energy 171 kcal | total fat 6 g | saturated fat 3 g | carbohydrate 24 g | fibre 1 g | protein 6 g | sodium 176 mg | good source of vitamin B12

condiments

almond butter

Use raw almonds with their skins, as they pack extra flavour and antioxidants. Spread this bold butter on toast or stir into oatmeal for a healthy, filling breakfast. Its deep flavour and thick texture make this naturally sweet nut butter perfect for indulgent treats.

INGREDIENTS

2 cups (500 ml) raw almonds with skins

Preheat oven to 375°F (190°C). Spread almonds in a single layer on a rimmed baking sheet and roast about 10 to 12 minutes until fragrant. Rotate baking sheet halfway through toasting. Transfer to a wire rack and let almonds cool slightly (about 10 to 15 minutes).

Run almonds through food processor for 10 to 20 minutes until smooth and creamy. Scrape down sides as necessary. Let food processor rest for 2 to 3 minutes from time to time.

Keeps for 2 to 3 weeks in a jar in the refrigerator.

Makes about 2 cups ‖ **NUTRITION** (per 2 tablespoons): energy 102 kcal | total fat 9 g | saturated fat 1 g | carbohydrate 4 g | fibre 2 g | protein 4 g | sodium 0 mg | excellent source of vitamin E

cashew butter

Don't give up on making this yourself. All it takes is 30 minutes of your time and a good food processor! This subtly sweet butter is versatile enough to bake into cookies or to swirl on top of brownies; it also pairs well with spicy flavours. Try adding it to Indian curries or stir-fry sauces for extra depth and a creamy texture.

INGREDIENTS

2 cups (500 ml) raw cashews
pinch of salt (optional)

Preheat oven to 375°F (190°C). Spread cashews in a single layer on a rimmed baking sheet and roast about 5 to 7 minutes until lightly golden and fragrant. Rotate baking sheet halfway through toasting. Transfer to a wire rack and let cashews cool slightly (about 5 to 10 minutes).

Place cashews and salt (if using) in food processor. Process for 15 to 20 minutes until smooth and creamy. Scrape down sides as necessary. Let food processor rest for 2 to 3 minutes from time to time.

Keeps for 2 to 3 weeks in a jar in the refrigerator.

Makes about 2 cups ‖ **NUTRITION** (per 2 tablespoons): energy 91 kcal | total fat 7 g | saturated fat 1 g | carbohydrate 5 g | fibre 1 g | protein 3 g | sodium 2 mg

sunflower seed butter

Nut-free and gluten-free, this seed butter is a fantastic alternative to traditional peanut butter and other popular nut butters. It has a mild yet rich taste and a smooth texture. (Plus, it is a lot less expensive than the store-bought version!) By the way, adding sugar and salt is optional.

Preheat oven to 325°F (160°C).

Spread sunflower seeds on a cookie sheet and bake about 15 minutes until golden and fragrant.

Transfer seeds to a food processor and blend for 2 minutes. Add oil and continue to process for 3 minutes. Add sugar and salt, if using, and process for 3 minutes more, scraping down sides, until smooth and creamy.

Keeps for 2 to 3 weeks in a jar in the refrigerator.

Makes 2 cups ‖ NUTRITION (per 2 tablespoons): energy 112 kcal | total fat 10 g | saturated fat 1 g | carbohydrate 4 g | fibre 2 g | protein 4 g | sodium 3 mg | excellent source of vitamin E | good source of folate

INGREDIENTS

2 cups (500 ml) unsalted hulled sunflower seeds
1 tablespoon (15 ml) canola oil
pinch of granulated sugar (optional)
pinch of salt (optional)

pear butter

Preheat oven to 400°F (200°C).

In a large casserole dish with a lid, mix the pears, juices, and honey. Cover and bake for 1 hour, stirring after 30 minutes.

Transfer pears and any juices to a food processor and add almond extract and cinnamon. Process until smooth and return mixture to casserole dish.

Reduce oven temperature to 350°F (180°C) and bake, uncovered, for about 1 hour in total, stirring every 20 minutes until thick (the consistency of jam). The pear butter will thicken slightly as it cools.

When cool, transfer to a jar and store for up to 2 to 3 weeks in the refrigerator.

Makes 1½ to 2 cups ‖ NUTRITION (per 2 tablespoons): energy 55 kcal | total fat 0 g | saturated fat 0 g | carbohydrate 15 g | fibre 2 g |protein 0 g | sodium 1 mg

INGREDIENTS

8 cups (2 L) very ripe pears (Bartlett or Anjou), peeled, cored, and coarsely chopped
½ cup (125 ml) fresh orange juice
½ cup (125 ml) fresh lemon juice
1 tablespoon (15 ml) honey
½ teaspoon (2 ml) pure almond extract
¼ teaspoon (1 ml) cinnamon

roasted coconut

If you love coconut, you'll also love how roasting it enhances its sweet, nutty flavour. Simple and quick to make, roasted coconut can be enjoyed as a snack or sprinkled on salad or cereal. It can also be used as a garnish on a vegetable dish or almost any dessert. Just be sure to take note of how much of it you are eating—as with potato chips, once you start it can be very difficult to stop.

INGREDIENTS

2 cups (500 ml) dried unsweetened coconut ribbons
½ teaspoon (2 ml) kosher salt
½ teaspoon (2 ml) granulated sugar

Preheat oven to 300°F (150°C).

Divide coconut ribbons between two rimmed baking sheets and spread in single layers. Bake about 2 to 4 minutes until toasted, watching carefully to prevent burning.

Remove from oven and lightly sprinkle with salt and sugar. Store at room temperature in an airtight container.

Makes 2 cups ‖ **NUTRITION** (per tablespoon): energy 36 kcal | total fat 3 g | saturated fat 2 g | carbohydrate 4 g | fibre 0 g | protein 0 g | sodium 48 mg

fried capers

INGREDIENTS

¼ cup (60 ml) capers, rinsed
2 tablespoons (30 ml) extra-virgin olive oil

Pat capers dry with clean dishcloths.

Heat oil in a skillet over medium-high heat. When oil is hot, stir-fry capers in batches for about 30 to 60 seconds until most of them open like flowers and become crisp and slightly browned.

Remove from heat and transfer to paper towel with a slotted spoon. Store at room temperature in an airtight container.

Makes ¼ cup ‖ **NUTRITION** (per tablespoon): energy 63 kcal | total fat 7 g | saturated fat 1 g | carbohydrate 0 g | fibre 0 g | protein 0 g | sodium 259 mg

hot mustard

Awesome and easy to make. You may never buy prepared mustard again. This mustard is our secret ingredient in the Not-So-Basic Vinaigrette recipe (see page 109).

INGREDIENTS

½ cup (125 ml) ground mustard powder
½ cup (125 ml) apple cider vinegar
1 tablespoon (15 ml) pure maple syrup
½ teaspoon (2 ml) prepared horseradish
1 teaspoon (5 ml) ground turmeric
½ teaspoon (2 ml) salt
¼ teaspoon (1 ml) freshly ground pepper

Mix mustard powder and vinegar in a small bowl. Cover and refrigerate overnight.

Transfer mustard mixture to a blender; add remaining ingredients and blend until smooth. Add water, a tablespoon at a time, if mustard is too thick.

Ladle into a jar and store for up to 1 month in the refrigerator.

Makes ⅔ cup ‖ **NUTRITION** (per tablespoon): energy 8 kcal | total fat 0 g | saturated fat 0 g | carbohydrate 1 g | fibre 0 g | protein 0 g | sodium 80 mg

tahini mustard sauce

INGREDIENTS

2 garlic cloves, peeled
2 tablespoons (30 ml) tahini
2 tablespoons (30 ml) fresh lemon juice
2 teaspoons (10 ml) tamari sauce
2 teaspoons (10 ml) Dijon mustard
2 teaspoons (10 ml) pure maple syrup
½ teaspoon (2 ml) grated fresh ginger
¼ teaspoon (1 ml) cayenne pepper
¼ cup (60 ml) olive oil

Mince garlic in a food processor or blender. Add remaining ingredients and process until smooth.

Ladle into a jar and store for up to 2 weeks in the refrigerator.

Makes ½ cup ‖ **NUTRITION** (per 2 tablespoons): energy 93 kcal | total fat 9 g | saturated fat 1 g | carbohydrate 3 g | fibre 1 g | protein 1 g | sodium 107 mg

tomato corn salsa

INGREDIENTS

⅓ cup (75 ml) fresh lime juice
1 tablespoon (15 ml) extra-virgin olive oil
3 tablespoons (45 ml) finely chopped fresh coriander or parsley
2 tablespoons (30 ml) finely chopped fresh mint
pinch of crushed red pepper flakes
1 ripe tomato, seeded and diced small
1 cup (250 ml) corn kernels, fresh or thawed from frozen
1 jalapeño pepper, seeded and very finely chopped
½ red or yellow bell pepper, stems and seeds removed, diced small
1 shallot, finely diced
1 garlic clove, minced
½ teaspoon (2 ml) kosher salt, plus more for seasoning
¼ teaspoon (1 ml) freshly ground pepper, plus more for seasoning

In a medium bowl, whisk together lime juice, oil, herbs, and red pepper flakes. Mix in remaining ingredients. Season with salt and pepper to taste. Let rest for 30 minutes before serving.

Makes about 1½ cups ‖ **NUTRITION** (per 3 tablespoons): energy 50 kcal | total fat 2 g | saturated fat 0 g | carbohydrate 8 g | fibre 1 g | protein 1 g | sodium 127 mg | good source of vitamin C

DR. JOE'S SMART FACT

Some people experience the "salsa sniffles" when they eat spicy foods. The runny nose is not caused by an allergy but by a response of nerve receptors in the mouth and nose to compounds found in certain spices.

avocado mango red onion salsa

INGREDIENTS

3 tablespoons (45 ml) fresh lime juice
1 tablespoon (15 ml) canola oil
1 tablespoon (15 ml) honey
1 avocado, peeled, pitted and diced medium
1 mango, peel and stone removed, diced medium
1 plum tomato, seeded and diced medium
¼ cup (60 ml) finely chopped red onion
2 tablespoons (30 ml) finely chopped fresh coriander or parsley
kosher salt and freshly ground pepper

In a medium bowl, whisk together lime juice, oil, and honey. Mix in remaining ingredients. Season with salt and pepper to taste. Let rest for 30 minutes before serving.

Makes about 1½ cups ‖ **NUTRITION** (per 3 tablespoons): energy 85 kcal | total fat 6 g | saturated fat 1 g | carbohydrate 10 g | fibre 2 g | protein 1 g | sodium 3 mg

stone fruit salsa

This salsa is best when stone fruits are in season.

INGREDIENTS

juice and finely grated zest from 1 lime
2 tablespoons (30 ml) finely chopped fresh mint or cilantro
1 teaspoon (5 ml) honey
2 to 3 peaches, nectarines, plums and/or apricots, diced medium
½ cup (125 ml) English cucumber, diced medium
1 large shallot, diced small
1 jalapeño pepper, seeded and finely chopped
1 teaspoon (5 ml) finely chopped fresh ginger
kosher salt and freshly ground pepper

In a medium bowl, whisk together lime juice, zest, mint, and honey. Mix in remaining ingredients. Season with salt and pepper to taste. Let rest 30 minutes before serving.

Makes about 1½ cups ‖ **NUTRITION** (per 3 tablespoons): energy 28 kcal | total fat 0 g | saturated fat 0 g | carbohydrate 7 g | fibre 1 g | protein 1 g | sodium 2 mg

INGREDIENTS

1 garlic clove, peeled

1 cup (250 ml) packed fresh
   basil leaves

¼ cup (60 ml) Vegetable or Chicken
   Stock (see pages 80 and 81)

⅓ cup (75 ml) freshly grated
   Parmesan cheese

2 tablespoons (30 ml) pine nuts

¼ teaspoon (1 ml) freshly
   ground pepper

1 tablespoon (15 ml) extra-virgin
   olive oil

INGREDIENTS

½ cup (125 ml) English cucumber,
   peeled, seeded, and very
   finely chopped

kosher salt, plus more for seasoning

1 cup (250 ml) low-fat plain
   Greek yogurt

3 scallions, white and light green
   parts only, finely sliced

½ tablespoon (7 ml) minced fresh
   ginger

2 tablespoons (30 ml) finely
   chopped fresh mint

1 tablespoon (15 ml) finely chopped
   fresh cilantro (optional)

½ teaspoon (2 ml) garam masala
   or cumin

pinch of cayenne pepper

INGREDIENTS

1 medium English cucumber, peeled

kosher salt, plus more for seasoning

1 cup (250 ml) low-fat plain
   Greek yogurt

1 tablespoon (15 ml) fresh
   lemon juice

4 garlic cloves, minced

2 tablespoons (30 ml) finely
   chopped fresh dill

2 tablespoons (30 ml) finely
   chopped fresh flat-leaf parsley

½ teaspoon (2 ml) freshly ground
   pepper, plus more for seasoning

low-fat pesto

Mince garlic in a blender or food processor. Add remaining ingredients (except oil) and pulse until incorporated. Slowly add oil through feed tube and process until smooth.

Transfer to a jar and store for up to 5 days in the refrigerator.

Makes 1 cup ‖ **NUTRITION** (per 3 tablespoons): energy 18 kcal | total fat 2 g | saturated fat 0 g | carbohydrate 0 g | fibre 0 g | protein 1 g | sodium 22 mg

raita

Raita is a condiment made with yogurt and is most often served alongside spicy Indian curries. It is also great as a sauce or dip and is very handy to have in your refrigerator.

Place cucumber in a sieve set over a bowl and sprinkle with salt. Allow to rest for 5 minutes and press out excess liquid. In a medium bowl, stir all ingredients together. Add more salt and cayenne pepper to taste.

Transfer to an airtight container and store for up to 5 days in the refrigerator.

Makes 1½ cups ‖ **NUTRITION** (per 3 tablespoons): energy 21 kcal | total fat 0 g | saturated fat 0 g | carbohydrate 3 g | fibre 0 g | protein 2 g | sodium 25 mg

low-fat tzatziki

This garlicky delight is great as a dip for vegetables, a sauce for fish, a spread for sandwiches, or a condiment for burgers.

Coarsely grate cucumber, sprinkle with salt, and drain well in a sieve set over a bowl. Allow to rest for 5 minutes and press out excess liquid. In a medium bowl, stir all ingredients together. Taste, adding more salt and pepper if necessary.

Transfer to an airtight container and store for up to 5 days in the refrigerator.

Makes 1½ cups ‖ **NUTRITION** (per 3 tablespoons): energy 25 kcal | total fat 0 g | saturated fat 0 g | carbohydrate 4 g | fibre 0 g | protein 2 g | sodium 24 mg

PART FOUR

extras

THE COOKBOOK TEAM

A personal thanks goes to Rosalind Goodman, who began with a dream and inspired us to translate that vision into this wonderful cookbook.

We wish to thank our amazing volunteers, whose un-equivocal enthusiasm and support were critical to the success of this project. Our vision became theirs, and theirs ours, and it is no lie to say we never could have succeeded without their unwavering commitment.

We would like to thank our Monday gang, who gave up their free time to cook and bake in order to test hundreds of recipes.

In addition, a special thank you to all the contributors who shared their favourite recipes with us.

We thank the staff of the Goodman Cancer Research Centre for their continued support and active involvement, the staff at Tango Photographie, Montreal, who turned each recipe into a work of art, and the team from McGill-Queen's University Press, who assisted with the production of *The Smart Palate*.

Above all, special thanks to our families, whose humour, advice, and support helped to make this all possible.

Tina and Gail

THE smart palate VOLUNTEERS

NUTRITION

Cindy Bassel Brown
Gail Goldfarb Karp
Sharyn Katsof
Tina Landsman Abbey
Samantha Morielli
Joe Schwarcz
Emily Shore

EDITORIAL

Marlene Chan
Rona Davis
Anna Dysert
Gail Goldfarb Karp
Rosalind Goodman
Farla Grover
Tina Landsman Abbey
Alita Leibovitch
Jewel Lowenstein
Christopher Lyons
Sandy Martz
Annette Novak
Gwendolyn Owens
Marla Schuster
Emily Shore
Petal Steele

PROOFREADING

Wendy Albert
Diane Altman
Cindy Bassel Brown
Felice Flegg
Sheila Fried
Sue Carol Isaacson
Gail Goldfarb Karp
Sharyn Katsof
Ruth Khazzam
Carol Koffler
Freema Lander
Tina Landsman Abbey
Kathleen Maher Wagner
Debra Mayers
Renee Pearl Sigler

RECIPE DEVELOPMENT AND TESTING

Wendy Albert
Diane Altman
Cindy Bassel Brown
Etty Bienstock
Mark Caplan
Ronda Diamond
Brigitte Eidelman
Felice Flegg
Sheila Fried
Gail Goldfarb Karp
Rosalind Goodman
Shawna Goodman Sone
Sue Carol Isaacson
Sharyn Katsof
Ruth Khazzam
Carol Koffler
Freema Lander
Tina Landsman Abbey
Alita Leibovitch
Kathleen Maher Wagner
Sandy Martz
Debra Mayers
Margaret Nachshen
Annette Novak
Renee Pearl Sigler
Bernice Shaposnick
Emily Shore
Marla Shuster
Yocheved Sonenberg
Petal Steele
Doris Steinberg
Arlene Sternthal

RECIPE CONTRIBUTORS

Erica Abbey
Wendy Albert
Gloria Bass
Thouria Bensaoula
Heidi Blaukopf
Mark Caplan
Pearl Caplan
Sharon Cohen
Rona Davis
Ronda Diamond
Nancy Ditkofsky
Felice Flegg
Estelle Fox
Carole Gilman
Gail Goldfarb Karp
Rosalind Goodman
Shawna Goodman Sone
Monique Gross
Avigyle Grunbaum
Judi Grunbaum
Tamara Haskin
Ashley Karp
Richard Karp
Terry Kaspi
Sharyn Katsof
Ruth Khazzam
Carol Koffler
Adriana Kotler
Freema Lander
Esther Landsman
Tina Landsman Abbey
Alita Leibovitch
Kathleen Maher Wagner
Bonnie Marcus
Eric Martz
Sandy Martz
Debra Mayers
Margaret Nachshen
Annette Novak
Ariana Ost Haber Martz
Renee Pearl Sigler

Linda Rosenbloom
Ruth Rotem
Ellie Rothstein
Betty Sandler
Sandy Schreter
Tovit Schultz Granoff
Joe Schwarcz
Lori Segal Burnett
Linda Seltzer
Bernice Shaposnick
Donna Shore
Emily Shore
Michael Smith
Petal Steele
Arlene Sternthal
Stacey Stivaletti Sarno
Josie Suissa Lupovich
Linda Sutherland
Melba Victoriano
Hainya Wiseman
Jennifer Wolfe

THANK YOU TO THE GENEROUS SPONSORS WHO MADE THIS PROJECT POSSIBLE

UNDERWRITER

Felicia and Arnold Aaron Foundation

BENEFACTORS

Atoka Cranberries Inc.
The Azrieli Foundation
Importfab Inc.
Sandra and Leo Kolber Foundation
The Irving Ludmer Family Foundation
The Blema and Arnold Steinberg Family Foundation
Leesa Steinberg
Sharon Steinberg

PATRONS

Trudy and Aaron Ain
Evelyn S. Alexander Family Foundation
David Amiel
Irwin Beutel
BP Biomedicals
Rita Mayo and Charles R. Bronfman
Heather Sara Sokoloff and Lev Bukhman
C & C Packaging Inc.
Canderel Management Inc.
Judith and Mark Caplan
Dr. Susan Wisebord and Steven Cummings
The Divco Foundation
Dovson Investments Inc.
Ruth and Avrum Drazin
Penny and Gordon Echenberg Family Foundation
Wendy and Elliot Eisen
Foundation for Biomedical Research
Shirley Garfinkle
Gelmont Foundation
Leo and Shirley Goldfarb Foundation
Lorraine and Arthur Goldstein
Perry and Marty Granoff
Linda and Ian Greenberg
Joan Ivory
Ellen and Peter Jacobs
Alissa and Barry Katsof
Carol Diane Koffler

Esther and Andre Landsman
Nan and William Lassner
Leacross Foundation
Marsha and Dr. Mortimer Levy
Terry and Sam Minzberg
Leila and Herb Paperman
Provencher Roy & Associés Architectes
Alice and Joel Raby
Dorothy and Cyril Reitman
Diane and Myer Richler
Jean Remmer and Marvin Rosenbloom
The Larry and Cookie Rossy Family Foundation
Linda Rutenberg
Marilyn Schiff
Eileen and Joel Segal
Pauline and Jeff Segel
Neysa and David Sigler
Tina and Max Smart
Ruth and David Steinberg
Doris and Richard Stern and Family
Merle and Bernard Stotland
Lillian Vineberg
Arlene Wise
Hainya and Murray Wiseman
Beverly and John Zbarsky

NICOLE BEAUCHEMIN, PHD

Position: Professor
Education: PhD, Université de Montréal
Place of birth: Montreal, Canada
Recipe recommended: Buckwheat-Coated Black Cod
Focus of research: Dr. Beauchemin's research deals with colon cancer and focuses on the molecular mechanisms of pathways involving the CEACAM1 molecule in cancer progression. CEACAM1 belongs to a family of adhesion proteins that allow cancer cells to grow and metastasize.
Awards:

- Fonds de recherche Santé Québec, Salary Award, 1988–2005
- Recipient of the Abbott Award for Research, International Society for Oncodevelopmental Biology and Medicine, 1999

MAXIME BOUCHARD, PHD

Position: Associate Professor; Canada Research Chair in Developmental Genetics of the Urogenital System
Education: PhD, Université Laval
Place of birth: Chicoutimi, Canada
Recipe recommended: Sesame Ginger Salmon
Focus of research: One of the main emphases of Dr. Bouchard's research program is the elucidation of the mechanisms underlying the development of organs such as the kidney. Interestingly, most crucial regulators of early development also play a role in cancer initiation or progression. Using mouse genetic models in combination with cellular and biochemical assays, his team is investigating the molecular mechanisms that underlie developmental and neoplastic diseases of the urogenital system, such as prostate cancer.
Lab website: http://bouchardlab.wordpress.com/
Award:

- Canada Research Chair in developmental genetics of the urogenital system, Government of Canada, 2007–2012

PHILIP BRANTON, PHD

Position: Gilman Cheney Professor
Education: PhD, University of Toronto
Place of birth: Toronto, Canada
Recipe recommended: Cinnamon Cashew Crunches
Focus of research: Dr. Branton's team is interested in using viruses as models to study and potentially treat human cancer.
Awards:

- Named inaugural Scientific Director of the Institute of Cancer Research of the Canadian Institutes of Health Research, 2000
- Fellow of the Royal Society of Canada, 2002
- R.M. Taylor Medal, Canadian Cancer Society and the National Cancer Institute of Canada, 2005
- Canadian Cancer Research Alliance Award for Exceptional Leadership in Cancer Research, 2011
- Queen Elizabeth II Diamond Jubilee Medal, 2013

THOMAS DUCHAINE, PHD

Position: Associate Professor
Education: PhD, University of Massachusetts Medical School; PhD, Université de Montréal
Place of birth: St. Eustache, Canada
Recipe recommended: Spinach Dill Stuffed Salmon
Focus of research: Recently, an important new class of molecules influencing cell behaviour was discovered: the microRNAs. MicroRNAs are profoundly altered in most if not all forms of cancer and can impede or contribute to tumor initiation and progression. Dr. Duchaine's research focuses on the underlying mechanisms of microRNAs, their impact on the functions of genes, and how they become misguided in cancer. For this, the research in Dr. Duchaine's laboratory relies on an integrated array of the most powerful tools in biomedical science, including biochemistry, genetics, genomics, and proteomics.
Lab website: http://thomasduchaine.lab.mcgill.ca/
Awards:

- Fonds de recherche Santé Québec, Chercheur-Boursier, (Junior 1, 2007–2011, and Junior 2, 2011–2015)
- Canada Foundation for Innovation Leader's Opportunity Award, 2009–2014

IMED GALLOUZI, PHD

Position: Professor
Education: PhD, Université Montpellier 2
Place of birth: Tunisia
Recipe recommended: Penne with Roasted Vegetables
Focus of research: Dr. Gallouzi's research concerns novel ways to trigger the death of cancer cells and to prevent cancer-induced muscle wasting (cachexia). One focus of his group's work is HuR, a protein involved in both cell growth and cell death. HuR has been shown to control cell survival; when cleaved, it can promote cell death. Dr. Gallouzi is interested in targeting HuR to enhance cleavage and promote cancer cell death.
Awards:
- Fonds de recherche Santé Québec, Salary Award (Junior 1, 2002–2006)
- Tier II Canada Research Chair in Cellular Information System, 2002–2012

VINCENT GIGUÈRE, PHD

Position: Professor
Education: PhD, Université Laval
Place of birth: Québec City, Canada
Recipe recommended: Flank Steak with Chimichurri Sauce
Focus of research: The Giguère Lab researches the roles played by members of the superfamily of nuclear receptors in development, adult physiology, and disease. For a number of years, they have studied how the classic estrogen receptors, and the closely related orphan nuclear receptors referred to as estrogen-related receptors, influence breast cancer cell growth and proliferation. Dr. Giguère has several rewarding research projects and has trained numerous graduate students and postdoctoral fellows who have gone on to obtain independent positions in academia, industry, and government.

PHILIPPE GROS, PHD

Position: Professor
Education: PhD, Massachusetts Institute of Technology; PhD, Harvard Medical School; PhD, McGill University
Place of birth: Cavaillon, France
Recipe recommended: Pecan-Crusted Beef Tenderloin
Focus of research: Dr. Gros' research focuses on the genetic and molecular mechanisms of pathways involved in the development of drug resistance and the genetic determinants involved in predisposition to cancer. His team uses chemical carcinogenesis to induce colorectal tumors in mice. They have screened several inbred strains of mice for differences in susceptibility to colorectal cancer induced by carcinogens, as measured by the type, number, and size of lesions detected in the colon. Using a unique set of mouse lines, they have determined that the genetic basis for this difference in susceptibility is caused by a single major locus. The genes in this locus are currently being investigated for their pattern of tissue- and cell-specific expression and for the presence of mutations in either normal tissues or in DNA from tumors emerging in susceptible animals.
Award:
- James McGill Professorship from McGill University, 2003–2010

MICHAEL HALLETT, PHD

Position: Professor
Education: PhD, University of Victoria
Place of birth: St. Catharines, Canada
Recipe recommended: Sweet 'n Savoury Crunchy Chicken
Focus of research: Dr. Hallett's research group is focusing their work on the development of bioinformatics and biostatistical tools and expertise to permit the analysis of larger-scale datasets (sequencing, gene expression) for numerous cancers, including breast cancer. His group has established a collection of human breast cancer–related expression profiles at various stages of tumor progression, in addition to a compendium of breast cancer mouse model profiles that allow researchers to interrogate the behaviour of sets of genes across these datasets.

RUSSELL JONES, PHD

Position: Assistant Professor
Education: PhD, University of Toronto
Place of birth: Penticton, Canada
Recipe recommended: Breakfast Burrito
Focus of research: Dr. Jones' laboratory is interested in the molecular mechanisms underlying cellular growth and proliferation and in how these processes are normally regulated in the immune system or regulated during tumorigenesis. The ability of a cell to successfully grow and divide depends on the cell having enough energy to complete the task. Cancer is essentially a disease in which cells lose the normal checks and balances that prevent them from growing out of control. However, part of the challenge that faces cancer cells is that they require increased amounts of energy to meet the demands of uncontrolled growth. To meet this challenge, cancer cells often display fundamental changes in energy generation or metabolism. Part of the metabolic shift seen in cancer cells is their increased dependence on sugars for energy production, a phenomenon known as the "Warburg Effect." This

phenomenon is the principle behind PET scans used in the clinic, which image tumors based on their increased ability to take up sugar.

Lab website: www.medicine.mcgill.ca/physio/joneslab/

Award:

- Canadian Institutes of Health Research New Investigator, 2009–2014

LUKE MCCAFFREY, PHD

Position: Assistant Professor
Education: PhD, University of Western Ontario
Place of birth: Collingwood, Canada
Recipe recommended: Peach Cranberry Crisp
Focus of research: Dr. McCaffrey's laboratory studies tissue remodelling during development and cancer progression. The correct development of epithelial tissues is essential for their proper function and requires the coordinated action of cell survival, growth, adhesion, differentiation, and motility. The coordination of these processes requires a high degree of organization within individual cells, which is coordinated between cells during development but is disrupted by cancer. Dr. McCaffrey's group is investigating how a protein complex called the Par complex acts as a crucial controller of cell and tissue organization to coordinate developmental processes, and how disruption of this complex cooperates with oncogenes to enable cells to survive, grow, and invade other organs during breast cancer progression and metastasis.

Lab website: http://mccaffreylab.mcgill.ca/McCaffreyLab.html

Award:

- Fonds de recherche Santé Québec, New Investigator, 2013–2017

WILLIAM MULLER, PHD

Position: Professor
Education: PhD, McGill University
Place of birth: Glasgow, United Kingdom
Recipe recommended: Kale Peanut Salad with Peanut Dressing
Focus of research: Dr. Muller's laboratory focuses on mouse models of breast cancer progression. The progression of the primary mammary epithelial cell to malignant phenotype involves multiple genetic events, including the activation of dominant activating oncogenes and inactivation of specific tumor suppressor genes. Dr. Muller's laboratory focuses on the roles of a class of receptor tyrosine kinases known as the epidermal growth factor receptor (EGFR) family in the induction of breast cancer. A major

objective of the team's work is to determine the relative contribution of the various EGFR family members and their coupled signalling pathways in ErB-2–induced mammary tumor progression.

Awards:

- National Cancer Institute of Canada, Research Scientist Award, 1989–1995
- Medical Research Council of Canada, MRC Scientist Award, 1996–2001
- Canada Research Chair in Molecular Oncology, McGill University, 2002–2016
- Fellow of the Royal Society of Canada, 2011

ALAIN NEPVEU, PHD

Position: Professor
Education: PhD, Université de Montréal
Place of birth: Montreal, Canada
Recipe recommended: Braised Snapper with Cherry Tomatoes
Focus of research: Dr. Nepveu's laboratory is interested in DNA repair. They are studying how defects in DNA repair can contribute to tumor initiation and how certain cancer cells become dependent on specific DNA repair pathways. Their goal is to apply this knowledge to increase the sensitivity of cancer cells to specific radiotherapeutic and chemotherapeutic treatments.

Award:

- James McGill Professor, 2005–2018

MORAG PARK, PHD

Position: Director
Education: PhD, Glasgow University
Place of birth: Edinburgh, Scotland
Recipe recommended: Salmon Burger
Focus of research: Dr. Park's research interests focus on the molecular mechanisms of oncogenic activation of receptor tyrosine kinases and mechanisms for cell transformation using the Met receptor, hepatocyte growth factor (HGF) and oncoprotein as a model. Her group and others have shown that the activity of the HGF receptor is frequently altered in human cancer, and they have proposed new models for its mechanism of oncogenic activation. Their current work is aimed at identifying the critical molecular signals regulated by the HGF/SF receptor, and by receptor tyrosine kinases in general, that contribute to tumor progression and are suitable targets for therapeutic intervention.

Dr. Park's research goals have now developed into a broader interest in understanding how multiple genetic alterations and epigenetic events synergize to promote tumorigenesis and progression in human breast cancer. This research interest will interface with a breast cancer translational research initiative formed through a collaboration with multiple basic researchers at McGill and the McGill University Health Centre (MUHC) and with surgeons, oncologists, and pathologists at the MUHC. Dr. Park and colleagues are forming a Montreal Breast Cancer Functional Genomics Group that will employ recent advances in strategies of genomics and proteomics from the McGill-based and worldwide research community to identify molecular determinants of tumor prognosis, diagnosis, and response to therapies.

ARNIM PAUSE, PHD

Position: Associate Professor
Education: PhD, McGill University
Place of birth: Münster/Westfalen, Germany
Recipe recommended: Leek Zucchini Pesto Flatbread
Focus of research: Dr. Pause's research is focused on the functional characterization of tumor suppressor genes during cancer development. Dr. Pause's research program is divided into two areas. (1) The Birt–Hogg–Dubé (BHD) syndrome is a hereditary human cancer syndrome that predisposes affected individuals to develop kidney cancer, as well as colon, skin, and thyroid tumors, caused by loss of function mutations in the FLCN protein. They are studying the FLCN gene product from mouse and human cells in transgenic mice and in the *C. elegans* worm model. (2) The HD-PTP gene is located in a region of the genome that is frequently deleted in human kidney, lung, breast, ovarian, and cervical tumors. Dr. Pause's laboratory has shown that loss of function of this gene leads to lung cancer and lymphoma in the mouse and that loss of HD-PTP leads to a more aggressive and metastatic cancer. They are studying the normal function of HD-PTP in the cell using human and mouse cells and transgenic mice.
Awards:
• Canada Research Chair in Molecular Oncology, 2003–2013
• The GE & Science Prize for Young Life Scientists, 1995

JERRY PELLETIER, PHD

Position: Professor
Education: PhD, McGill University
Place of birth: Saint-Jean-sur-Richelieu, Canada
Recipe recommended: Untraditional Caesar Salad
Focus of research: Dr. Pelletier's team is searching for new cancer drug therapy approaches in the following two

ways. One arm of the research program is focused on characterizing inhibitors of mammalian translation and their molecular targets. The lab has screened over 500,000 compounds for chemical inhibitors that specifically target the translation initiation phase. The other arm of the research program uses RNA interference (RNAi) to identify new anti-cancer targets. In principle, tumors can be attacked by targeting oncogenes or non-oncogene addiction pathways that occur as a consequence of the tumor progression. RNAi allows the selective diminishment of expression of target genes in cancer cells. The lab is undertaking RNAi screens against all components of the translation apparatus to identify synthetic lethal combinations that can be considered as new drug targets.
Award:
• James McGill Professor, 2005–2019

GORDON SHORE, PHD

Position: Professor
Education: PhD, McGill University
Place of birth: London, Canada
Recipe recommended: Cioppino
Focus of research: The Bcl-2 family of opposing cell survival and cell death proteins regulates pathways associated with apoptotic and non-apoptotic forms of cell death, as well as cellular macroautophagy (the breakdown of cellular waste), all of which are critical for both normal tissue development and various pathologies, including many forms of cancer. Family members of these proteins reside primarily at mitochondria and ER, where they regulate key structural and functional activities of these organelles as well as important inter-organellar dynamics. Dr. Shore's laboratory studies various aspects of this complex and unique biology, including the modulation of Bcl-2 family activity for potential therapeutic benefit in cancer.

PETER SIEGEL, PHD

Position: Associate Professor
Education: PhD, McMaster University
Place of birth: Markdale, Canada
Recipe recommended: Braised Lamb Shanks with Figs and Orzo
Focus of research: The most deadly aspect of breast cancer is the spread or metastasis of cancer cells from the primary tumor to sites throughout the body. When breast cancer cells metastasize, they primarily form metastases in specific organs and tissues, including the bones, lungs, liver, and brain. Dr. Siegel and his research team are interested in determining the molecular mechanisms engaged

by cancer cells that allow them to grow in these different metastatic microenvironments. His research group uses mouse models of breast cancer metastasis to identify and functionally test the role of specific proteins in the metastatic process. He also collaborates with clinicians, surgeons, and pathologists to clinically validate targets and uses clinical material from patients with metastatic cancer to identify novel targets that can be further explored in the pre-clinical animal models established in his lab.

Lab website: www.medicine.mcgill.ca/biochem/siegellab/index.htm

Awards:

- Research Scholar of the Canadian Cancer Society, 2004–2010
- Fonds de recherche Santé Québec, Research Scholar (Junior 2), 2010–2012

NAHUM SONENBERG, PHD

Position: James McGill Professor
Education: PhD, Weizmann Institute of Science
Place of birth: Wetzlar, Germany
Recipe recommended: Roasted Cauliflower Soup
Focus of research: Dr. Sonenberg's primary research interests have been in the field of translational control in health and disease. He discovered that eIF4E is a proto-oncogene whose protein levels are elevated in many different tumors. Subsequently, he showed that rapamycin (an anti-cancer drug) inhibits eIF4E activity. While generating eIF4E binding protein "knock-out" mice, he found that the protein plays important roles in metabolism, learning and memory, and innate immunity. Most recently, he discovered that eIF4E is implicated in autism.

Lab website: www.med.mcgill.ca/nahum/

Awards:

Dr. Sonenberg has been recognized at each stage of his scientific career by prizes and salary support awards that recognize his excellence as a cancer researcher.

- Killam Prize for Health Sciences, 2005
- Elected member of the American Academy of Arts and Sciences, 2006
- Elected member of the Royal Society of London, UK, 2006
- Gairdner International Award, 2008
- Officer of the Order of Canada, 2010
- Howard Hughes Medical Institute International Scholar Award, 2012
- Rosenstiel Award, 2012
- McLaughlin Medal, 2013
- Queen Elizabeth Diamond Jubilee Medal, 2013
- Wolf Prize 2014

JULIE ST-PIERRE, PHD

Position: Assistant Professor
Education: PhD, University of Cambridge
Place of birth: Montréal, Canada
Recipe recommended: Date Chocolate "Ice Cream" Tart
Focus of research: Dr. St-Pierre's research is concentrated primarily on understanding the metabolic regulation of cancer cells. Cancer occurs when cells divide uncontrollably. To proliferate, cells need a lot of energy to build all the components necessary for making new cells. It is therefore not surprising that cancer cells display metabolic reorganizations tailored to their high and rapid energy demands. However, this metabolic reorganization of cancer cells is poorly understood. The focus of Dr. St-Pierre's laboratory is to reveal the metabolic abnormalities, as well as the molecules driving them, during the development of the tumor state. To answer these questions, they are using a combination of unbiased screening approaches, namely genomics and metabolomics.

Award:

- Fonds de recherche Santé Québec, Salary Award, 2010–2014
- The Maude Abbot Award, 2014

JOSÉ TEODORO, PHD

Position: Assistant Professor
Education: PhD, University of Western Ontario
Place of birth: London, Canada
Recipe recommended: Cilantro Lime Shrimp
Focus of research: Dr. Teodoro's aim is to discover new mechanisms to inhibit blood vessel formation in tumors. Tumors must develop a network of blood vessels carrying oxygen and nutrients to their cells to enable their growth. This process, called angiogenesis, is absolutely necessary and is an ideal target point for new cancer therapeutics. Dr. Teodoro's laboratory has shown that, in humans, natural tumor suppressor mechanisms work in part by inhibiting tumor angiogenesis; one of the most important of those is the p53 protein. As a tumor suppressor, p53 stimulates the production of natural anti-angiogenic factors.

Lab website: http://teodorolab.mcgill.ca/Home.html

Awards:

- CIHR New Investigator Award, 2008–2013
- Fonds de recherche Santé Québec, Chercheur-Boursier (Junior II), 2008–2010

MICHEL TREMBLAY, PHD

Position: Professor
Education: PhD, McMaster University
Place of birth: Québec City, Canada
Recipe recommended: Soba Spinach Edamame Salad
Focus of research: Dr. Tremblay's laboratory investigates the functions of several members of the protein tyrosine phosphatase family (PTP) that control cell proliferation and can act as negative or positive regulators of cancer growth. Dr. Tremblay's research has clearly shown that many PTPs can function as oncogenes or positive modulators of cancer progression. Particularly important is the oncogenic role of PTP1B and PRL2 in breast and other cancers. Using gene knock-out technologies and other molecular approaches, they have generated various mouse models and assays for all these enzymes and demonstrated their functions in cancer and also in other human diseases. In addition to using animal models, the laboratory collaborates with chemists at McGill University and around the world in the development of ways to inhibit or regulate protein tyrosine phosphatases. They are screening small molecules in vitro and in cells for their specificity and efficacy to inhibit over 35 different members of the PTP family.
Lab website: www.medicine.mcgill.ca/cancercentre/tremblaylab/

Awards:
Dr. Tremblay has been recognized at each stage of his scientific career by prizes and salary support awards that recognize his excellence as a cancer researcher.

- Fonds de recherche Santé Québec, Chercheur-Boursier (Junior II), Investigator's award, 1994–1998
- Fonds de recherche Santé Québec, Chercheur-Boursier (Senior), Investigator's award, 1998–2002
- Medical Research Council, MRC Scientist Award, 2000–2005
- Ambassador, Université de Sherbrooke, Quebec, 2002
- McGill Medical Ambassador, McGill University, 2003
- James McGill Professor, McGill University, 2004–2010
- Fonds de recherche Santé Québec, Chercheur National, 2005–2010
- Jeanne and J.-Louis Lévesque Chair in Cancer Research, 2005
- Fellow, Royal Society of Canada, 2006
- Prix Michel Sarrazin 2012 du Club de Recherches Cliniques du Québec, 2012
- The Robert L. Nobel Award of the Canadian Cancer Society, 2013

YOJIRO YAMANAKA, PHD

Position: Assistant Professor
Education: PhD, Osaka University
Place of birth: Yokohama, Japan
Recipe recommended: Halibut with Grilled Pepper Anchovy Relish and Israeli Couscous
Focus of research: Dr. Yamanaka's research is focused on epithelial morphogenesis in early mammalian development and ES cells. The epithelia are a fundamental type of organized tissue that play various roles in development and adult homeostasis. Disruption of epithelia underlies the genesis of various diseases, including cancer, where disorganization of tissue structures is a hallmark of malignancy and often results in invasion and metastasis. Thus, understanding how an epithelium is generated and maintained will provide a foundation for understanding how diseases such as cancer are initiated and progress. Using live imaging techniques and genetics, Dr. Yamanaka is able to analyze dynamic cellular and molecular activities in individual cells during morphogenesis in developing mouse embryos and embryonic stem cells. Understanding dynamic cellular activities during morphogenesis in an in vivo 3D space will provide useful insight into development as well as into various diseases including cancer.
Lab website: http://blastocyst.mcgill.ca/Yamanaka_lab/Welcome.html

XIANG JIAO YANG, PHD

Position: Professor
Education: PhD, Chinese Academy of Sciences
Place of birth: Zhejiang, China
Recipe recommended: Eggplant Hummus
Focus of research: Dr. Yang's laboratory focuses on the molecular and epigenetic basis of cancer, stem cells, and animal development, especially with regard to how cell signalling regulates chromatin modification, gene expression, and other events in the nucleus. His research is focused on how chromatin modifications change between normal cells and cancer cells, how these changes modulate gene expression, and the molecular mechanisms that control these processes.

Award:
- Harold E. Johns Award from National Cancer Institute of Canada, 2002

MARIA ZANNIS-HADJOPOULOS, PHD
Position: Professor
Education: PhD, McGill University
Place of birth: Athens, Greece
Recipe recommended: Vegetarian Shepherd's Pie
Focus of research: Dr. Zannis-Hadjopoulos' laboratory focuses on the molecular mechanisms regulating the initiation of mammalian DNA replication in normal and cancer cells. All dividing cells must replicate or "make a copy" of their DNA. Rapidly growing cells are prone to making errors or creating mutations that lead to cancer. Dr. Zannis-Hadjopoulos' research has uncovered DNA sequences that define the "origins" of replication and key proteins that control DNA replication. These projects are directly pertinent to the underlying fundamental mechanisms of cell neoplasia, differentiation, development, and senescence.
Awards:

- University Researcher Award, Programme experimental de soutien à l'emploi scientifique, Fonds FCAC, Ministère de Science et Technologie, Gouvernement du Québec, 1983–1988
- Scientist Award, Medical Research Council of Canada, 1988–1993
- Prix DEKA Award for High Technology, Hellenic Board of Trade of Metropolitan Montreal, 2000

GEORGE ZOGOPOULOS, PHD
Position: Assistant Professor of Surgery and Attending Surgeon at the McGill University Health Centre
Education: MD (Toronto), PhD (McGill), General Surgery Residency (Toronto), Cancer Genetics Research Fellowship (Lunenfeld-Tanenbaum Research Institute), Hepato-Pancreato-Biliary & Abdominal Organ Transplant Surgery Fellowship (Toronto General Hospital)
Place of birth: Montreal, Canada
Recipe recommended: Berry Squares
Focus of research: Dr. Zogopoulos' clinical interests include the surgical treatment of pancreatic, hepatic, and biliary malignancies as well as abdominal organ transplantation. His research focuses on elucidating the genetics of pancreatic cancer, translating these findings to clinical care, developing clinical screening strategies for individuals at high risk for hereditary pancreatic cancer, and developing surgical treatment strategies for locally advanced pancreatic cancer. To pursue these research goals, he established and directs the Quebec Pancreas Cancer Study, a familial clinical research registry of patients with pancreatic cancer and related conditions.
Lab website: www.cancerpancreas.ca
Award:

- Fonds de recherche Santé Québec, Chercheur-Boursier, Clinicien, 2012–2016

GLOSSARY

Almond flour is made from raw blanched almonds that have been ground to a fine powder. It is gluten free and can be used as a replacement for breadcrumbs or for white flour in baked goods.

Banana pepper is also known as the yellow wax pepper or banana chili. It is a medium-sized member of the chili pepper family and has a mild, tangy taste.

Barley is a whole grain high in fibre and protein and low in fat. It has a mild, nutty taste. Hulled barley is the least processed type of barley available. The most common type of barley is pearl barley: barley grains that have been processed to remove their hull and bran for faster cooking. Pot barley has had only its outer layer removed with the bran layer left intact and so is higher in fibre and nutrients. It takes twice as long to cook and requires presoaking.

Brown rice is a whole grain rice with a mild, nutty flavour that is considered to be more nutritious than white rice. Short-grain brown rice is one of the most flavourful of all the rice varieties.

Brown sugar is actually white, refined sugar with molasses added back in.

Buckwheat is a grain unrelated to wheat and has a distinctive nutty flavour. Because it is gluten free, it is a suitable wheat replacement for those with a gluten sensitivity. Buckwheat seeds are dehulled, and the remaining part of the seed is called *groats* or *kasha*.

Bulgur and wheat berries come from the same source: whole-grain wheat. Bulgur is actually the partly hulled and cooked wheat berry.

Cardamom is a spice sold as pods, seeds, or a ground powder. It has a unique spicy-sweet flavour and often used in baked goods and curries.

Chervil is a tender herb that is similar to parsley but with a more delicate flavour and a hint of anise.

Chia seeds resemble poppy seeds. They are packed with omega-3 fatty acids and are a great source of protein and fibre. Chia seeds have a neutral flavour, which makes them a wonderful addition to many recipes and to cereal and yogurt.

Chai is a blend of black tea with herbs and spices that originated in South Asia.

Chimichurri sauce is a condiment from Argentina that is often served with grilled meats.

Cilantro is a herb with a potent flavour and strong aroma. Many people experience an unpleasant taste and smell from this herb and avoid it altogether. Italian flat-leaf parsley is often used as a substitute.

Coconut oil is nature's version of butter. Unlike animal-derived saturated fats, it is a plant-based saturated fat and has no cholesterol. Different brands of coconut oil vary in flavour intensity: some are mild and buttery, while others are richly tropical. Coconut oil is usually found in a white solid state that can be easily melted into a clear liquid.

Couscous is a granule made from 100% durum wheat semolina.

Cumin is a spice that has a very distinctive and warm taste with a touch of peppery heat.

Edamame beans are unripened green soybeans and are among the few plant-based foods that are considered a complete protein. They can be boiled or steamed in their pods and then shelled.

Farro is the Italian name for "emmer wheat," an ancient variety of hard wheat grown in western Asia. It is known for its roasted, sweet, and nutty flavour and its chewy texture.

Flax seed is a shiny brown seed with a mild nutty flavour and is noted for having one of the largest nutritional profiles. High in fibre, flax seeds should be ground to maximize their nutritional value and be properly digested. Flax seeds are sold whole or already ground into a meal. You can easily grind your own flax seeds by putting them through a spice or coffee grinder when needed; this will also keep them fresher longer.

Freekeh is made from green wheat with a nutty, smoky flavour and a crunchy texture. It is full of fibre and has a low glycemic index.

Garam masala is a blend of ground spices originating from Indian cuisine. It contains coriander, cumin, cardamom, cloves, black pepper, cinnamon, and nutmeg.

Green papaya is either red or orange papaya picked before it has ripened. If your local supermarket does not carry green papaya, look for it in Thai, Vietnamese, or Korean groceries. Green mango is a good substitute.

Hemp is a high-protein seed that contains all of the essential amino acids. It has a high percentage of protein and contains essential minerals such as potassium, iron, zinc, and magnesium. The oil of the hemp seed contains important essential fatty acids, including the heart-healthy omega-3. Hemp is also an excellent source of fibre.

Jalapeño pepper is a medium-sized chili pepper that delivers a mild to moderate amount of heat. For less heat, remove the seeds.

Jerusalem artichoke is, despite its name, a tuber native to North America. It is sweet and crunchy and can be boiled, braised, fried, or steamed.

Kale is a member of the cabbage family with a slightly bitter flavour. It is considered a nutritional powerhouse and can be eaten raw in salads, juiced, or cooked.

Kamut is a grain similar in appearance to farro with a mild, nutty, almost buttery taste and a chewy texture. It contains a higher concentration of protein and minerals than modern wheat.

Kosher salt is a coarse-grained variety of salt. It is a multi-purpose salt that can be used at the table as well as in most recipes, with the exception of delicate doughs and desserts. Unlike table salt, it is iodine free, and some brands are additive free.

Lentils are legumes that, unlike other beans, do not require presoaking. Both the green and red varieties are rich sources of protein and fibre and have a high concentration of antioxidants.

Marjoram is a perennial herb with the flavour of sweet citrus infused with pine. It can be used either fresh or dried to season soups, stews, poultry, dressings, and sauces.

Mirin is a sweet condiment used in Japanese cuisine. It is similar to sake but with a lower alcohol content. Mirin can be found in most major supermarkets.

Miso paste is a Japanese seasoning made from fermented soybeans, grains, or rice. It is a thick, full-bodied salty paste used to season sauces and spreads. White and yellow misos tend to be the lightest in flavour, while red miso has a very intense flavour.

Panko breadcrumbs are a Japanese type of breadcrumb made from crustless bread that has been ground coarsely into large airy flakes that remain crisp much longer than standard breadcrumbs. They are also available in a whole-wheat variety.

Pearl barley: see **Barley**

Pepitas are hulled pumpkin seeds.

Pesto is a sauce from northern Italy often used on pasta and in soups.

Piri piri (also known as peri peri) is the Swahili word for pepper. It is a very hot sauce made from crushed chilis.

Quinoa is a small round seed available in a hundred varieties—red, white, black, or purple, to name just a few. Quinoa is referred to as a "superseed" because it contains eleven grams of protein per half cup (uncooked). Quinoa is sweet and nutty, has a fluffy texture, and is gluten free. It must be rinsed before cooking to remove its bitter coating. To increase the nutty flavour, toast it for a minute or two before cooking.

Quinoa flour is packed with nutrients and provides all of the essential amino acids. When used to make cookies and cakes, it is best combined with an equal amount of unbleached flour.

Raita is a condiment made with yogurt and various spices. Often accompanying a spicy curry meal, it is used to cool the mouth.

Rice vinegar is made from fermented rice or rice wine. It is of Chinese origin and has a milder and sweeter taste than regular vinegar.

Serrano pepper is a hot chili pepper with a higher level of spicy heat than the jalapeño pepper. Native to Mexico, it is often used in guacamole and salsa.

Soba noodles are Japanese noodles made of 30% buckwheat.

Spelt flour is a popular non-wheat flour with a sweet and nutty taste. It is rich in fibre. Spelt flour can be substituted in equal proportions for white flour. Not all varieties are whole grain, so be sure to read the label.

Sriracha sauce is a hot sauce containing a blend of chili peppers, distilled vinegar, garlic, sugar, and salt.

Sweet potato noodles are a Korean noodle made from the starch of the sweet potato. The long chewy noodles have little flavour of their own but pick up their taste from the soups or stir-fries they are used in. They are gluten free and can be purchased in Asian food stores.

Tahini is a paste made from ground sesame seeds.

Thai or bird's eye pepper is a small, very hot chili known for its pungency. They are used to add pure heat to a meal without imparting a pronounced chili flavour.

Turmeric is a bright orangey-yellow spice with a peppery flavour and an earthy aroma. It is often used in curries and gives regular prepared mustard its bright yellow colour.

Wakame is edible seaweed with a subtly sweet flavour. It is most often used in soups and salads and is found in Asian food stores.

Wheat berries: see **Bulgur**

Wheat germ is the edible section of the wheat kernel and is a concentrated source of many essential nutrients.

INDEX